848
B

T

D1031734

Modern Critical Views

Modern Critical Views

Modern Critical Views

VICTOR HUGO

Edited and with an introduction by
Harold Bloom
Sterling Professor of the Humanities
Yale University

CHELSEA HOUSE PUBLISHERS
New York ◇ Philadelphia

Library of Congress Cataloging-in-Publication Data
Victor Hugo.
    (Modern critical views)
    Bibliography: p.
    Includes index.
    Summary: A collection of twelve critical essays on
the works of the nineteenth-century writer, arranged
chronologically in the order of their original publication.
    1. Hugo, Victor, 1802–1885—Criticism and interpreta-
tion.   2. Hugo, Victor, 1802–1885—Criticisim and interpretation.   3. French literature—History and criticism.
I. Bloom, Harold.   II. Series.
PQ2301.V498   1988   848 '.709   87–10086
ISBN 1–55546–290–1

Contents

Editor's Note

This book brings together a representative selection of the best modern criticism available in English on the writings of Victor Hugo. The essays are reprinted here in the chronological order of their original publication. I am grateful to Dani Morrow for her work as a researcher for this volume.

My introduction centers upon Hugo's stance as a poet in regard to his originality as the major French Romantic, with particular emphasis upon his later, visionary epic fragments. Georges Poulet begins the chronological sequence with his meditation upon Hugo's consciousness of negativity and the abyss.

A useful overview of Hugo's apocalyptic poetry is provided by John Porter Houston, after which W. D. Howarth does the same for Hugo's verse dramas. Patricia A. Ward studies the medievalism of *La Légende des siècles*, while Richard B. Grant reads *Les Travailleurs de la mer* as an approach to, rather than a Joycean or Proustian arrival at, an epic synthesis.

Les Contemplations, with its complex allegory, is considered by Suzanne Nash in terms of its tradition and its importance for future generations of poets. Hugo's novel *Notre-Dame de Paris* is analyzed by Jeffrey Mehlman, in the context of Marx, Freud, and Derrida, under the broad headings of revolution and repetition. In a very different kind of reading, Alexander Welsh finds decidable meanings for the opening and the close of *Les Misérables*.

Henri Peyre, dean of French Romanticists, enlightens us on Hugo's poetic visions of God from 1852 onwards. Sandy Petrey's reading of *Quatrevingt-treize*, Hugo's final novel, is a study of historical codes. A second essay by Suzanne Nash provides us with a study of *Notre-Dame de Paris*, after which the distinguished critic Victor Brombert concludes this book with an advanced analysis of *Les Misérables* as a visionary novel.

Introduction

In his *William Shakespeare* (1864), Hugo attempted to proclaim his own radical originality as the prophet of French Romanticism:

> The nineteenth century springs only from itself; it does not receive an impulse from any ancestor; it is the child of an idea . . . but the nineteenth century has an august mother, the French Revolution.

Even as Shakespeare had no poetic father (though one might argue for Chaucer, noting the link between the Wife of Bath and Falstaff), so Hugo, the nineteenth century incarnate, denied any precursor except the Revolution. It is true that the Bible and Shakespeare counted for more in Hugo's poetry than any French forerunners, at least once the early effect of Chateaubriand rapidly wore away. Blake, Wordsworth, Coleridge, Shelley, and Keats, turning themselves away from Pope, had the native tradition of Spenser, Shakespeare, and Milton to sustain them, but Hugo and his contemporaries could not see themselves similarly as a renaissance of the Renaissance. Boileau could be defied by Keats, charmingly and convincingly, but French literary culture can no more eliminate the influence of Boileau than French thought can cease to be Cartesian, despite the tyranny of German philosophy in France since the student upheavals of the late 1960s.

I myself always recall, with amiable zest, a train ride back from Princeton to Yale that I enjoyed a decade or so ago with the leading theoretician of Gallic deconstruction. We were recent friends, had encountered one another while lecturing separately at Princeton, and fell into cultural debate on the train. Deploring a belated French modernism that wholly absorbed my friend, I urged the poetic strength of Victor Hugo as against that of the more fashionable Mallarmé. In honest amazement, my philosophic companion burst forth, "But, Harold, in France Victor Hugo is a poet read only by schoolchildren!"

1

It seems safe enough to prophesy that Hugo, like Shelley, always will bury his undertakers. He goes into English about as well as Shelley goes into French, so that there are no adequate translations of Hugo's poetry, and there are not likely to be any. Yet curiously enough, Hugo is a poet who in some ways fits better into Anglo-American than into French literary tradition. He is, at his strongest, a mythopoeic or visionary poet, akin to Blake and Shelley, as Swinburne first saw. Unfortunately, Hugo has nothing like Blake's conceptual powers, and also he does not approximate the subtle, skeptical intellect of Shelley. Since he also lacked epic precursors in his own language, Hugo had the advantage neither of Blake's and Shelley's gifts, nor of their agonistic relationship to that mortal god John Milton. Hugo had to become his own Milton, with rather mixed results, one must sadly admit, thinking of *La Fin de Satan* and *Dieu*. Astonishing as those curious epics are, they lack the authority of Hugo at his strongest, in "A Albert Dürer" and "Tristesse d'Olympio," "Sonnez, sonnez toujours" and "Booz endormi," "A Théophile Gautier" and "Orphée," and so many others. This is the authority of a Sublime directness: "Qu'il m'exauce. Je suis l'âme humaine chantant, / Et j'aime."

Whether or not table-rappings with assorted spooks sometimes helped to sabotage Hugo's eloquent directness, after 1853, is not clear to me. Séances seem to have been more benign for W. B. Yeats and James Merrill than they were for the already dangerously theomorphic Hugo. The spirits were tricky with Yeats and are sometimes wicked with the urbane and kindly Merrill, but they seem to have been as thoroughly cowed by the overbearing Hugo as nearly everyone else was. Apocalyptic poetry is a dangerous genre, particularly if attempted at some length. Yeats shrewdly developed the dialectics of his eschatology in the two versions (1925, 1937) of his prose tract *A Vision* and then based apocalyptic lyrics like "The Second Coming" and "Leda and the Swan" upon the more sequestered exegetical work. Merrill, with insouciant audacity, follows Dante and Blake by incorporating his doctrinal speculations directly into *The Changing Light at Sandover*. Hugo is more puzzling, in that he never worked his preternatural revelations into a system, whether in prose or verse. Instead, he wrote titanic, fragmentary poems, that both expound and refuse to expound his cosmological imaginings. *La Fin de Satan*, *Dieu*, and much of *La Légende des siècles* form together the closest French equivalent to that great mode of English poetry of which *Paradise Lost* is the masterpiece, and Blake's *The Four Zoas*, *Milton*, and *Jerusalem*, Shelley's *Prometheus Unbound*, and Keats's two *Hyperion* fragments are the grand second wave.

La Fin de Satan began under the title of *Satan pardonné*, which is an oxymoron, since a pardoned Satan hardly could be Satan. But there is much that is oxymoronic in the design and the rhetoric of Hugo's epic fragments. This is accompanied by a consistent parataxis, doubtless biblical in its stylistic origins, but beautifully subversive in Hugo's later rhetoric, since his syntax thus refuses traditional distinctions between higher and lower orders, up and down, heaven and the abyss. Here is Satan in the Night, limning his best night-piece in *La Fin de Satan:*

> Jadis, ce jour levant, cette lueur candide,
> C'était moi.—Moi!—J'étais l'archange au front splendide,
> La prunelle de feu de l'azur rayonnant.
> Dorant le ciel, la vie et l'homme; maintenant
> Je suis l'astre hideux qui blanchit l'ossuaire.
> Je portais le flambeau, je traîne le suaire;
> J'arrive avec la nuit dans ma main; et partout
> Où je vais, surgissant derrière moi, debout,
> L'hydre immense de l'ombre ouvre ses ailes noires.

The cunning power of this is that Hugo's Satan, unlike Milton's, is no different in value before and after his fall. The syntax and the tropological pattern combine to make equal the rising light with its white glow and the supposedly hideous star that casts a white glow upon the boneyard. Satan as torchbearer or Lucifer is one with Satan trailing the winding-sheet and arriving with night in his hand. An archangel making all things golden is neither better nor worse than the being behind whom the great hydra of darkness opens its black wings. This Satan hardly requires pardon. It is as though, for the later Hugo, there are no opposites, provided that the Sublime be intense enough.

Texture rather than architectonics is the strength of the later Hugo in verse. The lack of an epic precursor in French, or at least one that he could recognize, cost him a great deal. I remember his apocalyptic poems as individual passages or moments, not as fully achieved designs. If he was not Blake or Shelley or Keats, he remains their peer in great, isolated fragments, visions of an abyss that he had found for himself. He wrote his own elegy partly in his lament for Gautier, where he hymns the departure (though in 1872) of his own century, the Romantic nineteenth:

> Passons; car c'est la loi; nul ne peut s'y soustraire;
> Tout penche; et ce grand siècle avec tous ses rayons
> Entre en cette ombre immense où pâles nous fuyons.
> Oh! quel farouche bruit font dans le crépuscule

> Les chênes qu'on abat pour le bûcher d'Hercule!
> Les chevaux de la mort se mettent à hennir,
> Et sont joyeux, car l'âge éclatant va finir;
> Ce siècle altier qui sut dompter le vent contraire,
> Expire . . .—O Gautier! toi, leur égal et leur frère,
> Tu pars après Dumas, Lamartine et Musset.
> L'onde antique est tarie où l'on rajeunissait;
> Comme il n'est plus de Styx il n'est plus de Jouvence.
> Le dur faucheur avec sa large lame avance
> Pensif et pas à pas vers le reste du blé;
> C'est mon tour; et la nuit emplit mon œil troublé
> Qui, devinant, hélas, l'avenir des colombes,
> Pleure sur des berceaux et sourit à des tombes.

The Hercules for whose pyre the great oaks are being filled so noisily is hardly Gautier, but is rather Booz (Boaz), whose eyes held light and grandeur, and who turned to God as naturally as he turned to himself, because the timelessness was already his own:

> Le vieillard, qui revient vers la source première,
> Entre aux jours éternels et sort des jours changeants;
> Et l'on voit de la flamme aux yeux des jeunes gens,
> Mais dans l'œil du vieillard on voit de la lumière.

GEORGES POULET

The Interior Distance: Hugo's Spatial Imagery

> On the plain
> A sound is born.
> It is the breath
> Of night.
> ("Les Djinns")

It is indeed in a vague sort of place that, emerging from a kind of night, there becomes visible this poetry which is, above all, a rumor made up of words and images. From the outset, the poetry of Hugo presents itself as something that vaguely takes shape in the total vacuity of thought. Of course in the youthful verse an already skillful rhetoric applies itself to concealing this void. It develops common places. But a common place is not an authentic place. It is a mental vacuum in which words drift and roll. Hugo will acknowledge it later: with him there is never an initial movement *of* thought; there is only a movement *in* thought; that is to say, within the void which constitutes it, the sudden appearance of a sort of nucleus formed of confused, undulating images that tend to spread out and multiply:

> One sees floating *in space or in one's own brain* something, one knows not what, vague and unseizable as the dreams of sleeping flowers.
>
> (*Les Misérables*)

> Then like an island of shadows drifting on the breast of nights . . .
>
> ("La Vision de Dante")

From *The Interior Distance.* © 1959 by the Johns Hopkins University Press, Baltimore/London.

An idea rises up in my mind, and passes.
Or some deep line of poetry winds through space,
As an undulating fish in midst of sleep.
                              (*Les Carnets de Victor Hugo*)

This undulating fish that glides about in the "aquarium of night," one must seize if one can. If the prey escapes, others will come by, an infinity of others. They are "floatings of forms in the darkness." They seem to drift in shoals, swimming in a turbid density; in what comprises for Hugo the ecstasies in broad daylight as well as the dreams of night:

What was I doing there? I no longer know . . . I wandered, I dreamed, I worshiped, I prayed. What was I thinking of? Don't ask me. There are moments, you know, when thought floats as if drowned in a thousand confused ideas.

                                                   (*Le Rhin*)

Nothing yet exists of thought, therefore, except a confused profusion. Before the mind knows what is the matter in hand, it is already a matter of something vast and multiple, of a throng. Thus it is for Quasimodo when he sees the army of vagrants arriving:

Thick as the gloom was, he saw the head of a column emerge at that street, and in one instant there spread over the square a crowd *of which one could distinguish nothing in the darkness except that it was a crowd* . . . He seemed to see advancing toward him a mist full of men, to see shadows stir in the shadows.
                                         (*Notre-Dame de Paris*)

It was a cloud and it was a host.
It scudded along, it flowed, it rose up like a swell.
                                         ("La Vision de Dante")

Multiple presence, agitated by the "inexpressible movement of the chimera," still anonymous and formless, but a presence which the simple exercise of the visionary power immediately transforms into a plurality of extraordinarily distinct figures:

There are no mists, there are no algebras,
Which resist, in the depths of numbers or skies,
The calm and deep fixity of eyes;
I gazed at that wall first confused and vague,
Where the form seemed to float like a wave,
Where all seemed vapor, vertigo, illusion;

> And, under my pensive eye, the strange vision
> Became less hazy and more clear.
>> ("La Vision d'où est sorti ce livre")

It is thus by a double amplifying movement that Hugolian poetry takes possession of its space. For on the one hand its figures seem endowed with a kind of instantaneous fecundity which makes them proliferate and multiply forthwith; and, on the other hand, as each of these figures becomes more distinct, it divides itself, so to speak, into all the perceptible elements that compose it; "immense shade with thousands of tiny carved leaves"; so that this multitude is as it were interiorly inflated by precision of detail and variety of aspect.

It is at first sight, or oftenest, an infinity of faces:

> Now and again upon the livid wall the lightning
> Made thousands of faces glitter all at once.
>> (*Ibid.*)

> So that the frightening space presented nothing now
> Save visages, living flux, living reflux,
> A soundless teeming of hydras, men, and beasts,
> And the depths of the sky seemed to me full of heads.
>> (*Dieu*)

Sometimes, as in *Les Orientales,* and indeed nearly everywhere, edifices, Babels, whole silhouettes of cities rise up, curiously etching their contours upon the same depth of emptiness:

> There are Alhambras, high cathedrals,
> Babels, thrusting their spirals to the skies.
>> (*Les Feuilles d'automne,* 27)

> Some Moorish city, dazzling, wonderful,
> Which, like a rocket expanding in showers
> Rends the opacity with its shafts of gold!
>> ("Rêverie")

Or again there are visions of features, of bodily movements, of limbs, of costumes; then murmurings of all sorts, the sonorous volume of which multiplies and thickens the visible volume of the apparition:

> A ray issues forth from the fullness,
> And the creation, misshapen multitude,
> Appears before me; and I hear noises, footsteps, voices.
>> (*Dieu*)

Crowd without name! Chaos! voices, eyes, footsteps.
("La Pente de la rêverie")

Thus the nebulous core is at once condensed and deployed within a mass and within a number. It is like a sea, a sea of details. Everything is agglomerated into a moving unity which has in no wise the character of a mental construction and which will never be able to attain it. Everything is gregarious. Everything is at the same time distinct and alike, absolutely definite and totally absorbed in the whole. Nothing can be classified, or ordered elsewhere, than at the point of happenstance where it is numbered within the number. Such is the aspect concrete things present when one sees them flung one upon another, piled up pell-mell.

Images pell-mell:

All of light that the infinite is able to hurl
At once breaks to pieces pell-mell in the air.
("Le Sacre de la femme")

Pell-mell also of the words that express them; for words are things and are images:

Yes, all of you must understand that words are things.
They roll pell-mell into the dark gulf of prose.
(*Les Contemplations*)

Finally a pell-mell of the whole creation, as it appears from below, for example, to the Devil:

You cannot imagine the effect, from below,
This enormous train of disasters has,
Chaos, plagues, planets, globes, stars,
Pell-mell.
(*Les Carnets de Hugo*)

Hence the universe which delineates itself in the eyes of Hugo seems from the first to be reduced by who knows what disruptive force to its dislocated elements. It is less a universe than the colossal and still-smoking residue of some cosmic catastrophe:

One sees in the air no more than splendid ruins,
Confused accumulations, glittering heaps
Of coppers and brasses crumbling upon one another.
("Au bord de la mer")

> Instead of a universe, it was a cemetery;
> Here and there rose up some lugubrious stone,
> Some standing pillar, no longer supporting anything;
> All the truncated centuries lay there; no more linkage.
>   ("La Vision d'où est sorti ce livre")

No more linkage between centuries, places, beings, things; and the consequent impossibility of reconstructing them or of setting them in order. A world returned to chaos, to brute, to bulk, to undifferentiated unity. And yet this fallen world has, by very virtue of its shapelessness, an extraordinary stability. Whatever be the collapses and upheavals which never cease to happen, whatever be the vast eddies which incessantly displace things therein, it is nonetheless true that things persist there, tangible, concrete, with that fundamental capacity things have of occupying place, of making volume, of piling themselves into a heap:

> Like a Babel with approaches obstructed
> By turrets, by belfries, by slender spires,
> Buildings constructed to fit all minds;
> Enormous piling up of stone and intelligence,
> Vast amassment.
>   (*Les Rayons et les ombres*, 35)

Hugo's universe is nothing other than that: an immense piling up of perceptible forms, reflected by this other amassment, that of works and of words:

> This is one immense horizon of ideas barely glimpsed, of pieces of work begun, of rough drafts, of plans, of drawings hardly started, of vague lineaments, dramas, comedies, history, poetry, philosophy, socialism, naturalism, *a heap of floating works* into which my thought plunges without knowing whether it will return.

This note relating to the rough copy of 1846 goes as well for the final so-called finished works. For even the totalities of *La Légende des siècles* and *Les Misérables* are still rough drafts. Hugo can never do anything except add and enlarge; add to the multitude of detail, enlarge the mass of the whole. But whatever he adds to it, this totality remains forever sketchy. Inexhaustible cascade of words that fall, incalculable heap of images that pile up, the work of Hugo is a discrete plurality, without dimension, in which nothing is linked to anything else, but in which the Nothing becomes Everything, and the void, mass:

Who then will measure the dark from one end to the other,
And life and the tomb, unheard of spaces
Where the pile of days dies under the heap of nights?

(L'Année terrible)

II

It is under the firmament
A kind of strange and mournful heaping up.
(Dieu, "Les Voix")

Dark and moving mass of meditations!
(Les Chants du crépuscule, 13)

This mass is never anything but a mass. Nevertheless it is a *moving* mass. It stirs. It swarms. It grows. And the vast movement that animates it and that continually traverses its formidable framework from one end to the other is not solely an internal movement of growth and the development of parts; it is a movement of translation by means of which the huge mass displaces itself and becomes still more huge, because, coming all the time nearer and nearer, it more and more fills the field of vision:

And this ominous, heavy mass arisen and flowing toward us,
Dismal, livid, huge, with an air of rage about it,
Rolled on and increased, driven by stormy gales.
("La Vision de Dante")

The monster grew larger and larger without cease,
And I no longer knew what it was. What was it,
A mountain, a hydra, a deep abyss, a city,
A cloud, a shadow, the immensity?
(Dieu, "L'Esprit humain")

To this enlargement in space there corresponds an analogous enlargement in time:

I saw suddenly arise, sometimes from the breast of the waves,
Beside the living cities of two worlds,
Other towns with strange façades, unheard of,
Ruined sepulchers of vanished times.
("La Pente de la rêverie")

All peoples having for tiers all times . . .
All towns, Thebes, Athens, all the layers
Of Rome upon the heaps of Tyres and Carthages.
("La Vision d'où est sorti ce livre")

Time is only then a second space; that is to say an extent in depth in which all the images of the past are disposed and amassed and out of which they can be drawn forth by our gaze like images of space. At any instant from the depths of forgetfulness, there can "pour forth pell-mell like smoke two thousand years of memories." Pell-mell, that is to say torn up out of chronological order, detached from historical continuity, and by consequence immediately susceptible of being added to the actuality without disparity or contradiction. Hugo's universe is ageless for it indifferently comprises all the ages. Like the "wall of centuries," with which the "Vision d'où est sorti ce livre" opens, it is a plane upon which are entangled together figures and styles that belong simultaneously to all times, and upon which the play of light and shadow makes now one epoch, now another appear:

There were intercrossings of flame and of cloud,
Mysterious playings of splendor, throwbacks
Of shadows from one century to another.

So Hugolian duration is radically discontinuous, made up of a perpetually renewed accumulation of anachronistic images between which incongruous meetings occur; and in that respect, on an infinitely vaster scale, and on the plan of a cosmic and not an individual history, it presents an unexpected resemblance to Proustian duration. For, like the latter, it is full of sudden encounters between epochs which do not follow each other but which nevertheless touch and even collide with each other. And actually there are passages in the work of Hugo in which the typical operation of the "involuntary memory" is most outstandingly revealed. For example this passage from *Alpes et Pyrénées,* in which, by means of the miracle of the affective memory, Hugo suddenly meets on the way into Spain the child he had been thirty years before:

It is July 27, 1843, at half past ten in the morning, that, at the moment of entering Spain, between Bidart and Saint-Jean-de-Luz, at the doorway of a wretched inn, I saw once more an old Spanish oxcart. I mean by that the little cart of Biscaye, with its team of oxen, and the two stout wheels that turn with the axle and make a frightful noise such as one hears a league away in the mountains.
Never smile, my friend, at the tender care with which I so

minutely record this memory. If you only knew how charming for me is that din so horrible to anyone else! It recalls blessed years to me.

I was very small when I crossed those mountains and when I heard it for the first time. The other day, as soon as it struck my ear, just to hear it I suddenly felt young again, it seemed to me that my whole childhood suddenly came back to life within me.

I would not know how to tell you by what strange and supernatural effect my memory was as fresh as an April dawn, everything returned to me at once; the slightest details of that happy epoch appeared clear and luminous to me, lighted up by the rising sun. The closer the oxcart approached with its savage music, the more distinctly I saw once more that ravishing past, and it seemed to me that *between that past and today there was nothing . . .*

Bless him, the poor unknown ox-driver who had had the mysterious power to make my thought *radiate* and who, without knowing it, summoned up this magical evocation in my soul!

Is not this sudden radiation of a past until then obscurely buried in the "interior gulf" the same phenomenon that Proust has described in a famous passage? And does not the noisy sound of the axle play the same evocative role as the *madeleine* in the cup of tea? In both cases the retrospective leap is made with the same suddenness and fullness, enveloped by the same feeling of freshness and joy. And if, in the work of Proust, there are other places where the affective resurrection remains incomplete, half sunk in oblivion, by the same token it is possible to find in Hugo recollections which are unachieved or only glimpsed in the depths of time. Does not perhaps the true meaning of the "Tristesse d'Olympio" lie in this imperfect vision, "in a dark coil where all seems to end," of a memory which remains veiled and which one feels to palpitate without the power to awaken it from its sleep?

Here, as many times in Proust, the total radiation of the past has been on the point of being accomplished; but the "mysterious play of splendor" by which the Hugolian memory operates, has not this time succeeded in making it rise up, in making it *radiate*.

For "memory," says Hugo, "is a radiation":

> O memories! treasure growing in the darkness!
> Somber horizon of bygone thoughts!

Precious glimmer of vanished things!
Radiation of a past that has disappeared.
("Un Soir que je regardais le ciel")

As in Gautier, as in Nerval, as later in Flammarion and Renan, there is thus in Hugo the belief in the indefinitely luminous life of images. Scattered throughout a universe of shadows where they set up their hearth of light, they cast into this temporal space more or less strong rays which can be caught by the mind. Just as the images of the present dilate themselves, as all sounds reverberate, as everything that occupies a place in the spatial universe tends to become larger or to move up to first rank, so in the extents of duration everything continues to radiate, that is to say, to palpitate, to project light, to reproduce itself, to tend to approach the actual. And the property of the poet is precisely to further by the act of his retrospective vision all this confused movement by which the past strives to become the present again. One always has the impression, in a poem of Hugo's, of a vast vanguard of images, like that of an army on the march toward the actual. As in the thought of Bergson, it seems as if the entire past occupies the whole length of the line of the horizon. But in this case the progress toward the present and toward the future does not possess the Bergsonian character of a continuous glide; indeed on the contrary it is a chaotic outburst, a loose bundle of disparate flashings in which all is confounded and confused: "Our memory, a kind of forest," says Hugo; and in the preface to *Les Contemplations:*

> These are all the impressions, all the memories, all the realities,
> all the vague phantoms, pleasant or dismal, which a conscious-
> ness can contain, recurring and recalled, gleam by gleam, sigh by
> sigh, *intermixed in the same cloudy swarm.*

Once again we observe that astonishing relationship in Hugo between clarity of detail and massiveness of ensemble. It is the reason why, disparate as memories may be, and violent as the shock of their reality may be against the reality of the actual, there is no fundamental difference in Hugo's world between what one remembers and what one imagines, no more than between what one imagines and what one sees. All is simply form, and form upon form; and all simultaneously serves, by the same activity, for the edification of the same Babel: a vast structure which unfolds in height as in breadth, in the centuries as in space, but of which each block, that is to say each word and each image, whatever its origin, has the duly assigned present task of supporting the immense ensemble in its actuality:

It was like a great building
Formed of accumulations of centuries and places;
One could not find the sides or the center of it;
At all heights, nations, peoples, races,
A thousand human workers, leaving their traces everywhere,
Labored night and day.

("La Pente de la rêverie")

A simultaneous labor in which all the imaginations, perceptive, retrospective, prospective, collaborate in the same task: the enlargement and the drawing closer of a nebulous core which now occupies all space and all time, all space-time; "mounting flood of ideas that invades you little by little and that almost submerges the intelligence."

III

And you wish that, under the *pressure* of all these concentric gulfs at the bottom of which I am, bah! I should curl up and roll myself into my ego! . . . You want me to say to all that is: I am not of it! You want me to deny my adhesion to the indivisible!

(*Post-scriptum de ma vie*)

Thus for Hugo the self is found amongst an engulfing reality. The Hugolian being comes suddenly to consciousness when the formidable mass of things breaks over him and he feels everywhere its moving and multiple contact. "The pressure of darkness exists";—therefore I exist!

There is nothing more fundamental to the thought of Hugo than this discovery. One can even say that if there is a "thought of Hugo," it is thanks to this discovery. Before the discovery occurred, Hugolian thought was only vision and spectacle. It was that anonymous point of view from which the eye embraces what there is to see. Nothing existed for it except a regarding of the immense field from which the radical objectivity of things unrolls.

And suddenly the object is no longer an object, and the spectacle is no longer a spectacle. How can one describe this situation in which a human being appears all at once to himself, not in the sanctuary of his consciousness, not in a solitary thought which assures him of his sole existence, but in so total an envelopment and penetration by things that he cannot detach himself from them, cannot distinguish himself from them, cannot abstract himself from them? He *is,* but he is *in* things. He is *athwart* things, and things are athwart him. He is, but like a wrestler so tightly entwined with his adversary that the same heat and the same lock seem to animate both of them. There is nothing so different from the state of the spectator one was just beforehand. There is no longer on the horizon a growing mass of external images which one watches approach with the same detachment one has in seeing clouds scud across the sky, forerunners of a storm. Now the storm is here, everywhere, in all the ways of access to me, and in my very self. It is "storm under the skull." One discovers oneself at the center of a whirling world which is an enormous pressure and an enormous presence. One ceaselessly experiences "the obscure thrust of an inexpressible encounter" or "the monstrous weight of the whole." "The incommensurable cosmic synthesis overwhelms and crushes us." It is like "a sort of seizure of our mind." One is, and one feels oneself to be, solely in the feeling of a total and forced participation in a reality which encroaches upon us because it is *all* and consequently also *us*:

> One feels caught. One is at the discretion of this shadow. Evasion is impossible. One sees oneself enmeshed, one is an integral part of an unapprized All, one feels the unknown within oneself fraternize mysteriously with an unknown outside oneself.
>
> (*Les Travailleurs de la mer*)

There is in the strict sense, therefore, neither individual thought nor even individual existence:

> The world is an ensemble in which no one is alone.
>
> (*Dieu*)

> All is confounded with all, and nothing exists apart.
>
> (*Ibid.*)

No one has lived more intensely than Hugo this primary experience in which there is discovered the solidarity of the self and the world. The one exists only *with* the other, mingled with the other. There is no otherness because there is really no personality:

> Then is this the life of a man? Yes and the life of other men too. None of us has the honor of having a life to himself. My life is yours, your life is mine, you live what I live . . . Ah! madman, you who believe that I am not you!
>
> (Preface to *Les Contemplations*)

And so for Hugo, as for Bradley later, there are no *external relationships*. There is only the internal relationship of an all to a self and of a self to an all; immediate co-penetration of the mind and the world; simulta-

neous presence of anything to anybody, upon which rests the substantial
unity of the real and the thinkable. In a certain sense, everything I appre-
hend is myself; and in another sense, everything I imagine is to be found
outside myself, in things, because I bring pressure to bear upon things as
things bring pressure to bear upon me:

> The dream one has within oneself, one finds again outside oneself.
>
> (*William Shakespeare*)

The world is then composed not only of what I see in it, but of what I
imagine in it, and as a consequence of what my imagination really makes my
eyes see in it. I unceasingly dispose within surrounding space the real and
visible form of my thoughts, as a thing which I place among things. And
therefore I see myself, objectively and subjectively at one and the same time,
within myself and in that exterior outside myself:

> And in the lugubrious vision *and in myself*
> *Which I beheld as in the depths of a pale mirror,*
> Boundless life expanded its misshapen branches.
>
> ("La Vision d'où est sorti ce livre")

In contemplating the universe, Hugo contemplates himself:

> He fathoms the destinies and contemplates the shadows
> Which our dreams form when thrown among things.
>
> ("Saturne")

Hence the impossibility for Hugo of regarding himself as simply a
self-thinking consciousness and of considering himself, even in his own eyes,
as a pure subjectivity. If he never analyzed or poured out his soul, if we
never distinguish in him, contrary to other romantics, the feeling of interior
solitude and the taste for introspection, it is because consciousness for him
is not a thought that withdraws itself, that isolates itself and situates itself
within itself, outside the object. Hugo always places himself within the
object, or at least *alongside* it. For him all consciousness of being is a
consciousness of being in common with something and indeed with everything. He does not set himself apart. He does not belong exclusively to
himself. He belongs to an existence that is the cosmic existence.

And in this vast existence he regains all the elements of his own. Not
only of his present existence, but of his past existence as well as his future
existence. By means of his memory, by means of his imagination, he perpetually encounters, outside himself, a being which he was or will be. If
Hugo's affective resurrections are as profound as Proust's, they never in-
volve him, however, in a solitary and internal search for lost time. Time is

never lost. It is there, outside, among things. To remember is not to find within oneself, in the presence of a certain object which plays the role of "recollecting sign," an interior world which is that of our memories; it is to see in the object something of oneself which one has placed in it and which one finds there again. For Hugo, if we recognize objects, they also recognize us. Depositories of our states of mind, they know they must return to us one day the deposit we have entrusted to them:

> God lends us for a moment the meadows and springs,
> The great shuddering woods, the deep rumbling rocks,
> And the azure skies and the lakes and the plains,
> To *place there* our hearts, our dreams, our loves.
> ("Tristesse d'Olympio")

Thus the drama of the "Tristesse d'Olympio" is that for once nature does not restore to us that part of ourself which she had in keeping, and that is because having herself changed, she does not recognize us as her depositor. But inversely one can find in the work of Hugo numerous cases in which this recognition takes place and in which restitution is integral. The instance developed at greatest length relates to the journey to Spain in 1843. It must be cited in its entirety:

> I am in Pampelune, and I should not know how to say what I am experiencing here. I had never seen this town, and it seems to me that I recognize every street in it, every house, every doorway. All of the Spain which I saw in my childhood appears before me here as on the day when I heard the first oxcart pass by. Thirty years of my life are effaced; I become a child again, the little Frenchman, *el nino, el chiquito frances,* as they called me. A whole world that was sleeping awakens within me, lives again and teems in my memory. I thought it was almost entirely blotted out; and now it is more resplendent than ever. . . .
>
> I have spent two delightful hours tête-a-tête with an old green small-paneled shutter that opens in two sections in such a way as to make a window if one opens half of it, and a balcony if one opens all of it. This shutter had been for thirty years unsuspectedly in some corner of my thought. I called out: Look! There is my old blind!
>
> What a mystery the past is! And how true it is that *we deposit ourselves in the objects that surround us!* We think them inanimate, yet they live; they live with the mysterious life we have given them. At each phase of our life we cast off our entire being

and forget it in some corner of the world. All that entirety of inexpressible things which was ourself *remains there* in the shadow, *making one with the things upon which we have imprinted ourselves without our knowledge.* Finally one day, by chance, we see those objects again; they abruptly rise up before us and, all at once, with the omnipotence of reality, *restore our past to us.* It is like a sudden light; *they recognize us, they make themselves known to us, they bring us back, complete and dazzling, the consignment of our memories,* and they render to us a charming phantom of ourself, the child who played, the young man who loved.

(*Alpes et Pyrénées*)

Nothing could be more striking than this passage, first because in it Hugo passes, without being aware of it, from the classic conception of an *internal* memory ("That shutter was in some corner of *my* thought"), to the prelogical and primitive conception of a purely *exterior* memory; and in the next place because this particular theory of memory clearly appears here for what it is, that is to say an application of the more general theory which Hugo was forming of his relations with the universe. Memory is projected into outside objects; in them it lives a semi-objective existence. It is regained *within* this world of objects, inextricably mingled with them and participating in their life. It is *my* memory, but it is mingled, as I myself am, in an ensemble. It is made, of all the world, into all the world.

But this propensity of Hugo's to place memory in the object rather than in the subject, leads to another curious result. The object tends to become subject, that is to say, the center of spiritual life, capable not only of preserving and reflecting thoughts and feelings, but also of producing them in its turn. Things are animate. They simultaneously live the life we have given them and their own life. They think, they suffer, perhaps they even remember obscurely on their own account. Their own recollections are mingled no doubt with our own; so much so that in putting ourselves in communication with them, we become vaguely conscious of this double level. Behind personal memory, then, there appears an historical memory, a cosmic memory. There is always, disseminated throughout the universe, a sort of "legend of the centuries" which adheres to objects and beings, and which, if one observes carefully, reveals, linked to the present image, the image tenfold of a "vertiginous past":

I stared at the pebbles in the empty road. I gazed at nature, serene as a good conscience. Little by little the specter of things superimposed itself in my mind upon present realities and effaced them like old writing that reappears on a badly bleached page in the midst of a new text; I thought I saw the bailiff Gessler lying bleeding on the empty road, on those diluvian pebbles fallen from Mount Rigi, and I heard his dog barking in the woods at the gigantic shadow of William Tell standing in the underbrush.

From perception the mind passes without transition to the memory of facts and then to the recreative evocation. It is thus impossible to distinguish in Hugo what is the part of memory and what of imagination. From a certain point of view everything is memory, since everything is directly suggested to the mind by the object. Together with its sensory appearance, the object delivers up to him its historical depth. But from another point of view everything is imagination; since any memory, whatever it may be, is immediately covered by new layers of images. Hugo never experiences pure memory or isolated memory. Nothing can remain isolated in the Hugolian universe. And also memory, like the rest, appears at the heart of a tumultuous plurality which changes its perceptible aspect, its affective tonality, and finally invests it with an epic grandeur. The perspective recession enlarges the image instead of diminishing it:

> Objects loom larger in the imaginations of men like crags in mists, in proportion as they move into the distance.
> (*Littérature et philosophie mêlées*)

Hugo can never, in the strict sense, remember. He can only imagine, and imagine himself.

IV

And so the whirling universe, at the center of which whirls the thought of the poet, appears now as continuously enlarged and expanded by a genuinely creative operation. It is not only, as previously, a sort of amassing of things which proliferate. It is a world into which there is constantly thrust the alluvial deposit of an imagination that never ceases to invent its forms for itself. It is a creation to which is superadded another creation, that of the mental forms of the mind. Hugo is clearly aware of the fact that the real is incessantly and really augmented, not only by its own fecundity, but by a sort of condensation of dreams into living matter. The universe is not simply a universe of the real, it is also a universe of the possible which realizes itself:

The Possible is a formidable matrix. The mystery is concretized into monsters. Some fragments of darkness emerge from this mass, immanence, break away from it, detach themselves, roll, float, condense themselves, borrow from the ambient blackness, undergo unknown polarizations, take life, create for themselves out of the obscurity one knows not what form and out of the miasma one knows not what soul, and go forth, larvae, through life. It is something like shadows made animals.

(Les Travailleurs de la mer)

A chimerical reality appears in the indistinct depths. The inconceivable takes form a few paces away from you with a spectral clarity . . . Cavities of night, things become haggard, taciturn profiles that vanish as one approaches, obscure dishevellings, irritated wisps, livid puddles, the doleful reflected in the funereal, the sepulchral immensity of silence, unknown possible beings, bendings of mysterious branches, frightening torsos of trees, diffuse bunches of quivering grass, one is defenseless against all that. There is no one so fearless as not to tremble and to sense the proximity of anguish. One experiences something hideous, as if the mind were amalgamated with darkness.

(Les Misérables)

There is thus not only what one sees; there is also what one glimpses; and behind what one glimpses, there is that which one fancies. All that is possible *can* exist; all that is imaginable already exists if it is imagined. The enveloping mass is not made up solely of realities, but of possibilities which one has himself simply by the act of his imagination summoned into matter:

Contemplation becomes vision. One knows not what whirlpool of the hypothetic and the real, that which can be complicating that which is, our invention of the possible deluding even ourself, our own conceptions mingled with the obscurity, our conjectures, our dreams and our aspirations taking form, all chimerical no doubt, all perhaps true.

(Post-scriptum de ma vie)

As a consequence, as in the mentality of primitives, which has been rightly compared with that of Hugo, a strange amalgam of the real and the possible takes place. Any line of demarcation disappears between what one dreams and what one perceives:

> One meditates, bewildered by possible things;
> All borders are erased, one sees invisible ones.
>
> *(Toute la lyre)*

Everywhere things are seen which are there because they *are;* but everywhere also are detected things which, although they *are not,* are nevertheless also there because there somewhere exists a thought that has dreamed them. When Claude Frollo saw the cathedral transformed first into a crowd of human figures, then into a gigantic animal on the march, it was still only an isolated attack of fever and madness, so intense "that the exterior world was now no more for the poor unfortunate than a sort of visible, palpable, frightful Apocalypse." But precisely this Apocalypse existed solely *for* the poor unfortunate, and within himself. For the Hugo of maturity, on the contrary, each human thought is capable of engendering an Apocalypse for everybody else. Thus when one wanders through a sleeping city, one is surrounded by a crowd of phantoms created by the thought of the sleepers:

> The discomposed thought of those asleep floats above them, a vapor that is both living and dead, and is combined with the possible, which quite likely also thinks in space. *As a consequence there are entanglements.* The dream, this cloud, superimposes its thicknesses and its transparencies upon that star, the mind. Above those closed eyelids within which vision has replaced view, a sepulchral disaggregation of silhouettes and aspects dilates within the impalpable. A dispersion of mysterious existences is amalgamated with our life by means of this margin of death that sleep is.
>
> *(L'Homme qui rit)*

There is thus added to the dilation of the real the dilation of the dream. The two mingle or become neighbor one to another in an "unfathomable promiscuity," co-penetrate one another in order to form a complicated space which the imagination furnishes with a vertiginous fourth dimension, the "extent of the possible."

But where is this extent? Is it without or within? It is at once external and internal, felt and dreamed. It is the exterior world in which the things that are seem to open up or to draw aside in order to make room for the things that are not; and it is also the "dark inner immensity," in which thought is continually assailed, oppressed, and penetrated by phantoms from without. "All that is in the abyss is in man." There is only one selfsame space without, within, comprised by the same tangle of crisscrossing forms. By dint of everywhere disposing intersection points and meeting places, of laying trajectories crosswise, of ramifying and joining certain growths, in the course of confronting everywhere the ugly and the beautiful, the darkness and the light, the grotesque and the terrible, one ends by delineating, without as within, in thought as well as outside of thought, a penetrable and innumerable entity which has the appearance and the density of forests:

> A forest for thee is a hideous world.
> The dream and the real are mingled there together.
>
> ("A Albert Dürer")

This forest is the world; and it is also thought. World and thought are for Hugo the same entanglement:

> Knowest thou the true, the possible,
> All the *network* of the invisible?
>
> (*Toute la lyre*)

> This *entanglement* of stars and universes.
>
> (*Religions et religion*)

> O dark *intercrossing* of gulfs and dreams,
> Sleep, white aperture of apparitions.
>
> (*Dieu*)

> As if all the invisible threads of being
> *Crossed* in my breast which the universe penetrates!
>
> (*Les Quatre Vents de l'esprit*)

> In the strange *forest* one calls thought,
> Everything exists.
>
> (*Ibid.*)

To this cosmic and psychic entanglement there corresponds also an entanglement of words. The Hugolian sentence is constructed under the form of the tangle, the network, or the web. It multiplies the branchings-off, contrives the intersecting of terms and incidents, seeks to create a kind of sonorous and visual volume by the double density of modulations and perspectives. It makes "the verse roar, stormy forest."

But a forest is not composed solely of tree trunks, branches, and foliage. Dense as it may be, there is always depth in its mass and daylight in its foliation. A forest is a lattice. Things pass, and the gaze passes, through its meshes.

Such again is the Hugolian universe. The mass of forms which constitute it do not check the gaze like a curtain. Into the tangle of things the restless gaze, uneasy as to what lies beyond, can on all sides penetrate deeply. Farther off than what one sees, there is always something one merely glimpses; and beyond what one glimpses, there are gaps in which there seems to be nothing, gaps in the void, in which one's gaze is lost:

> frightening holes, torn from the infinite, with enormous stars in
> their depths, and wonderful gleams.
>
> (*Post-scriptum de ma vie*)

> Like the gigantic shafts of a temple in ruins,
> *Allowing glimpses of the abyss* between its broken walls.
>
> ("La Vision d'où est sorti ce livre")

Behind the amplitude there is a void. Behind number, behind mass, within the depths, in the interstices and amid the thousand apertures of a network-world which cannot succeed in keeping out space, there is this space, a space-gulf: "Such are the precipices we call space."

And once again, as a consequence, everything changes its nature. The tangle of things no longer appears as an edifice, a Babel, as the construction of a world, as the approximation of a plentitude:

> Something unheard of, gigantic, incommensurable; an edifice
> such as no human eye has ever seen;
>
> (*Notre-Dame de Paris*)

all becomes hollow, porous, penetrable; "all becomes uncertain and vague." Everything passes through everything. The world is now nothing more than one vast coming-and-going of atoms in the darkness, a series of ebbings and flowings which range from the infinitely great to the infinitely small:

> The forms of night come and go in the darkness.
>
> (*Les Contemplations*)

In vast cosmic exchanges, universal life comes and goes in un-known quantities, rolling everything along in the invisible mys-tery of its effluviums.

> (*Les Misérables*)

> Frightening aspects are seen everywhere;
> The ghost vibrio equals the phantom sun;
> A world more profound than the star is the atom;
> When under the thinker's eye the infinitely small
> Is placed upon the infinitely great, it engulfs it;
> Then the infinitely great remounts and submerges it . . .

> All being, whatsoever, is the milieu of the gulf . . .
> This is why man, a prey to so many dark tumults,
> Dreams, and *fingers space,* and desires a point of support,
> Fearing the tragic night round about him.
>
> ("A l'homme")

Thus the colossal and massive construction of a universe full of images is broken up. Its scattered elements, whether stars or atoms, roll on, lost in the vacuity of a space more vast and more real than they are. Instead of appearing in one single compact mass which intercepts the horizon and fills up the expanse, they pass at frightful distances from one another,

> Ghost worlds . . . ,
> These, faint, rolling in the gloomy depths,
> Those, almost engulfed in the boundless infinite.
>
> ("Explication")

Suddenly, above as below, as in the depths of itself, there is only one selfsame gulf in which everything rises up, floats, revolves, decreases, pales, and is effaced,

> space
> In which the formless floats forever, passes and repasses.
>
> (*Toute la lyre*)

There is no longer anything but a space that one vainly fingers in search of a point of support:

> O cistern of darkness! O livid depths!
> Plenitudes are equal to voids.
> Where then is the support?
>
> (*Dieu*)

To the immense effort of the imagination to establish itself in the number, in the plenum, in the thickness and in the whole, there succeeds, in the general dissolution of things, a feeling of vertigo and anguish. One is deserted by the universe. One is alone, teetering at the edge of an abyss.

Among all the effects of contrast which constitute the work of Hugo, there is none more striking than that to be found between the motion by means of which the images first appear, surge up, accumulate, and fill all the horizon; and on the other hand, the movement by which, having passed through thought, they decrease, disaggregate, and are lost in the distance:

> Soon all around me the shadows increased,
> The horizon was lost, forms disappeared,

> And man and thing, and being and mind
> Floated away on my breath; a shudder took me.
> I was alone.
>
> ("La Pente de la rêverie")

> Then, as in a chaos which would withdraw a world,
> All is lost in the folds of a thick mist.
>
> ("Que la musique date du XVIe siècle")

> Everything has but to rise, float and disappear.
>
> ("Magnitudo Parvi")

Such is the double movement, everywhere repeated, in *Les Contempla-tions,* in the *Légende,* in *Dieu,* in all the great works of maturity. It is ·already, as Baudelaire was the first to remark, the subject of the "Pente de la rêverie," which dates from 1830. But it was already the subject of the "Djinns," which dates from 1828. All the poetic effort of Hugo consisted in trying to condense into a void—the void of thought—a vaporous core of images in order to make out of them a reality, all reality. And at first this attempt seems to succeed. Images concretize and amalgamate themselves, a world is formed in which thought finds, situates, and supports itself. But this imaginary reality soon appears fantastic. Its very fecundity ends by becom ing the principal agent of its destruction. For it exists only by a continual invention which always lures thought beyond that which is directed toward what can be. It is like a sort of vicious circle in which it is unceasingly necessary for the imagination to produce new forms in order to shore up those it has already imagined. But the more of them it produces, the more unreal this superabundance appears. There is

> So much reality that all becomes phantom.
>
> ("Le Titan")

The Hugolian creation ends by resembling the delirium of a demented crea-ture:

> The abyss appears mad beneath the hurricane of being.
>
> ("Magnitudo Parvi")

> Being is prodigious to such a point—I shudder at it!—
> That it resembles nothingness; and All gives at intervals
>   The same vertigo as Nothing!
>
> (*Dieu*)

It is a chaos that returns to chaos and nothingness, not by deficiency but by plethora. One could say that in its rush toward existence it is incapable of halting at a mysterious and infinitely delicate point of the spiritual universe, the point where thought and image can subsist in themselves, affirm themselves viable and durable. The very fury with which the thought of Hugo wants to realize itself in an avalanche of forms makes it overshoot the mark. He is incapable of stopping this hurrying motion of the fancy which passes within him and throughout him, in order to lose itself in the impalpable. What he says of one of his characters he can say of himself:

> His brain had lost the power of retaining his ideas, they passed like waves, and he held his forehead in his two hands in order to stop them.
>
> (Les Misérables)

After the passage of ideas, of images, there is nothing left but a universal void, the very void in which they took shape. Nothing remains except space:

> All flies,
> All passes;
> Space
> Effaces
> The sound.
> ("Les Djinns")

V

Come, I shall teach thee all: *There is a gulf.*—
As if he had said all in this word, the owl
Paused; then resumed:—When? why? how? where?
All is silent, all is shut, all is deaf, all withdrawn,
All lives within the fathomless and fatal twilight.

If, in this episode of the poem *Dieu,* Hugo attained the highest summit of his poetry, it is because in no place is his own thought more adequately expressed. Almost everywhere else, as we have seen, this thought either does not exist, or is found engaged with things, hemmed in by forces, grappling at close quarters with a multiple reality from which it cannot distinguish itself; or simply absorbed with the enormous task of fomenting a world. But in the movement of Hugolian thought, there is a moment, a single moment in which this thought is shown naked, disencumbered of its creations, given over to itself. A frightful moment, for it then discovers itself in the void. And it is in this void, in this absence of any image or idea, that the thought of Hugo is made manifest to itself, such as at very bottom it is: no longer creator of images, no longer participator in a cosmic drama, but anxious, terrified thought, conscious of its powerlessness and of the enormity of the questions it asks itself.

No doubt the image of a Hugo "leaning over the crumbling edge of the bottomless problem," somewhere on the coast of Guernsey, or on "the promontory of thought," is marred for us by the final emphasis with which he retrospectively described himself in the pose of the "thinker." But the true Hugo is not this optimistic and sovereign being who "talks with God" and who is represented emblematically in his poem by Eagle, Griffon, Angel, or even Light. Far from that, he is simply the Owl, that doubter, bird of night, the scared creature who in the dark vouches for the immensity of the void and the misery of human thought:

> I am the formidable regarder of the pit;
> I am he who wishes to know why; I am
> The eye the tortured in the torture opens . . .
> This world is the abyss, and the abyss my cave.
> Mournful, I dream in the cavern-universe; and darkness
> Buffets my forehead with its great somber branches . . .
> I have for spectacle, in the depths of these haggard limbos,
> For aim of my mind, for goal of my regards,
> For meditation, for reason, for madness,
> The extraordinary crater of immense blackness;
> And I have become, having neither light nor sound,
> A kind of horrible vase of the night
> Which chimera and dream slowly fill up,
> Aspects of gloom, the shoreless depth,
> And, on the threshold of the void with its indistinct hollows,
> The rugged shuddering of dismal escarpments.

Neither Goya, nor Piranesi, nor De Quincey ever attained to such effects, the very effects which the most modern poetry seeks for. And what is more disconcerting is the fact that Hugo achieves them by the very reverse of his habitual procedure. For image here is simply image. It no longer creates a form. It no longer establishes an illusory reality. It is simply a pure symbol, and *the symbol of nothing*. Hugo attains to the highest poetry, not when he tries to fill his mental space with a forest of pseudo-real forms, but when he succeeds in expressing, by means of forms of which each in its turn acknowledges itself to be hollow and empty, the very reality of the void. Before Mallarmé, Hugo had discovered negative poetry.

A poetry whose descending spiral glides down into a gulf over the edge of which Hugo has for a long time been leaning:

> Reverie is a hollowing.
> (*Post-scriptum de ma vie*)

Vertiginous spirals of the mind returning upon itself, which make thought seem like a snake.

> (*Quatrevingt-treize*)

> Wells of India! tombs! constellated monuments!
> You whose interior offers to confused glances
> Only a turning mass of stairs and ramps . . .
> Chaoses of walls, of rooms, of landings,
> Where collapses at random a staircase-gulf! . . .
> Before your depths I have often grown pale
> As when looking down into an abyss or a furnace,
> Dreadful Babel that Piranesi dreamed! . . .
> —O dreams of granite! visionary caves! . . .
> You are less profound and hopeless
> Than fate, this den inhabited by our fears,
> Where the mind hears, lost in frightful labyrinths,
> The billows of days with a thousand dull sounds
> Fall to the dark depths of an unknown gulf!
> (*Les Rayons et les ombres*, 13)

Here again there is revealed in Hugo that poetry which is the inverse of his habitual poetry. For the *turning masses,* the *chaoses* of things were precisely the materials with which he expressly strove to erect the Babels of his positive poetry. But here we find ourselves in the presence of "Babels turned upside down" which plunge themselves into the subterranean world that leads, by degrees, and deeper and deeper, into a negative universe.

A universe over the edge of which one leans, but also perchance one slips off the edge. No theme had haunted Hugo more than that of the swallowing up, or of the fall:

> He had the sensation of someone who loses his footing.
> (*L'Homme qui rit*)

> It seemed to him . . . that he found himself slipping over an incline in the middle of the night, upright, shuddering, recoiling in vain from the extreme edge of an abyss.
> (*Les Misérables*)

To fall in the silence and the mist forever!
At first some brightness of luminous pinnacles
Lets you distinguish your desperate hands.
One falls, one sees pass frightened forms,
Mouths open, foreheads bathed in sweat,
Hideous faces that a glimmer lights up,
Then one sees nothing more.

                              ("La Vision de Dante")

One sees nothing more because there is nothing more to see. Hugo's
most tragic experience consists in this interior fall of thought in which one
feels oneself progressively removed from all that once was the object of
one's vision—images, figures, perceptible events, concrete things—in such a
way that nothing remains perceptible or thinkable except the selfsame place
in which the mind situated all that it saw and thought.

But this place is "the double sea of time and space." When the mind is
stripped of all concrete forms, when nothing remains, within it or around it,
of the universe of figures and movements which it distributed over the
expanse and the duration, that expanse and that duration continue nonetheless to remain in the mind, as the first and last forms of its intuition, but
an intuition which now can no longer be exercised upon anything else but
itself. It seems that in this supreme experience Hugo had attained to the
"dark underside" of thought, the place where one can, so to speak, see
function naked what Kant calls the a priori forms of human perception. He
saw running on no load the fundamental gearing of spiritual activity. A
terrifying experience, in which space is now no more than a yawning gulf,
and time nothing else than a continuous shipwreck.

The experience of space:

                        And when my eyes were reopened, I saw
The shadow; the hideous, unconscious, fathomless shadow,
Formidable vision of the invisible Nothing,
Without form, without contour, without floor, without ceiling,
Where into obscurity obscurity is melted;
No stairway, no bridge, no spiral, no ramp;
The blind shadow unlighted by any lamp;
The dark of the unknown, undisturbed by any wind;
The shadow, frightening veil of the specter eternity;
Who has not seen that has seen nothing of the terrible.
It is yawning space, impossible expanse,

> A thing of affright, confusion, and wreckage
> That flies through all the senses before the distracted eye.
>
> ("La Vision de Dante")

The experience of time:

> The abyss was being blotted out. Nothing had form.
> The gloom seemed to swell its enormous wave.
> It was something submerged, one knew not what;
> It was what is no more, the vanished and silent;
> And one could not have told, in this horror profound,
> If this frightening residue of a mystery or a world,
> Like the vague fog in which the dream escapes,
> Called itself shipwreck or called itself night . . .
> And the archangel knew, like a mast that founders,
> That he was the drowned of the deluge of the shadow.
>
> (*La Fin de Satan*)

This experience is agony. Pure time and space are what still subsist when nothing else subsists. But they are also what ceases to subsist because nothing else any longer subsists. It is what dies in the last place. Beyond there is nothing. There, one touches "the place where Everything is no longer": "One is in absence. One feels himself dying. One desires a star."

But as in the extraordinary poem of the "Titan," in which one sees the overwhelmed giant, in order to flee from the vengeance of the gods, plunge himself deeper and deeper into the earth and suddenly emerge under the open sky of the antipodes, it is in the depths of his spiritual agony that Hugo discovered his certitude and regained the optimistic energy that allowed him to begin again to create worlds. There is still a page that must be cited here; it is the passage in *L'Homme qui rit* in which one sees a hanging on a plain. And this sinister spectacle seems at first to engender in the mind the same descending and dissolving movement as everywhere else: "One felt around him as it were a diminution of life going into the depths." Everything is drained and obliterated in the consciousness of something boundless enveloping this central point of vision. But this boundlessness can no longer be conceived as something negative, as a space without forms and a time without events: "The boundless, limited by nothing, neither by a tree nor a roof-top, nor a passer-by, was around about this death. When the *immanence* hangs over us, sky, gulf, tomb, eternity appear *patent;* it is then that we feel the whole as inaccessible, immured. When the infinite opens, there is no closing more formidable." At the moment then when thought, having been stripped not only of all forms but even of the principle of those forms, finds itself in the presence of the total void, it is in this very negation that it suddenly finds an infinite presence and affirmation. It is then that in a kind of sacred horror one has the experience of a "Me-gulf," me, "into whom all the me's fall." Divine immanence is the immanence of a transcendence. It is at once something that opens and something that closes. It is that limitless plenitude which can only be perceived as a limitless gulf.

> The latent me of the patent infinite, that is God.
> God is the evident invisible.
>
> (*William Shakespeare*)

Thus at the depths of the interior void to which one attains by means of a sort of negative theology, in a feeling of inexpressible awe, of "horror of God," one arrives at an absolute evidence. Thought and the universe are in a gulf. But that gulf is God. Consequently all is saved. All is sustained: "The universe hangs, nothing falls."

Nothing falls except in God, toward God. There now remains only to imagine that procession of beings in the abyss, their gradations in spaces, their eternal progress in the divine. Including Satan himself, all creatures infinitely draw near to God across the spaces of the future.

JOHN PORTER HOUSTON

Hugo's Later Poetry

We have already seen the breadth of Victor Hugo's imagination in the early period of his verse. Between the poems written before 1840 and those first published during his exile from France it appears that he wrote less and less verse but extended his interest in occultism and religious philosophy. The peculiar strains of private vision that we remarked on [elsewhere] now swell to occupy the whole foreground of his poetry, and his range of vocabulary greatly increases. Finally, when he went into exile, Hugo ceased to be the court-poet figure we have commented on and began a unique poetic career as estranged prophet of God and of the conscience of his country. The late poems are shot through with meditations on God and evil, the fate of France, the nature of the universe and its ultimate destiny. Our principal concern will be with *Châtiments, La Fin de Satan, Dieu,* and *La Légende des siècles,* for these are the most characteristic works of Hugo's great burst of creative energy in the 1850s.

Since all these books are remarkable in their detail and dissimilar—and often weak—in overall structure, I propose to examine them in the following manner: first, general comments on each (with the exception of *La Légende*), especially with reference to style; then a summing up of high points of innovation in Hugo's later diction; next comes a further examination of *Châtiments, La Fin de Satan,* and *Dieu* as large-scale poetic schemes and Hugo's failure to sustain them. Finally, we must probe the reasons of sensibility which prevented Hugo from creating the theodicy he aspired to. We shall conclude with some observations on *La Légende des siècles.*

From *The Demonic Imagination: Style and Theme in French Romantic Poetry.* © 1969 by Louisiana State University Press.

Shortly after his exile, Hugo published his first volume of verse in over
ten years, and all of it recent. It consists of diatribes, lyrics, and prophetic
utterances against the government of Louis Napoleon, which had ostensibly
exiled him. Furthermore, *Châtiments* (1853) is unlike its earlier companion
works both in having a general theme and in being structured into a series
of separate but linked parts; before *Les Fleurs du mal,* Hugo thought of
arranging shorter poems into a large design. The first six sections have for
titles such Bonapartist political slogans as "La Société est sauvée," "L'Ordre
est rétabli," "La Stabilité est assurée," and contain an intermittent poetic
history of various aspects of the Coup d'Etat and the establishment of the
Second Empire. "L'Autorité est sacrée," the center of the work, deals with
Napoleon the First and the contrast between the two regimes. The seventh
and ironically titled concluding book, "Les Sauvers se sauveront," foresees,
in prohetic tones, the fall of Louis Napoleon. Thus *Châtiments* embodies an
imaginative pattern of history.

The opening sections are dominated by images of night and urban filth,
as Hugo scourges not only Louis Napoleon and his henchmen, but all
Frenchmen who passively accepted the Coup d'Etat. The following lines
concern the President of the Assembly, "colui che fece per viltà il gran
rifiuto," having abdicated his authority to the usurper:

> Si par hasard, la nuit, dans les carrefours mornes,
> Fouillant du croc l'ordure où dort plus d'un secret,
> Un chiffonnier trouvait cette âme au coin des bornes,
>   Il la dédaignerait!
>
>   (4.8)

Night is personified in an unusual image:

> Le jour parut. La nuit, complice des bandits,
> Prit la fuite, et, traînant à la hâte ses voiles,
> Dans les plis de sa robe emporta les étoiles
> Et les mille soleils dans l'ombre étincelant,
> Comme les sequins d'or qu'emporte en s'en allant
> Une fille, aux baisers du crime habituée,
> Qui se rhabille après s'être prostituée!
>
>   (1.5)

Dawn has apocalyptic associations and will mark the end of the Empire:

> Et le monde, éveillé par cette âpre fanfare,
> Est pareil

> Aux ivrognes de nuit qu'en se levant effare
> Le soleil.
>
> (7.15)

The spiritual low point of the work occurs perhaps in a description of the sewers of ancient Rome, but the theme of regeneration emerges at the end, where the Tree of Life becomes a major image:

> L'arbre saint du Progrès, autrefois chimérique
> Croîta, couvrant l'Europe et couvrant l'Amérique,
>   Sur le passé détruit.
> Et, laissant l'éther pur luire à travers ses branches,
> Le jour apparaîtra plein de colombes blanches,
>   Plein d'étoiles la nuit.
>
> Et nous qui serons morts, morts dans l'exil peut-être,
> Martyrs saignants, pendant que les hommes, sans maître,
>   Vivront, plus fiers, plus beaux,
> Sous ce grand arbre, amour des cieux qu'il avoisine,
> Nous nous réveillerons pour baiser sa racine,
>   Au fond de nos tombeaux.
>
> ("Lux," 5)

Châtiments is, clearly, a cyclic work in which night yields to dawn, urban ugliness to a vision of nature, decadence to rebirth. The thematic material is a variation on the return of the Golden Age and not basically very different from the pattern of certain *Chimères* [of Nerval].

Whatever we think of the success of this verse, it is obvious that Hugo is doing something quite new; the work is ordered around archetypal symbols of good and evil, and its meaning transcends that of any single piece of verse in the volume. Despite many references to Second Empire notables, *Châtiments* tends to break loose from its historical context and, like biblical poetry, to strive toward the condition of prophetic myth. Although the work was hastily written and thus stylistically uneven, it is clear that, with it, Hugo was moving in a new poetic direction.

If *Châtiments* is remarkable, the posthumous *Fin de Satan* (written 1854, 1859–60), is even more so; in it Hugo tried to cope with the Christian concept of evil. The book is one of those odd nineteenth-century works, like *Faust* or *La Tentation de Saint Antoine*, whose form seems to owe a good deal to the idea of drama, without really achieving theatrical viability. Rather than the traditional sequence of epic books, it consists of an alternance between Satan's scenes, whose rubric is "Hors de la Terre," and earthly

ones; both shift between narrative and dialogue or soliloquy. We are struck
equally by the particular terrestrial episodes in which Hugo depicts the
moral history of man, and by his Satan, whose eloquence and theological
capacities match the gifts of Milton's Prince of Darkness. Hugo's selection
of episodes is curious, especially if we compare it with Milton's orthodoxy:
he depicts Satan's plummeting into hell, Nimrod's attack on heaven (a tale derived from the medieval Persian poet Firdausi), Christ crucified, and Satan's
change from an absolute devil to a fallen angel susceptible of redemption.

   The crux of this poem lies in "Hors de la Terre" 3, a lengthy monologue in which Satan, after expressing his ambivalent feelings toward God and
creation, makes the discovery that he loves God. The greatest poetic difficulties are involved here: Satan's emotions must have some analogy to human
ones, while, at the same time, he can be rendered neither as an insignificant
inferior spirit nor as the hero of a stoic tragedy, in the manner of Milton; Hugo
had to avoid motive and psychology in his presentation of Satan in order to
make of him the expression of the universe's longing to be reintegrated into
godhead. Hugo solved this problem by making Satan experience not pride,
but spite, and suffer not Miltonic fires, which burn without scathing, but the
absence of repose. The underlying theme of "Hors de la Terre" 3 is Satan's
constant awareness and painful vigil, his incapacity for sleep:

>   Encor si je pouvais dormir!
>
>   Si seulement
>   Une heure, une minute, un soupir, un moment,
>   Le temps qu'une onde passe au fond du lac sonore,
>   Fût-ce pour m'éveiller plus lamentable encore,
>   Sur n'importe quels durs et funèbres chevets,
>   Si je pouvais poser mon front! si je pouvais,
>   Nu, sur un bloc de bronze ou sur un tas de pierres,
>   L'une de l'autre, hélas! rapprocher mes paupières,
>   Et m'étendre, et sentir quelque chose de frais,
>   De doux et de serein, comme si je mourais!
>   Si je pouvais me perdre un moment dans un songe,
>   Apaiser dans mon flanc ce qui remue et ronge,
>   Aspirer un fluide étrange, aérien,
>   Impalpable, et flotter, et n'entendre plus rien,
>   Ni mon aile frémir, ni battre mon artère,
>   Ni ces cris dont je suis la cause sur la terre.
>   ("Hors de la Terre" 3.9)

The marvelous richness of Hugo's syntax and rhythms is evident here: the periodic sentence form is not in the least imprisoned by the alexandrine couplet, while its grammatical elaboration can equal any long passage in French verse. The last line of the quotation suggests another extraordinary aspect of the "Hors de la Terre" sections in *La Fin de Satan:* faced with representing hell after Virgil, Dante, and Milton, Hugo chose to represent it, not as a subterranean compartment with its own geography and inhabitants, but as sheer solitary darkness and emptiness, peopled only by Satan's own sensations, his insomnia, his all-seeing, and the sounds that continuously reach him. In short, Satan is no longer Milton's earth-wanderer seeking mischief to work, but the nadir of the world-soul:

> Je suis sous cette voûte,
> Je regarde l'horreur profonde, et je l'écoute.
> Pas un être ne peut souffrir sans que j'en sois.
> Je suis l'affreux milieu des douleurs. Je perçois
> Chaque pulsation de la fièvre du monde.
> Mon ouïe est le centre où se répète et gronde
> Tout le bruit ténébreux dans l'étendue épars;
> J'entends l'ombre. O tourment! le mal de toutes parts
> M'apporte en mon cachot sa triste joie aiguë;
> J'entends glisser l'aspic et croître la ciguë;
> Le mal pèse sur moi du zénith au nadir;
> La mer a beau hurler, l'avalanche bondir,
> L'orage entre-heurter les foudres qu'il secoue,
> L'éclatant zodiaque a beau tourner sa roue
> De constellations, sombre meule des cieux,
> A travers le fracas vaste et prodigieux
> Des astres dont parfois le groupe énorme penche,
> A travers l'océan, la foudre et l'avalanche
> Roulant du haut des monts parmi les sapins verts,
> J'entends le pas d'un crime au bout de l'univers.
>
> ("Hors de la Terre" 3.9)

The spatial imagery is especially remarkable in this passage. Satan occupies the earth's core, and, by analogy with the principle of gravity, the geocentric universe presses on him with the weight of its evil. (The equating of weight with evil is not, for Hugo, merely a constant metaphor but a real theological concept.) Once Satan's position as the object of all gravity is established, Hugo then evokes the surface of the earth (asp, hemlock, and ocean) and finally the spectacle of the night sky, pushing Satan's perceptions farther and farther out from a center. Circles and circular movement dominate (zenith, wheel, sliding stars, rolling avalanche), for Hugo is trying to convey the feeling that concentric rings of matter spin about the fixed point that is Satan. The sky he paints is therefore not serene but full of portentous objects and savage motion. As is so often the case, Hugo's spatial imagination strikes us as far more complex than that of most poets; he envisions not merely a flat earth domed with sky, but huge cosmological configurations— something especially rare in an age which had not yet known the experience of airplanes, much less of spacecraft.

Just as Hugo used a sophisticated cosmology in which there is no fixed point where heaven is located, he correspondingly abandoned the traditional myth in which Satan is King of the Damned and God is that of the Angels and the Elect. All the trappings of the divine and demonic kingdoms are eliminated, which permits Hugo to face squarely what was for him the essential problem of Christian theology: How can Satan endure eternally "cast into the lake of fire and brimstone . . . for ever and ever," as St. John affirms (20:10)? Such a doctrine denies, above all, God's omnipotence:

> Oui, c'est l'énigme, ô nuit, de tes millions d'yeux :
> Le grand souffrant fait face au grand mystérieux.
> Grâce, ô Dieu! Pour toi-même il faut que je l'obtienne.
> Ma perpétuité fait ombre sur la tienne.
> Devant ton oeil flambeau rien ne doit demeurer,
> Tout doit changer, viellir et se transfigurer.
> Toi seul es. Devant toi tout doit avoir un âge.
> Et c'est pour ta splendeur un importun nuage
> Qu'on voie un spectre assis au fond de ton ciel bleu,
> Et l'éternel Satan devant l'éternel Dieu!
>
> ("Hors de la Terre" 3.6)

This argument is the crux of *La Fin de Satan:* Can evil be eternal? Satan finally wills his own redemption and, as Lucifer, is rejoined with God. The problem of dualism, which, as we have seen, haunted Baudelaire, was likewise fundamental to Hugo's imagination, but he tried to overcome this obsessive vision by creating the myth of Satan's reunion with godhead, which, in turn, is symbolic of mankind and the universe's absorption into divinity.

Dieu is a further attempt to order Hugo's thoughts on good and evil, but this time patterned after biblical prophecy rather than epic or drama. The opening vision of a strange creature from which voices emerge owes something to Ezekiel, while scriptural reminiscences are not infrequent. "Les Voix" is a remarkable series of poetic fragments; they express in bitter, somber, or ironical tones the remoteness or absence of God, Job being the obvious prototype. Frequently they are constructed around a striking image:

> Quelle pensée as-tu d'allumer ton esprit
> Au bord du noir problème où la ràison périt?
> Pourquoi ne pas laisser les grandes ailes d'ombre,
> Songeur, so déployer sur cet univers sombre?
> Pourquoi vouloir leurrer d'un feu follet qui fuit
> L'antique Adam, errant dans l'insondable nuit?
>
> . . . .
>
> La blanche aurore est morte, et l'homme est dans la nuit.
> Il lui restait encor, dans le temple où Dieu luit,
> L'effrayant chandelier dont la flamme constante
> Pendant qu'ils écrivaient, éclaira les Septante;
> Mais il n'a même plus ce foyer du vrai jour;
> Les sept vices de l'homme ont, chacun à leur tour,
> Eteint un des flambeaux de la lampe à sept branches;
> Maintenant c'est fini. L'abîme où tu te penches,
> L'obscurité lugubre aux vagues épaisseurs,
> Le firmament formé de toutes les noirceurs,
> Cet océan de nuit où l'esprit flotte et sombre,
> Rit de te voir risquer ta lanterne en cette ombre
> Où dans la main de Dieu s'est éteint le soleil.
>
> (Quinzième fragment)

We have seen precedents for this somber deity, whose hand is the world's prison and whose dead sun sheds night. The importance of "Les Voix," however, lies not in any dialectic of theology, but in its stylistic brilliance; unordered and incomplete as it is, the density and inventiveness of the language is compelling. In the passage quoted above, metaphor and comparison in the traditional sense have vanished, to be replaced by the literalness of mythopoeia. Hugo does not attempt to create an imaginary scene based on the ordinary elements of vision and enriched by metaphor; instead, all the images must be taken at face value. The "wings of shadow" are not part of an analogy between night and a bird; they are the sinister living presence of darkness. In the same way, the "ocean of night" which "laughs" is a truly mythic conception. Furthermore, the chaotic spatial relations must be understood literally: underlying the whole passage is an inverted cosmology in which the reaches of heaven are replaced by an abyss; up and down have become interchangeable.

"Ascension dans les Ténèbres," the second part of *Dieu*, consists of a series of visions, based on a biblical pattern. The poet first contemplates a symbolic object (cf. the beginning of Amos), which then utters prophecy or dogma. The objects belong largely to the romantic bestiary: a bat, an owl, a raven, a vulture, an eagle, a griffon, an angel, and Light personified. These correspond, furthermore, to stages (pseudo-logical or historical) in the development of religion: atheism is followed by skepticism, dualism, polytheism, Judaism, Christianity, and nineteenth-century occultism, in that order.

The language of certain passages demonstrates perhaps a greater audacity of metaphor than any other work of Hugo's. In "La Chauve-souris" a fantastic, evil spring is compared to a wet-dream, an analogy hardly to be expected in a nineteenth-century poet:

> Le printemps, le soleil, les bêtes en chaleur,
> Sont une chimérique et monstrueuse fleur;
> A travers son sommeil ce monde effaré souffre;
> Avril n'est que le rêve érotique du gouffre,
> Une pollution nocturne de ruisseaux,
> De rameaux, de parfums, d'aube et de chants d'oiseaux.
> L'horreur seule survit, par tout continuée.
> Et, par moments, un vent qui sort de la nuée
> Dessine des contours, des rayons et des yeux
> Dans ce noir tourbillon d'atomes furieux.

Discreet reference is made to the atheist Lucretius's doctrine of atoms, which is presented as a pattern of ceaseless, infernal movement. It is not farfetched to see in Hugo's evocation of spring the demonic version of the Latin poet's invocation to Venus Genitrix, for a passage in his critical writings shows how sinister Hugo felt *De Rerum Natura* to be. The ancient theory of atomic motion becomes, in "La Chauve-souris," an image of idle swirling, and this is accompanied by a demonic vision of the Great Chain of Being:

> Les cailloux sont broyés par la bête de somme,
> L'âne paît le chardon, l'homme dévore l'homme,
> L'agneau broute la fleur, le loup broute l'agneau.
> Sombre chaîne éternelle où l'anneau mord l'anneau!

The chain does not lead upward but becomes a closed circle—the infernal counterpart to the perfect circle which traditionally symbolizes godhead.

"La Chauve-souris," which has as its theme the inexistence of God, is dominated by images of destruction, dissolution of appearances, and nothingness. In the following section, "Le Hibou," the theme changes to doubt and fear about the nature of God, and here the very meaning of the universe is questioned. "Le Hibou" contains some of the most splendid mythopoeic verse in French: poetry in which the animate and inanimate are one, in which landscape is penetrated with life. The following lines offer a fine example:

> On a peur quand l'aube qui s'éveille
> Fait une plaie au bas des cieux, rouge et vermeille;
> On a peur quand la bise épand son long frisson;
> On a peur quand on voit, vague, à fleur d'horizon,
> Montrant, dans l'étendue au crépuscule ouverte,
> Ramper le scarabée effroyable du soir;
> On a peur quand minuit sur les monts vient s'asseoir!

Here the cosmos is not a flickering illusion as in "La Chauve-souris," but a dreadful manifestation of life and will. The sequence of images is especially masterful: the "wound" inflicted by dawn complements the personification of midnight later on; dawn and night, like the breeze, are impalpable but shifting and present. On the other hand, the most developed image, that of the beetle, has a horrifying concreteness; Hugo was one of the first of those modern writers such as Dostoyevski or Sartre to feel that insects represent life in its most inhuman and repellent form. Of the highly organized creatures they seem the most blindly and most mechanically intent on survival, and blown-up representations of them thus occupy so large a place in the sinister iconography of recent art and literature. In these lines the scarab symbolizes the huge, destructive powers of sundown.

As we progress to the later sections of "Ascension dans les Ténèbres," and as Hugo speaks of established religious doctrines, his language changes in character: rather than the awesome visions of "La Chauve-souris" and "Le Hibou," he gives us odd, complicated metaphors in which the attempt to poetize theology is apparent:

> C'est le vivant, le vaste épanoui!
> Ce que contemple au loin le soleil ébloui,
> C'est lui. Les cieux, vous, nous, les étoiles, poussière!
> Il est l'oeil gouffre, ouvert au fond la lumière,
> Vu par tous les flambeaux, senti par tous les nids,
> D'ou l'univers jaillit en rayons infinis.

Il regarde, et c'est tout. Voir suffit au sublime.
Il crée un monde rien qu'en voyant un abîme.
Et cet être qui voit, ayant toujours été,
A toujours tout créé de toute éternité.

("La Lumière")

Hugo construes godhead as a cone reaching upward to an eternal eye, from which creation radiates along the Great Chain of Being. The metaphor is the old one of God as light, supported by the occultist theory of the universe as emanation. This, however, is a *schema*, a rhetorical figure, for we know that not even for Hugo was God literally an eye. In short, *Dieu* concludes with demonstrations of godhead rather than intuitions of deity, unlike the earlier sections.

In our cursory examination of passages from *La Fin de Satan* and *Dieu* we have seen gorgeous elaborations on a number of themes, but it remains now to attempt a summary of Hugo's later stylistic practices, a discussion of his notions about language, and, finally, a comparison of Hugo's poetic style with others we have been considering [elsewhere].

Certain tendencies in Hugo's later style can readily be seen in the examples of it we have quoted. With the exception of the passage on insomnia from "Satan dans la nuit," all are characterized by parataxis, by the juxtaposition of relatively simple sentence structures. At most an occasional relative clause relieves their syntactic identity. (Differences in length and rhythm, however, compensate for grammatical sameness.) Although adjectives and participles abound, it would be difficult to call this style phrasal in the same way as Vigny's or Baudelaire's: it breaks with the rhetorical principle that verse-paragraphs, like prose, need the variety created by frequent subordination. While short relative clauses are common enough in his late style, Hugo's peculiar and characteristic grammatical device is to build up his sentences by reduplication of subject or object and by apposition, in short, to create a primarily nominal syntax. One is especially struck by the scarceness of adverbial clauses, which express logical and temporal relationships, as they do in certain *Chimères*. Instead we find abundant examples of identification and parallel action, the patterns of meaning most associated with parataxis and enumeration of nouns. An especially good example of the lengths to which Hugo would go in lengthening an otherwise simple sentence by mere accumulation of nouns occurs in "Les Voix":

L'espace, ici flot vague et là cratère ardent,
Le grand fond immobile et sourd, la violence
Des visions mêlées à l'éternel silence,

Rien et Tout, le roulis gigantesque des cieux
Dans on ne sait quel vent lugubre et monstrueux,
Des tours d'ombre dont l'oeil ne peut compter les marches,
Des déluges roulant d'inexprimables arches,
La pluie immense au loin rayant les infinis,
Des lueurs blanchissant des masques d'Erynnis,
Des passages subits de méduses, frappées
D'une clarté pareille à des reflets d'épées,
Des ponts difformes, noirs, allants hors du réel,
Sinistres, bleuissant vaguement près du ciel,
L'ascension sans but et la chute sans bornes;
Voilà ce que voyaient ces contemplateurs mornes.

("Les Voix," Cinquième fragment)

The range of verbal resources is remarkable, both in the way of individual words and their combinations: there are proper nouns (*Erynnis*), concrete ones frequently coupled with blurring modifiers (*tours d'ombre dont l'oeil ne peut compter les marches*), semi-abstract nouns (*fond immobile*), and completely abstract ones (*Rien et Tout*). Above all, Hugo uses verbal nouns (*roulis, passages, chute, ascension*) along with present participles to suggest hazy forms of motion, bare outlines of the immaterial. This preference for verbal nouns and participles, with their sometimes peculiar inchoative or frequentative aspects (*bleuissant, passages*) is a stylistic trouvaille which was to be a mannerism in later poets and prose writers, but in Hugo it serves the special function of creating a dense fusion of impressions. Image adjoins image with no connective words of sequence or relation.

Frequently, Hugo resorts to two other devices in order to confront nouns with one another. One is a radically antithetical use of the copula and predicate nominative: "la fange est cristal" (*Dieu*, "La Lumière"). Expressions like this one are not simply ultra-concise analogies like "Vous êtes un beau ciel d'automne . . ." (Baudelaire, "Causerie"), but have a metaphysical, incantatory character. "Mire is crystal" attempts to make a philosophical assertion or prophecy. Hugo's other idiosyncratic handling of nouns lies on the extreme confines of French syntax. He often yoked two nouns together as a single unit: the "oeil gouffre" in the passage quoted from "La Lumière" is an example, and a particularly good one, since eyes and depths have similar and dissimilar connotations. Elsewhere we find more normally affective linkings, such as "la fosse silence," but, in any case, this construction rarely occurs in ordinary French except for commercial expressions like *fermeture éclair*. It is significant that Hugo, whose grammar is on the whole conservative, should depart so much from normal usage. This device confirms the implications to be drawn from his fondness for the predicate nominative: Hugo's deepest tendency is toward a syntax of nouns, the magic, naming part of speech.

Hugo's feelings about language were rarely set down, yet, with the few indications of them we have, it seems safe to say that after 1850 he moved beyond his fellow romantics into an evocative theory of language which anticipates that of certain symbolists. The *verbe,* which is St. John's *logos* in French, is seen as an entity, above and beyond the reality of things in a poem from *Les Contemplations,* "Suite." A further curious text about words, which was published only posthumously, maintains that letters have implicit connotations of color and emotion—all this long before the corresponding affirmations of Rimbaud and Mallarmé. Like these poets, Hugo seems to have arrived at the idea that words, *logoi,* generate a transcendent world, superior to the normal one we flounder in. However extreme the theory may be as a general view of language, it still commands respect because of the great poetry which was written in conjunction with it. And, as a matter of fact, when we examine certain manipulations of words in Hugo's later verse, it becomes clear that this theory of language is not divorced from certain semantic effects.

The peculiar relationships which Hugo establishes among substantives invite some analysis of his use of specific words. The words which most obviously take on new values in Hugo's later verse are those which are primarily visual in sense. The largest number of them refer to darkness or the abyss: *abîme, gouffre, obscurité, sombre, ombre,* and *noir.* It is not just in overtly visionary poems like *Dieu* that those words obtrude; they are the constants of Hugo's imagination. In his earlier poetry they retain their customary connotations and use and are contrasted with light imagery in the tradition of Dante and Milton. However, *Dieu* and *La Légende des siècles* present us with a new and peculiar handling of the imagery of darkness: it is constantly used in a figurative way which defies visualization. A character in the *Légende* is called "ce noir rêveur," although he has a "front de neige" ("Le Comte Félibien"). In *Dieu,* which contains numerous visions of the world as godless or governed by an evil god, Hugo creates an arsenal of ambiguous symbols suggesting at once the divine and the demonic. "Sombre azur" is an example of this; it occurs in a passage which describes the destruction of him who seeks God:

> Aveugle de trop voir et sourd de trop entendre,
> Dans l'éblouissement du ciel toujours plus blanc,

Effaré, désormais plus emporté qu'allant,
Ivre de tout ce sombre azur qui le pénètre,
Sentant l'écrasement de l'abîme sous l'être,
Respirant mal l'air vierge et fatal du zénith,
Il avance, et blanchit, et s'efface; et finit
Par se dissoudre, avec son doute ou sa prière,
Dans une énormité de foudre et de lumière.

                              ("Les Voix," Sixième fragment)

These lines are a remarkable demonstration of spatial imagery and demonic symbolism in Hugo's later poetry: the godseeker ascends toward godhead as in traditional cosmology, but sound and sight create a feeling of pressure rather than one of weightlessness—heaven is chaos rather than illumination, despite the white light—and, later, the air "penetrates" him with its deadly weight. All this could symbolize a trial, were it not for the seeker's being sucked up (*emporté*), without so willing, into the *sombre azur*. This oxymoron either expresses the sinister quality of the inviting blue sky or else represents a sudden darkening of it in its threatening upper regions. We are confronted with a problem of the metaphoric or literal value of a word; one suspects here that in this kind of phantasmagoria of language Hugo hardly distinguished the two. "L'écrasement de l'abîme sous l'être" has contradictory implications: an "abyss" beneath one cannot "crush"; however, right from the beginning of *Dieu,* the poet speaks of an abyss stretching upward, a demonic vision of the sky. If *l'être* designates here, as it does elsewhere in *Dieu,* all visible creation, the line would seem to contain a paradox about up and down, lightness and weight. Finally, the bright light which traditionally symbolizes godhead is presented in a demonic modality: it becomes destructive lightning, and union with God is equated with death. Sinister white light thus becomes a symbolic equivalent to Hugo's "affreux soleil noir d'où rayonne la nuit" (*Les Contemplations,* "Ce que dit la bouche d'ombre").

Hugo's abundant use of substantives assures a richness of visual detail, but when they are coupled in such expressions as *azur noir* we cannot compare this poetry to the physical act of seeing. Indeed, if poetry wishes to be an act of creation totally divorced from mimesis, it should not allow comparison with the experience of the senses; one *sees* the world about one, but the visions of poetry are seen only in a metaphorical sense. Thus Hugo's visionary poems are paradoxically unsusceptible of complete visualization. His poetry escapes plastic definition; the images conflict with one another, vanish, or are blurred by abstract words and adjectives:

Le fantôme géant se répandit en voix
Qui sous ses flancs confus murmuraient à la fois,
Et, comme d'un brasier tombent des étincelles,
Comme on voit des oiseaux épars, pigeons, sarcelles,
D'un grand essaim passant s'écarter quelquefois,
Comme un vert tourbillon de feuilles sort d'un bois,
Comme, dans les hauteurs par les vents remuées,
En avant d'un orage il vole des nuées,
Toutes ces voix, mêlant le cri, l'appel, le chant,
De l'immense être informe et noir se détachant,
Me montrant vaguement des masques et des bouches,
Vinrent sur moi bruire avec des bruits farouches,
Parfois en même temps et souvent tour à tour,
Comme des monts, à l'heure où se lève le jour,
L'un après l'autre, au fond de l'horizon s'éclairent.
Et des formes, sortant du monstre, me parlèrent.

(*Dieu*, "L'Esprit humain")

The five similes attempt to give outline to the apparition, but adjectives like *informe* and *confus* dispel their effect. The voices which emanate from the phantom are of uncertain materiality; they appear *vaguement*. Finally, they are called *formes*, a word which implies visibility without describing. The poet is glimpsing something, but the object will not remain still long enough to be really contemplated. It continually recedes into the blackness, which, as the typical background of Hugo's visionary poetry, always defeats the attempt to see. As Georges Poulet puts it:

Such is . . . the Hugolian universe. The mass of forms which constitutes it does not stop the glance like a curtain. The eye, uneasy at what lies beyond, can pierce the labyrinth of things in all directions. There is always, farther than what one sees, something that one glimpses, and, beyond what one glimpses, there are still holes where there is nothing more, it seems, openings onto emptiness, where one's glance loses itself.

(*La Distance intérieure*)

Thus Hugo's poetry turns away from the ordinary realities of sight to erect a flickering, crepuscular vision, which tantalizes because one cannot quite seize it. It plays with one's sense of the visual by offering dense and massive imagery, but always cheats the eye in the end.

At the same time, however, we should qualify Poulet's very evocative description of Hugo's visionary cosmos. Against the dark background and amidst the flickering images we can distinguish certain recurrent geometrical forms: the circle, point of irradiation of light or gravity, cone of vision, and closed-in space. There is a continual conflict between chaos and pattern. Often these geometric designs break down into architectural elements, among which towers, walls, and arches are frequent. A keen sense of line seems to be dictating these images projected onto nothingness. Furthermore, the feeling of position in space is curious and original in Hugo's visionary poems: the angle of vision ranges from looking up from a low central point to the dizzying glance from on high of *survol.* The relativity of spatial relations is acutely rendered in this poetry, and one feels in it a more real conception of the cosmos than in Dante or Milton, whose pictures of hell and heaven are essentially, if not theoretically, derived from a flat, layered picture of the universe. At the same time, Hugo is not a poet whose vision is earth grounded, like that of Baudelaire or other contemporaries; his imagination soars, veers, plunges, but never confines itself to simple geocentric notions of up and down, high and low. Hugo's capacities for visualizing are, in short, totally exceptional insofar as he invented a personal morphology of the cosmos which symbolizes his conceptions of good and evil.

When we compare the style of *La Fin de Satan* and *Dieu* to that of *Les Chimères, Les Fleurs du mal,* or *Les Destinées,* the most essential difference seems to be that the authors of the latter works were stanzaic poets, while Hugo was not. By this I do not mean that Hugo never wrote stanzas, far from it, but that the characteristic verse forms of Nerval, Baudelaire, and Vigny, unlike those of Hugo, imply a great concern with regular metric units: Nerval's sonnet, Vigny's *septain,* and Baudelaire's great gamut of *quintils,* refrains, and false sonnets demand a kind of prosodic thought which is foreign to Hugo's inspiration. The comparison with Baudelaire is especially instructive, since he and Hugo were the most abundantly gifted of the French romantic poets. Baudelaire loved the sonnet in all its possible variations, while Hugo wrote but three of them, and those late in life; Baudelaire most often used quatrains, constructed so as to make of them distinct metaphoric structures, whereas Hugo's stanzas, varied as they are, show no signs of any aesthetic peculiar to them. Finally, after 1830 Hugo generally ignored important stanzaic discoveries of the nineteenth century, such as terza rima and other old or exotic forms: none of his great poems are so metrically unusual as Baudelaire's "Harmonie du soir" or "Litanies de Satan." The conclusion seems to be that, while Hugo was the greatest innovator in displacing accents in the alexandrine line, his prosodic imagination was otherwise conservative.

Where Hugo's style was quite unconservative is in the domain of analogy and vocabulary. There are, of course, certain Hugolian mannerisms—such as the abundant use of words like *ombre, sombre,* and *abîme*—which anyone can recognize and which make it easy to parody his later style. However, the range of analogy of which Hugo was capable thoroughly surpasses that of any other French romantic poet. It frequently happens that a passage in which Hugo's habitual vocabulary dominates is made memorable by some rare expression or image; the following lines from *Dieu,* which contain a pantheist's diatribe against medieval theology, demonstrate this:

> Jette de la logique à sa grève déserte,
> Mais sans finir par donc ni commencer par certe.
> L'ombre est un grand hymen, l'abîme est un grand lit;
> L'Etre emplit l'étendue et l'emplit et l'emplit;
> . . . .
> L'air frémit, l'arbre croît, l'oiseau chante, l'eau fuit,
> Et des lumières vont jusqu'au fond de la nuit;
> L'illusion serait étange, que t'en semble,
> De voir dans ce splendide et redoutable ensemble,
> Dans ce flot de la vie et dans ce noir torrent,
> Un docteur de Sorbonne énorme pérorant.
>
> ("Les Voix," Vingt-deuxième fragment)

The nature imagery is not very interesting in terms of vocabulary, except perhaps for the rather erotic connotations of the concrete bed; otherwise Hugo reiterates, without any great freshness, such constants of his imagination as the word *être,* taken in the rather vague sense of godhead and substance, and the spatial conception of light radiating. But what makes the passage extraordinary is the completely original image of God as a medieval professor and the attendant use of *donc* and *certe.* Balancing Hugo's almost ritual use of *hymen, flot, abîme,* is a kind of inventive power which no other French romantic had except Baudelaire, and he, because his production was small, devised only in a limited number of cases such unusual comparisons.

Sometimes Hugo draws marvelous effects from a relatively ordinary word, placed in a peculiar context. Such is the case of *l'être* in the following lines:

> Le fond de l'être est clos par un nuage obscur,
> Traversé de lueurs, aux prodiges semblable,
> Voile de l'insondable et de l'incalculable,

Sans limite, sans fin, sans contour, sans milieu;
C'est ce nuage noir que l'homme appelle Dieu.
("Les Voix," Neuvième fragment)

As we have seen, *l'être* is a frequent and vague term in Hugo's later poetry; its very imprecision gives it remarkable auras of connotation. While sometimes, as in an earlier quoted passage, *l'être* seems to be identifiable with divine presence, here is designates creation. (This ambiguity stems from the usage of articles in French and might be compared with the English expressions "Supreme Being" and "Being," the latter indicating quite a variety of concepts.) The notion of matter being closed off at one end, as expressed in the above lines, is an extraordinary variant of the image we have in Vigny and Baudelaire of the world as prison cell or box, but here the contours of the cell are dimmed, and the universe takes on the amorphous shape of a container with a blurred center of focus. Nothing in the way of vocabulary is particularly arresting here, but the spatial concept created is eerie.

If Hugo's late visionary style has no analogue in the works of other French romantics, they share with him an essential concern for religious philosophy; none of the French romantic poets seems to have been without a private theology, and the interlocking theme of their verse is the existence and nature of God, as well as the problem of the very notion of godhead in a post-Christian world.

We have already alluded to Hugo's professed occultist ideas—they closely resemble the philosophy expressed in the *Aeneid,* book 6, which is the locus classicus of esoteric belief: along the Great Chain of Being souls are gradually rising, through metempsychosis, toward an eventual reunion with godhead. Christianity's seemingly eternal hell is rejected as a denial of God's omnipotence and perfection, for Hugo espouses the cabalistic notion that creation is a flaw in God, an area from which his omnipresence receded. Briefly, Hugo's theology rejects dualism in favor of the idea of a cycle: creation begins with necessary imperfection, for it is not part of godhead, but eventually will lose its materiality and be reintegrated into deity.

There are perhaps practical reasons why this philosophy should be difficult to represent in an epic or dramatic poem, but we need not explore them, since any great poet might at any time show that our preconceived notions of suitability of subject are purely theoretical. The fact remains, however, that Hugo finished neither *Dieu* nor *La Fin de Satan,* which seems to indicate some conflict between his poetic capacities and his avowed beliefs. I have already tried to show the stylistic magnificence evident in large portions of these poems; now, it seems to me, with some closer analysis of the shape and theme of each poem, we may be able to determine the imaginative check which prevented either from being completed.

The opening of *La Fin de Satan* is a selective reworking of themes from Genesis, legend, and paleontology: the fable of Lucifer precedes the creation of a universe of monsters, the world of the pre-adamites, which, in turn, is covered by the Flood. (Hugo's narrative style here is less effective than elsewhere.) The Adam and Eve myth is omitted, but Cain is alluded to at the point where Isis saves the three instruments of his crime: a nail, a stick, and a stone. These three provide the origins for the episodes of Nimrod and his sword, the Cross, and the Prison. Hugo evidently wishes to represent the world as beginning in pure evil, not in Eden. The first episode is thus that of Nimrod, who constructs a flying machine in order to wage war on God. Up to this point, the poem seems rather static in theme; there is little variation in the uniform mood of despair and horror.

The second "Hors de la Terre" section announces the birth, from a feather of the fallen Lucifer, of the Angel Liberty. The allegory appears to have been suggested by Vigny and seems to belong to another poetic order than what precedes and follows, for as we shall see, there is an odd mixture of conventions in *La Fin de Satan*. This second interlude has no bearing on what follows, which is an account of the Crucifixion. "Le Gibet" is Hugo's equivalent of the demonic gospel we have encountered in Vigny, Baudelaire, and Nerval. Yet the sinister implication in Hugo's poem is not that God is absent, but that the Passion and Christ are meaningless; for Hugo, Christ is merely a noble man victimized by judicial murder: the fact that Christ's death was necessary, according to orthodox theology, does not occur to him, since he did not believe in salvation through Christ or in the importance of the Resurrection. As a result, the whole episode takes on a lurid color, quite absent from the Gospel, where the story of Jesus ends on a serene, Paschal note. Hugo sees the Crucifixion purely in physical, human terms as a kind of ancient version of the horrors of the Inquisition. The almost bombastic tone of the style is suggested by the following passage in which Barabbas contemplates the Cross:

> Tout en marchant, il heurte un obstacle; il le touche.
> —Quel est cet arbre? où donc suis-je? dit Barabbas.
> Le long de l'arbre obscur il lève ses deux bras
> Si longtemps enchaînés qu'il les dresse avec peine.
> —Cet arbre est un poteau, dit-il. Il y promène
> Ses doigts par la torture atroce estropiés;
> Et tout à coup, hagard, pâle, il tâte des pieds,

Comme un hibou surpris rentre sous la feuillée,
Il retire sa main; elle est toute mouillée.
Ces pieds sont froids, un clou les traverse, et de sang
Et de fange et de fiel tout le bois est glissant.
Barabbas éperdu recule; son oeil s'ouvre,
Et, par degrés, un blême et noir linéament
S'ébauche à son regard sous l'obscur firmament;
C'est une croix.

("Le Gibet," 21)

While "Le Gibet" is not, by and large, one of the best composed or subtly written parts of *La Fin de Satan*, it tells us a good deal about Hugo's religious sensibility: he could no more understand Christ as a redeemer than he could accept the Pope as Christ's Vicar. The metaphysical superstructures of orthodoxy had no immediacy for him; Hugo had to feel the forces of good and evil more directly, in concrete examples of suffering and joy.

The long third "Hors de la Terre" section I have already quoted from; in it Hugo is free from the requirements of narration and can indulge in rich cascades of imagery as Satan surveys his attitudes toward God and the world. This is the true turning point of the poem, and it would perhaps have been better if Hugo had omitted all the terrestrial episodes to focus on Satan; he might have, working on the plane of pure myth, written a very eloquent poem based on his occultist philosophy. But unfortunately Hugo did not feel his Satan was an adequate exponent of the balance of Good and Evil; he introduced the Angel Liberty and Lilith (previously Isis in the poem) to struggle over him. Liberty wins and here Hugo faced a problem which he never solved: how, once Liberty has rescued Satan, can the final reconciliation with God be represented.

Other epic poets have managed to depict man's regeneration under God or the approach of a Golden Age in various ways. For example, through Anchises' prophecy in the *Aeneid*, book 6, Virgil convincingly suggested that, with the Pax Romana, his contemporaries stood at the threshold of a great era. Such prophecies are more commonly conveyed, however, in symbolic terms: Shelley, at the end of *Prometheus Unbound*, and the biblical apocalyptist both suggest an end to man's tribulations. Hugo chose, on the other hand, to balance the Crucifixion by mankind's redemption during the French Revolution, an event neither situated in the future nor in the mythic past. Here one's sense of recent history will allow no suspension of disbelief; nor did it for Hugo, since he never wrote more than a few lines of the episode. This inability or unwillingness to finish "La Prison" suggests one observation; it seems impossible to confer mythic dimensions on recent events, unless it is demonic myth which is being created, for decline and fall are more readily imagined than regeneration. (In regard to the unfinished French Revolution episode in *La Fin de Satan,* it might do to recall the thematic structure of *Châtiments:* there Louis Napoleon's Coup d'Etat is treated as God's punishment visited on Napoleon the First for his own arrogation of power. This is, of course, a myth of decadence following a Golden Age—a tenuous parallel to Solomon and his descendants—and might seem to work out poetically, but a careful reading of the central poem, "L'Expiation," reveals considerable ambivalence about the role of Napoleon: his epoch is not an unqualified Golden Age.)

In *Dieu* we are no longer dealing with mythic narrative but with a series of prophecies, revelations. They are juxtaposed with no principle of continuity save the beginning formula of each: "Et je vis au-dessus de ma tête un point noir." It strikes us immediately that Hugo has two ways of writing about godhead. The first involves much description of Nature's awesomeness: the creator is intuited through his creation, just as in the book of Job. The poet does not simply reflect on his own feelings and thus arrive at the idea of God by subjective means as, say, Pascal did; he can only understand God in terms of the spectacle of the universe. The difference from Job, however, is that he finds the monstrosity of the universe ("Canst thou draw out leviathan with a hook?") to be a sign not only of God's power but of his malevolence as well. The biblical voice out of the whirlwind is refuted by its own device of rhetorical questions:

> Vision! la mer triste entrechoque en grondant,
> Sous les nuages lourds que les souffles assemblent,
> Ses monstrueux airains en fusion, qui tremblent;
> Les flots font un fracas de boucliers affreux
> Se heurtant, et l'éclair sépulcral est sur eux.
> Quelle est la foi, le dogme et la philosophie
> Que cette impénétrable horreur nous signifie?
>
> ("Le Hibou")

The implied answer is that the universe is the work of an evil deity, and the image we have so frequently encountered of the sky as shroud or weighty ceiling confirms this implication. Hugo's representation of the world as the kingdom of a sadistic tyrant is superbly rich in poetry; the sense of terror before the manifestations of nature is conveyed in the above lines by battle imagery, which, however, does not degenerate into simple personifications of the sky and earth.

The other way in which Hugo writes about God, toward the end of *Dieu,* belongs to the domain of pure verbal affirmation; God is not here deduced to be evil, but declared to be light, good, and the point to which the whole universe aspires. This is apocalyptic, not mystical or devotional poetry, such as the following:

> All manner of things shall be well
> When the tongues of flame are in-folded
> Into the crowned knot of fire
> And the fire and rose are one.
>
> (T. S. Eliot, "Little Gidding")

Instead of having a basic body of Christian symbols to draw on like T. S. Eliot, Hugo must invent a language to reveal his own conception of God. Here, for example, is a grandiose passage on the Great Chain of Being and the movement of souls upward along it toward God:

> Rien n'existe que lui, le flamboiement profond,
> Et les âmes,—les grains de lumière, les mythes,
> Le moi mystérieux, atomes sans limites,
> Qui vont vers le grand moi, leur centre et leur aimant;—
> Point touchant au zénith par le rayonnement,
> Ainsi qu'un vêtement subissant la matière,
> Traversant tour à tour dans l'étendue entière
> La formule de chair propre à chaque milieu;
> Ici la sève, ici le sang, ici le feu;
> Blocs, arbres, griffes, dents, fronts pensants, auréoles;
> Retournant aux cercueils comme à des alvéoles;
> Mourant pour s'épurer, tombant pour s'élever,
> Sans fin, ne se perdant que pour se retrouver,
> Chaîne d'êtres qu'en haut l'échelle d'or réclame,
> Vers l'éternel foyer volant de flamme en flamme,
> Juste éclos du pervers, bon sorti du méchant,
> Montant, montant, montant sans cesse, et le cherchant,
> Et l'approchant toujours, mais sans jamais atteindre,
> Lui, l'être qu'on ne peut toucher, ternir, éteindre,
> Le voyant, le vivant, sans mort, sans nuit, sans mal,
> L'idée énorme au fond de l'immense idéal!
>
> ("La Lumière")

What is particularly noticeable here is a depersonalization of the notions of both God and the soul: the former is an "idea," the latter an "atom" or

"myth." The whole process of redemption—if that be the proper term for
Hugo's theology—assumes the aspect of a play of beams of light in movement, a mechanical spectacle. In this attempt to avoid representing God in
anthropomorphic terms, Hugo offers us a conception of Him as abstract as
that of the exploding universe. By contrast, we might compare, in terms of
poetic effect, a passage from the *Purgatorio* on the relation of God and the
soul:

> Esce di mano a lui che la vagheggia
>> Prima che sia,—a guisa di fanciulla
>> Che piangendo e ridendo pargoleggia,—
> L'anima semplicetta, che sa nulla,
>> Salvo che, mossa da lieto fattore,
>> Volentier torna a ciò che la trastulla.
>>> (16.85–90)

The homely comparison and the strongly anthropomorphic Creator suggest
immediately a certain feeling about God, although Dante knew, of course,
that this is poetic metaphor and not theology. But it connects God with
human life in a way the passage from Hugo does not. On the other hand,
when Dante must represent a vision of God at the end of the *Paradiso,* he
simply resorts to the highly symbolic description of three rings of light,
which is very evocative in the context of Christian tradition. Hugo's
flamboiement profond is an equally rich, almost mystical symbol of God,
but he is not satisfied with it and adds epithet after epithet until God is
merely abstracted into an "idea."

The difficulty Hugo experienced in finishing *Dieu* seems to have lain in
his inability to reach a final statement or evocation of God. He heaps image
upon image, as if never feeling that he has definitively expressed his thoughts.
The poem breaks off with the speaker's death, but continuations were
sketched out. The most thorough editors of *Dieu* have suggested not only
that doubt does not really yield to faith in the course of the poem, but even
that the somber "Voix" may have at one time been intended as a conclusion, to follow the visions of God as light. In that case, the cyclic structure
of *Dieu* would have risen from the atheistic "La Chauve-souris" to an
intimation of God, only to fall back into somber intuitions of deity's indif-
ference. In any event, Hugo's manuscripts and notes do not seem to indicate
any final point of certainty about godhead or its nature.

If we contrast the last part of *Dieu,* however, with the earlier suggestions of a tyrannical God, we realize that only the latter hold together
poetically; they are not empty affirmations about an "idea," but visions of

man in his universe attempting to pierce the mystery of it. In short, Hugo's gifts are at their fullest when his imagination is at its most demonic. We can better understand this cleavage in Hugo's prophetic poetry if we recall that from an early point in his career the sinister fascinated him, while his occultist theology developed only later. Furthermore, his particular form of occultism is rationalistic, as befits its roots in late antique thought, rather than oriented toward myth and symbol. It is difficult to imagine how this theology could be reconciled with demonic myth in an extended poem, and the proof is that neither *Dieu* nor *La Fin de Satan* seems to be informed by a dialectic pattern. In *La Fin de Satan,* the universe is first evil and, then, after Satan's change of heart, good. This is simple antithesis. Similarly, *Dieu* is made up of visions of the world under the sway of evil or nonexistent gods, which are simply juxtaposed to affirmations of God's goodness. There is no dialectic progression from one view to the other, no synthesis arrived at in stages. Vigny failed to write his projected *Fin de Satan* through perhaps similar incapacities, and Baudelaire escaped from dualism, as a poet at least, only when he wrote "Le Voyage" for the second edition of *Les Fleurs du mal.* But Hugo's poetic imagination could not bridge his gap of faith. Probably the only nineteenth-century French poet who succeeded in working out a perfectly articulated mythic poem on good and evil was Rimbaud, in *Une Saison en enfer.*

Despite his failure to bring *Dieu* and *La Fin de Satan* to conclusion, however, no other French romantic wrote such hallucinatory poems on the intimation of evil as Hugo; this achievement is unrelated to his inability to complete his long prophetic poems and confirms our contention that the demonic cast of imagination, in one form or another, dominates much of the best of French romantic verse. Hugo tried harder than any other to believe in an omnipotent God of goodness and justice, but his poetic powers never allowed him completely to express this. Nevertheless, in his last work, *La Légende des siècles,* he managed to suggest at least that God is an avenger, and, thereby, of course, the more primitive Judaeo-Christian conceptions of Him.

La Légende des siècles is largely a series of romances and myths with, here and there, a piece of prophetic poetry or apocalyptics inserted. The work promises, for the most part, no ultimate revelation of godhead, but consists of "little epics" or epic fragments, in which the conflict of good and evil is represented in heroic and legendary terms. Here Hugo is working in conventions which, if they do not produce such brilliant poetry as the best parts of *La Fin de Satan* and *Dieu,* allowed him at least to complete his task. Both God and Satan appear in *La Légende* in traditional mythic forms. In

"Puissance égale bonté," for example, God and Eblis, the Islamic devil, make a wager over the extent of their creative powers (one recalls the beginning of Job); Eblis creates the spider, which he then offers to God as raw material:

> Et Dieu prit l'araignée et la mit au milieu
> Du gouffre qui n'était pas encor le ciel bleu;
> Et l'Esprit regarda la bête; sa prunelle,
> Formidable, versait la lueur éternelle;
> Le monstre, si petit qu'il semblait un point noir,
> Grossit alors, et fut soudain énorme à voir;
> Et Dieu le regardait de son regard tranquille;
> Une aube étrange erra sur cette forme vile;
> L'affreux ventre devint un globe lumineux;
> Et les pattes, changeant en sphères d'or leurs noeuds,
> S'allongèrent dans l'ombre en grands rayons de flamme;
> Iblis leva les yeux, et tout à coup l'infâme,
> Ebloui, se courba sous l'abîme vermeil;
> Car Dieu, de l'araignée, avait fait le soleil.

The metamorphosis, a common enough mythic pattern in Hugo's later poetry, is particularly successful here: the strange association between spider and sun is of the sort critics are wont to call pre-surrealist, although it is typical of the sinister high romantic imagination. God's creative powers, we must also note, do not lie in His hands, in accordance with the Psalmist's notion of His handiwork, but in His eye. God is the eye which peers into the darkest corner: "L'oeil était dans la tombe et regardait Caïn" ("La Conscience"). In "Le Titan," when the Titan has broken the bonds imposed on him by the Olympians, he crawls through the earth to the other side, where he contemplates infinity:

> Il sent en lui la joie obscure de l'abîme;
> Il subit, accablé de soleils et de cieux,
> L'inexprimable horreur des lieux prodigieux.
> Il regarde, éperdu, le vrai, ce précipice.
> Evidence sans borne, ou fatale, ou propice!
> O stupeur! il finit par distinguer, au fond
> De ce gouffre où le jour avec la nuit se fond,
> A travers l'épaisseur d'une brume éternelle,
> Dans on ne sait quelle ombre énorme, une prunelle!

The counterpart to God's all-seeing is His power to make Himself invisible. In "Suprématie," God appears before the lesser deities of the Hindu pantheon, and, in answer to the claims of Indra, the sky god, to seeing all creation, asks:

> —Vois-tu ce brin de paille?"
> Dit l'étrange clarté d'où sortait une voix.
> Indra baissa la tête et cria : "Je le vois.
> Lumière, je te dis que j'embrasse tout l'être;
> Toi-même, entends-tu bien, tu ne peux disparaître
> De mon regard, jamais éclipsé ni décru!
>
> A peine eut-il parlé qu'elle avait disparu.

Invisibility is, of course, merely a variant on the theme of darkness. It is useful to compare the God of *La Légende*, who appears as an eye or else withdraws from sight, with the symbolism of the earlier part of *Dieu*. There, God's refusal to be contemplated or to be figured in any stable way implies His sinister character, His enmity to mankind. But in *La Légende*, God's inaccessibility represents His omnipotence with no sinister overtones. Darkness is a sign of His majesty: in the closing line of the last poem He declares, "Je n'aurais qu'à souffler et tout serait de l'ombre" ("Abîme"). This does not imply that God is a menacing figure but simply bespeaks His power, as set above that of natural forces and inferior deities.

The Satan of *La Légende des siècles* is not the supreme deity of the early parts of *Dieu* nor God's antagonist as in *La Fin de Satan*. He now appears on earth, lurking behind evildoers or identified with false gods. His presence is especially felt in the lurid medieval tales whose very landscape suggests demonic conspiracy. "Les Conseillers probes et libres" will serve as an example. A warlord of some vague medieval epoch has summoned his vassals:

> Sont présents cent barons et chevaliers, la fleur
> Du grand arbre héraldique et généalogique
> Que ce sol noir nourrit de sa sève tragique.
>
> . . . .
>
> Dans ce réseau de chefs qui couvrait l'Italie,
> Je passe Théodat, prince de Trente; Elle,
> Despote d'Avenzo, qu'a réclamé l'oubli;
> Ce borgne Ordelafo, le bourreau de Forli;
> Lascaris, que sa tante Alberte fit eunuque;
> Othobon, sieur d'Assise, et Tibalt, sieur de Lucque.

The rich interplay of proper names and epithets gives a condensed feeling of
the darker ages and their brutal, picturesque history. These personages, and
many others, assemble before the cathedral:

> Derrière eux, sur la pierre auguste d'un portail,
> Est sculpté Satan, roi, forçat, épouvantail,
> L'effrayant ramasseur de haillons de l'abîme,
> Ayant sa hotte au dos, pleine d'âmes, son crime
> Sur son aile qui ploie, et son roc noir qui luit
> Dans son poing formidable, et, dans ses yeux, la nuit.

The council has been convoked to divide up spoils and plan further rapine.
The city in which it is held is itself an occupied one:

> Dans Ancône, est-ce deuil, terreur, indifférence?
> Tout se tait; les maisons, les bouges, les palais,
> Ont bouché leur lucarne ou fermé leurs volets;
> Le cadran qui dit l'heure a l'air triste et funeste.
>
> Le soleil luit aux cieux comme dans une peste.

After the sycophantic speeches by which the Holy Roman Emperor is greeted,
each lord present is meted out a fief to plunder and terrorize, while church-
men condone the proceedings and receive their own sinecures. Finally,

> Pendant que le conseil se tenait de la sorte,
> Et qu'ils parlaient ainsi dans cette ville morte,
> Et que le maître avait sous ses pieds ces prélats,
> Ces femmes, ces barons en habits de galas,
> Et l'Italie au loin comme une solitude,
> Quelques seigneurs, ainsi qu'ils en ont l'habitude,
> Regardant derrière eux d'un regard inquiet,
> Virent que le Satan de pierre souriait.

"Les Conseillers probes et libres" suggests rather well the peculiar coloring
of so many poems of *La Légende*. These are emphatically not "historical"
poems, such as Leconte de Lisle was writing; they do not give the impression
of highly researched attempts to recreate any specific period of history.
Instead, they evoke a fantastic past, whose meaning is more anagogical than
sociological. Hugo did not really care about sound historiography, and the
proof is that, living in the first great age of historical study, he principally
relied for inspiration on the already quaint, outmoded seventeenth-century
encyclopedic dictionary of Moreri. Hugo merely needed a certain amount of
information or lore about which his imagination could then play freely.

The epic fragments of *La Légende des siècles* tend to follow certain patterns. They present the conflict of good and evil in political terms: kings, knights, tyrants, and new gods rising to overthrow the old ones are typical figures. The central theme of the collection might be defined as the revelation of power, since the tales are commonly built around the appearance of an avenging hero or deity come to mete out justice. The world of *La Légende* is thus seen to stand between the domain of realism and the absolute, anagogical realm of God and Satan presented in *Dieu* and in parts of *La Fin de Satan,* thereby lessening the poetic problems. In the latter poems, the difficulty lies partly in the fact that deity is more a presence than an actor; here Hugo could depict men and gods in action. While Hugo failed to complete his equivalents of the *Commedia* or *Paradise Lost,* the less ambitious genre of the legend proved to be an excellent vehicle for his need to express both visions of evil and the intimation of a benevolent supreme being. Furthermore, *La Légende* finally provided Hugo with a new and appropriate thematic use for the fantastic architectural imagery which . . . obsessed him from a very early point in his career. The introductory poem of the collection sets the tone:

> Et qu'est-ce maintenant que ce livre, traduit
> Du passé, du tombeau, du gouffre et de la nuit?
> C'est la tradition tombée à la secousse
> Des révolutions que Dieu déchaîne et pousse;
> Ce qui demeure après que la terre a tremblé;
> Décombre où l'avenir, vague aurore, est mêlé;
> C'est la construction des hommes, la masure
> Des siècles, qu'emplit l'ombre et que l'idée azure,
> L'affreux charnier-palais en ruine, habité
> Par la mort et bâti par la fatalité,
>
> .   .   .   .
>
> Ce livre, c'est le reste effrayant de Babel;
> C'est la lugubre Tour des Choses, l'édifice
> Du bien, du mal, des pleurs, du deuil, du sacrifice,
> Fier jadis, dominant les lointains horizons,
> Aujourd'hui n'ayant plus que de hideux tronçons,
> Epars, couchés, perdus dans l'obscure vallée;
> C'est l'épopée humaine, âpre, immense,—écroulée.
>
> ("La Vision d'où est sorti ce livre")

The imagery of sinister ruined buildings becomes a suitable symbol of the past; labyrinthine convolutions represent not only the concrete remnants of the ages but also the mysterious complexity of fate and freedom, good and evil. With *La Légende* a number of Hugo's favorite themes and images converge in a harmonious whole: the eye of heaven, night, strange architecture, God's remoteness, vengeance, and revelation all combine to create an atmosphere heavy with suggestions of evil but illuminated here and there with apocalyptic warnings.

In discussing Hugo's later poetry I have not gone further than *La Fin de Satan, Dieu,* and *La Légende des siècles,* although there is much of poetic interest to explore, because none of it would add a great deal to the questions of theme and symbolism which we have been investigating. These three works are without doubt Hugo's most ambitious poetic projects in the sense that they were conceived of as great wholes, whereas a book like *Les Contemplations* is simply a series of poems of varying inspiration put together with some semblance of thematic order. (The same charge of miscellany might be brought against the later additions to *La Légende* but, by and large, they reinforce the tone of the original series.) Furthermore, as Hugo pointed out in the 1859 preface to *La Légende,* he thought of it as forming with *Dieu* and *La Fin de Satan* an even greater whole which would give a comprehensive account of the Great Chain of Being: evil or the subhuman, mankind in its diversity, and God or the concept of the infinite. Of course, these three books, as they stand, are related only insofar as they are the work of one powerful imagination. Anyone who has examined Hugo's notes and worksheets knows that he strove constantly to arrive at syntheses without ever working out the necessary articulations. The failure to achieve a dialectic in *Dieu* or *La Fin de Satan* is merely a particular case of his incapacity for putting an entire building behind his peristyle, to borrow a metaphor from the preface to *La Légende,* in which Hugo argues desperately that his mythic poems are not fragments but will eventually be seen as a coherent whole. Whatever we may think of the unity of Hugo's thought and poetic practice, however, *La Fin de Satan, Dieu,* and *La Légende* still remain the most persistent and successful attempt in nineteenth-century French poetry to see, in epic scope, the universe, past, present, and future.

We have seen that much French romantic poetry can be interpreted as a series of questions or propositions about good and evil, with the awareness of evil becoming especially dominant. The poets speak of God and Satan with varying degrees of literalness: for Vigny or Petrus Borel, God is merely a figure to designate Christianity or the bourgeois mentality, while for Baudelaire and Hugo, God and Satan have genuine theological meaning. These last two poets were consequently the most obsessed by dualism. Nerval is another matter: his conception of godhead is completely cyclic, with Christianity as a temporary eclipse of the true gods. All these writers share, moreover, a post-Christian view of the world, for even Baudelaire uses only fragments of traditional religion, and Hugo's God coincides but now and then with that of Christianity. The feeling that the cycle of history is at an end can be found in Gautier and even Musset (as in the beginning of "Rolla"), while in other poets, especially Nerval and Hugo, the themes of apocalypse and regeneration occur.

The symbolism which supports theological themes in French romantic poetry grows out of traditional archetypes, but it is frequently given realistic, contemporary reference or even constitutes a demonic mode of the familiar symbolism of godhead. For example, the nineteenth-century city is sinister, as in Sainte-Beuve or Vigny, while the very notion of architecture is associated for Hugo with the labyrinths of hell: Satan's Pandemonium rather than the New Jerusalem is the relevant archetype. Baudelaire carries perhaps farthest, with his rich use of commonplace detail, the identification of a real contemporary metropolis with the demonic citadel of tradition. At the same time, he created a new version of the terrestrial paradise: in his verse the tropics have intense emotive connotations which are without analogue in other French romantic poets. They rarely conceived of an earthly form of heaven, with the possible exception of Nerval, whose Mediterranean landscapes fulfill much the same function.

Complementing the symbolism of place is that of motion: movement and immobility are recurrent themes, and either may express serenity or despair. There is a demonic circular movement in *Les Destinées* and demonic aimless movement in *Dieu*. At the same time, Hugo's Great Chain of Being is a variant of the divine circle, its fixity suggesting lack of change, while the immobility of Satan in *La Fin de Satan* implies imprisonment and suffering.

But the most persistent image is doubtless the sky, which can represent paradisiacal light, as often in Baudelaire, or the dividing and indifferent blue which torments the godseeker of *Dieu*. The converse of the bright sky is a dark prison-like lid, with the attendant image of a black sun pouring forth shadow. The dark sky, which shuts man off from the God who traditionally lies behind it, provides the characteristic backdrop for a demonic gospel, in which the good news is ironically that God has withdrawn from mankind.

Many changes can, of course, be wrought within these patterns. In Vigny, nature is no longer opposed to the city, but becomes equally hostile, and in Hugo, the landscape inspires panic. Nerval opposed the consoling bowels of the earth, the traditional hell, to the evil sky, while considering nature as belonging to the former. Baudelaire, finally, could use almost any symbol—sky, ocean, city, wildwood—in either a divine or demonic sense.

But it is perhaps Hugo who carried farthest the principle of the anagogical ambiguity of any image: in the early part of *Dieu,* Satan's and God's traditional attributes are inextricably mingled, while in *La Légende des siècles* both, though remaining distinct, are vested with the power of darkness.

Regardless, therefore, of the comparative merits of each poet or poem, it appears that demonic symbolism reached its most complex form with Hugo—and to a lesser extent, with Baudelaire—about the middle of the century. Leconte de Lisle, who was almost Baudelaire's contemporary, attempted in "Qaïn" and "La Fin de l'Homme" to rework the demonic interpretation of Genesis which goes back to Byron, but his pessimism was more literary than theological. It is only with Rimbaud and *Une Saison en enfer* that the dialectics of God and Satan received a final statement and solution in French poetry, for Rimbaud drew together the various strands of divine and demonic imagery that had run through the French romantics and devised an issue from their dualism: he equated Christian good and evil and thereby rejected both of them.

Although the history of the demonic imagination in nineteenth-century French poetry ends, for our purposes, with Hugo, certain dominant themes of the symbolists consist of further variations on the satanic: the rejection of life for the artifact, the worship of sterility as opposed to nature, and the obsession with nothingness all derive clearly, however altered in context, from romantic concerns. The symbolists, insofar as they were "decadents," took a rather perverse delight in elaborating, without any theological *inquiétude,* the anti-natural visions of the romantics in which minerals replaced trees, death reproduction, imagination reality. Finally, the wheel came full swing, and in Proust the true life of art, as opposed to the vile everyday one, leads again to resurrection and salvation: aestheticism has become a new Way of the Cross, replacing the old Christian one. Satan's attributes become redemptory. But that is the subject of another book.

W. D. HOWARTH

Hugo and the Romantic Drama in Verse

HERNANI

In view of the prominence we have given [elsewhere] to the novelty of Hugo's dramatic formula as defined in the *Préface de Cromwell*, perhaps the most important critical question to consider with regard to *Hernani* is the success with which that formula is embodied in the play. As far as structure and dramatic craftsmanship are concerned, the new play certainly marks a significant advance on *Cromwell*: how well does it illustrate the theory of the *Préface*?

To begin with, unlike *Cromwell*, *Hernani* is irregular in structure: that is, it infringes the unities both of time and place. Hugo here claims considerable freedom, and the scene ranges from Saragossa and the mountains of Aragon to Aix-la-Chapelle; while the time span must be at least sufficient to allow for journeys from Spain to Aix and back (according to history, the death of Maximilian, reported in act 1, and the election of Charles V [act 4] were separated by five months). Hugo had referred in the *Préface* to the unity of action as "la seule vraie et fondée"; and although commentators may debate whether the subplot in *Hernani* does, or does not, technically conform to the notion of a "unified" action, the play possesses a tight, coherent structure. There is a close interlinking of plot (the love of three men for Doña Sol) and subplot (Carlos's ambitions for the Empire), while the subtitle (*L'Honneur castillan*) may be seen as indicating the source of the various *péripéties*, the relations between the three men being determined by the interplay of their love and honour, as follows:

From *Sublime and Grotesque: A Study of French Romantic Drama*. © 1975 by W. D. Howarth. George Harrap & Co., 1975.

Act 1 is almost entirely expository. We learn that Doña Sol is loved by three men, each of whom has something in his favour: Don Carlos, royal power; Don Ruy Gomez, the fact that she is due to marry him; Hernani, the fact that she returns his love. There is little development, though Hernani's desire for vengeance on the King is revealed, as is Carlos's ambition to be elected to the Empire. A rendezvous is arranged between the lovers for the following evening, and at the end of the act Carlos saves Hernani from detection by Ruy Gomez.

In *act 2* Carlos impersonates Hernani at the rendezvous, and tries to abduct Doña Sol. Hernani spares Carlos's life.

Act 3. Hernani offends against the code of honour by making love to Doña Sol after accepting Ruy Gomez's hospitality; but Ruy Gomez saves his life by refusing to hand him over to the King. Carlos abducts Doña Sol instead. Hernani accepts that his life is forfeit to Ruy Gomez, but demands a chance to avenge himself on Carlos; he offers to lay down his life when Ruy Gomez claims it.

In *act 4* Hernani refuses Ruy Gomez's offer of his life in exchange for the right to kill Carlos. But Carlos's election as Emperor is announced, whereupon he pardons the conspirators (including Ruy Gomez and Hernani), reinstates Hernani in his rank and titles, and bestows Doña Sol on him. Hernani accepts, abandoning his desire for vengeance.

Act 5 opens with the marriage celebrations. But Ruy Gomez arrives, reminding Hernani of his promise, and claiming his life. The lovers die together; Ruy Gomez kills himself.

The interplay of these two forces leads to the crisis (4.3), which is resolved by an apparently happy ending with the removal of the material obstacle to the marriage. The hidden obstacle remains, however, and Ruy Gomez's implacable jealousy brings about not only the deaths of the two lovers, but also his own.

But structural cohesion, while it may make for dramatic effectiveness, is no guarantee of other, more valuable qualities: the fortunes of the term "well-made play" show clearly enough that dramaturgical competence on its own cannot redeem mediocrity of content. It has often been said of *Hernani* that it is like Pixérécourt's plays: well constructed, "good theatre," but vitiated by absurd or arbitrary données of characterization or plot. Certainly many contemporaries thought so, and this view is popular among modern commentators.

At first sight, *Cromwell* certainly appears the more serious of the two plays, the more ambitious. It is easier to recognize in the dramatic treatment of a major historical subject like that of *Cromwell* that moral purpose which Hugo was later to insist on as an essential feature of "drame": despite some of the bizarre elements—the Puritans, the clowns—surrounding Cromwell himself, the portrait of the Protector remains a responsible and a recognizable one. That of Don Carlos, by comparison, is much more difficult to accept. The gratuitousness of the first scene spent in a cupboard, and the striking contrast between the King of acts 1–3 and the same man as Emperor in acts 4 and 5, appear to do violence to all credibility; and although Hugo prepared the ground before the first performance with the following text:

> Il est peut-être à propos de mettre sous les yeux du public ce que dit la chronique espagnole de Alaya . . . touchant la jeunesse de Charles-Quint, lequel figure comme on sait dans *Hernani*: "Don Carlos, tant qu'il ne fut qu'archiduc d'Autriche et roi d'Espagne, fut un jeune prince amoureux de son plasir, grand coureur d'aventures, sérénades et estocades, sous les balcons de Saragosse, ravissant volontiers les belles aux galants et les femmes aux maris, voluptueux et cruel au besoin. Mais, du jour où il fut empereur, une révolution se fit en lui (*se hizo una revolucion en el*), et le débauché Don Carlos devint ce monarque habile, sage, clément, hautain, glorieux, hardi avec prudence, que l'Europe a admiré sous le nom de Charles-Quint,"
>
> (*Grandezas de España,* descanso 24)

no trace has ever been discovered of the authority here referred to, and one can only conclude that this was an example of deliberate *mystification*. Whatever Hugo may claim about the serious historical foundations of the play:

> Par le sens historique, . . . *Ruy Blas* se rattache à *Hernani*. Le grand fait de la noblesse se montre, dans *Hernani* comme dans *Ruy Blas,* à côté du grand fait de la royauté. Seulement, dans *Hernani,* comme la royauté absolue n'est pas faite, la noblesse lutte encore contre le roi, ici avec l'orgueil, là avec l'épée; à demi féodale, à demi rebelle. En 1519, le seigneur vit loin de la cour, dans la montagne, en bandit comme Hernani, ou en patriarche comme Ruy Gomez. Deux cents ans plus tard, la question est retournée. Les vassaux sont devenus des courtisans
>
> (Preface to *Ruy Blas*)

these are really of the vaguest. The "sens historique," like the Spanish local colour, which, according to *Victor Hugo raconté par un témoin de sa vie*, derived from the poet's childhood memories, is either very approximative, or else reflects secondhand *idées reçues* about Spain and the Spanish.

If the moral earnestness which Hugo claims hardly seems to be justified by an examination of the historical sources, is it possible instead to see in *Hernani* a more topical message, addressed to his politically-minded contemporaries? The preface to the play contains this stirring call:

> Le romantisme ... n'est ... que le *libéralisme* en littérature ...
> La liberté dans l'art, la liberté dans la société, voilà le double but
> auquel doivent tendre d'un même pas tous les esprits conséquents
> et logiques; voilà la double bannière qui rallie ... toute la jeunesse
> si patiente et si forte d'aujourd'hui ... Les *Ultras* de tout genre,
> classiques ou monarchiques, auront beau se prêter secours pour
> refaire l'ancien régime de toutes pièces, société et littérature;
> chaque progrès du pays, chaque développement des intelligences,
> chaque pas de la liberté fera crouler tout ce qu'ils auront
> échafaudé.

—and it was hardly a coincidence that less than three months after publication of this text (dated March 9, 1830) the July Revolution had taken place and Charles X been forced to abdicate. At first sight, one might be tempted to compare *Hernani* with Schiller's *Die Räuber,* as expressing the political idealism which animated many of the "Jeunes-France," as of the "Stürmer-und-Dränger." But Hernani is no Karl Moor: although like Schiller's hero he is a "noble bandit," his quarrel is with his King, Don Carlos, not with society. He is motivated by a personal vendetta, and once Carlos has decided to mark his election to the Empire by a signal act of clemency, the bandit-chief is ready enough to renounce his way of life, accept the Order of the Golden Fleece, and settle down to married bliss as a "grand d'Espagne." It would be difficult not to conclude that the literary affinities with Corneille's Cinna are stronger than any ideological link with Schiller's Karl Moor. Indeed, if we are looking for reflections of topical ideas in *Hernani,* the most obvious example is provided, not by Hernani himself as a representative of the ideology of the 1830 Revolution, but by Charles V, saluting Charlemagne as an embodiment of the Napoleonic legend:

> Quoi donc! avoir été prince, empereur et roi!
> Avoir été l'épée, avoir été la loi!
> Géant, pour piédestal avoir eu l'Allemagne!

Quoi! pour titre césar et pour nom Charlemagne!
Avoir été plus grand qu'Annibal, qu'Attila,
Aussi grand que le monde.

(ll. 1495–1500)

But both topical allusion and historical reference are of subsidiary importance: it is above all contemporary literary influences that the play reflects. The central theme, "l'honneur castillan," had come into fashion with the recent revival of Spanish themes and motifs: Mérimée's Clara Gazul plays had been one notable example of this, while Hugo himself says in the Preface to *Hernani* that "le *Romancero general* est la véritable clef [de ce drame]." G. Lote declares confidently: "En dehors du *Romancero,* presque toute la documentation historique d'*Hernani* sort des pièces du théâtre espagnol et du livre de Sismondi: *De la littérature du Midi de l'Europe*"; and if the source of one important scene (act 3, scene 6, the "scene des portraits") has been shown to be a contemporary English tragedy set in Italy, the twist given to the original by Hugo in order to accommodate it to the currently fashionable "honour theme" seems just as significant as the English borrowing itself.

Into this Spanish framework, of highly conventional character, has been placed a hero who is the very embodiment of that romantic fatalism which is often ascribed to Byron's influence (but which had already been seen in such heroes as Chateaubriand's René or Nodier's Jean Sbogar—to say nothing of eighteenth-century precursors such as Crébillon's Rhadamiste or Prévost's Des Grieux); and those young romantics among Hugo's supporters who identified themselves with Hernani seem less likely to have done so because he represented a political or social ideal, than because they saw in him a fellow-sufferer from *le mal du siècle.*

If we analyse Hernani's particular form of *mal du siècle,* we can easily see that he expresses no coherent philosophy: neither nihilistic resignation, nor committed antisocial individualism. Although, as we have noted, he has not irrevocably turned his back on society, he feels himself to be an outcast, "[Un] malheureux que tout abandonne et repousse" (l. 48). He neither finds consolation in religious faith nor feels the anguish of rejection by God: his despair is quite without metaphysical overtones, and it is "le ciel"—nature—not "le Ciel" which provides the bare necessities of the life of hardship to which he is reduced:

Je n'ai reçu du ciel jaloux
Que l'air, le jour et l'eau, la dot qu'il donne a tous.

(ll. 121–22)

Though the challenge from the King rouses him at the end of act 1 to a
positive expression of the one dynamic passion—the desire for vengeance—
by which he is animated, elsewhere, even in his relationship with Doña Sol,
his despair makes of him a predominantly passive character. He may attribute to himself daemonic qualities:

> Je suis une force qui va!
> Agent aveugle et sourd de mystères funèbres!
> Une âme de malheur faite avec des ténèbres!
> Où vais-je? je ne sais. Mais je me sens poussé
> D'un souffle impétueux, d'un destin insensé.
> Je descends, je descends, et jamais ne m'arrête.
>
> (ll. 992–97)

—but what he actually displays is more like a brooding melancholy. In his
extreme absorption in his own sufferings, now he insults Doña Sol, doubt-
ing her constancy, now he indulges in an orgy of masochistic self-abasement:

> Tu vis et je suis mort. Je ne vois pas pourquoi
> Tu te ferais murer dans ma tombe avec moi.
>
> (ll. 971–72)

The change in his fortunes at the end of act 4 leaves Hernani—almost
literally—speechless; then for a brief spell, in act 5, scene 3, he enjoys the
opposite extreme of exalted euphoria, before the appearance of the masked
Ruy Gomez plunges him into the depths of fatalistic despair.

What we have here, therefore, is not so much the coherent expression
of an attitude to life, as an impressionistic succession of moods. Hugo's
conception of character is poetic, not rationalistic: he shows a poet's intuitive grasp of essential human feelings, and expresses these, like Shakespeare
in his soliloquies, in a manner which transcends the particular and the
contingent, to achieve an appeal that is truly universal. Those critics who
fault Hugo on the minutiae of character-portrayal, taking as their criterion
the rationalistic concept of realism, fail to understand the true nature of his
poetic drama. George Steiner has expressed very clearly the position of the
romantic poet in this respect:

> Until the advent of rational empiricism the controlling habits of
> the Western mind were symbolic and allegoric. Available evi-
> dence regarding the natural world, the course of history, and the
> variety of human action was translated into imaginative designs
> or mythologies . . . After Shakespeare the master spirits of west-
> ern consciousness are no longer the blind seers, the poets, or

Orpheus performing his art in the face of hell. They are Descartes, Newton, and Voltaire. And their chroniclers are not the dramatic poets but the prose novelists.

The Romantics were the inheritors of this tremendous change. They were not yet prepared to accept it as irremediable. Rousseau's primitivism, the anti-Newtonian mythology of Blake, Coleridge's organic metaphysics, Victor Hugo's image of the poets as the Magi, and Shelley's "unacknowledged legislators" are related elements in the rearguard action fought by the Romantics against the new scientific rationalism.

(The Death of Tragedy)

Even the tragedy of Corneille had abandoned the poetic, the suggestive: its appeal had been to the spectator's reason, not to his imagination. The rhetoric and the dialectic of eighteenth-century tragedy, while not excluding a strong appeal to the sensibility of the spectator, made few demands on his imagination: their domain was the prosaic domain of the rationalist, not that of the poet. It may well be true that in his conception of character Hugo shares something of the primitivism of Pixérécourt and other popular dramatists: his characters, like theirs, remain relatively unsophisticated. But whereas in prose melodrama the banality of the language, or the turgid sentimental clichés, add nothing to these elementary données, in Hugo at his best the simplicity of this basic concept of character is embroidered with the rich texture of his imagery, so that—the comparison with Shakespeare is not entirely out of place—generalizations about love, death, old age or honour become, not banal commonplaces, but moving, evocative or exciting poetic utterances.

In any case, Hugo's characterization, however systematic, does not reproduce the naive black-and-white confrontations of a Pixérécourt. True to the spirit of the *Préface de Cromwell*, he seeks the dramatic opposition between contrary elements not in pairs of contrasting characters, but within the same character; thus, each of the three male protagonists exhibits some conflict between the instinct of love and the principle of honour. In Carlos, the debauched monarch gives way to the magnanimous Emperor; Ruy Gomez's proud refusal to betray Hernani contrasts with the vengeance dictated by his jealousy; and Hernani's noble bearing is compromised by the deceit that he practices in act 3. But such contrasts are less crudely systematic than in some of the later plays; and while the same antithetical principle of the contrast between sublime and grotesque does clearly underlie Hugo's conception of his characters (bandit and outlaw / "grand d'Espagne"; king hiding in cupboard / emperor at vigil in Charlemagne's tomb), it is not applied in *Hernani* in such a doctrinaire fashion.

With Hugo, rationalistic concepts of plausibility of characterization are not really appropriate. In this play perhaps more than anywhere else in Hugo's theatre, characters are above all vehicles for poetic developments of a lyrical, elegiac, or satirical nature. It is impossible not to be struck, from this, the first of Hugo's major plays, onwards, by the distinctly *operatic* character of Hugo's dramatic writing. For the playwright has rejected the linear plot-development of the traditional serious drama of the rationalist neoclassical era, in which even soliloquies normally fulfilled a dialectical function; in place of this, we have a structure in which "plot" is a framework for a series of solos and duets, arias and recitatives, of a very much more static nature. Static, because—unlike the case of the classical soliloquy, which although it may slow down the action in a physical sense, does advance the psychological action—here the dramatic context is often only a pretext. Instead of being intensely inward-looking like the classical hero, bounded by the confines of his particular predicament, Hugo's characters, like Shakespeare's, look outward from the particular to the universal; their imaginative flights transcend the limitations of context, and it is the function of the imagery, like that of the music in opera, to give memorable, striking form to these passages, which are poetic rather than strictly speaking dramatic, at any rate in the conventional sense of the word.

The lyrical quality of Hugo's writing in *Hernani* has often been appreciated—but usually as if it were a question of isolated passages which constitute a superficial adornment and help to redeem the triviality, or absurdity, of the rest of the play. On the contrary, the kind of imaginative writing exemplified by such varied passages as Hernani's lyrical description of the bandit's life (ll. 125–46), his invective against Carlos (ll. 381–414), Ruy Gomez's elegy on old age (3.1), Carlos's act 4 monologue, or the marvellous love-duet of the last act, is no superficial decoration; it permeates the whole of Hugo's drama. As in romantic opera, these virtuoso passages—together with the flow and sparkle of imaginative writing, in lower key, throughout the play—are what really count. Hugo offers us, not the logical conviction of a chain of events leading up to an intellectually satisfying catastrophe, but the intuitive recognition of the poetic power of universal tragic themes. The irrational romantic death-wish, the poignant self-knowledge of old age, young love doomed to early death: these may be clichés, and there is no doubt something arbitrary in the way Hugo presents them to us; but it is by his "operatic" treatment of these perennial themes, which denotes a concept

of drama totally different from the worn-out neoclassical formula, that
Hugo the tragic poet has succeeded in creating a new "sublime":

> Quand pâsse un jeune pâtre—oui, c'en est là!—souvent,
> Tandis que nous allons, lui chantant, moi rêvant,
> Lui dans son pré vert, moi dans mes noires allées,
> Souvent je dis tout bas:—O mes tours crénelées,
> Mon vieux donjon ducal, que je vous donnerais,
> Oh! que je donnerais mes blés et mes forêts,
> Et les vastes troupeaux qui tondent mes collines,
> Mon vieux nom, mon vieux titre, et toutes mes ruines,
> Et tous mes vieux aïeux qui bientôt m'attendront,
> Pour sa chaumière neuve et pour son jeune front!
> Car ses cheveux sont noirs, car son œil reluit comme
> Le tien, tu peux le voir, et dire: Ce jeune homme!
> Et puis, penser à moi qui suis vieux. Je le sais!
> Pourtant j'ai nom Silva, mais ce n'est plus assez!
> Oui, je me dis cela. Vois à quel point je t'aime!
> Le tout, pour être jeune et beau, comme toi-même!
> Mais à quoi vais-je ici rêver? Moi, jeune et beau!
> Qui te dois de si loin devancer au tombeau!
>
> (ll. 735–52)

The effects are simple, as befits all true lyric verse, based on the requirements of oral delivery. But it is these simple devices—the repetitions (*que je
vous donnerais, / Oh! que je donnerais; Mon vieux nom, mon vieux titre; et
toutes mes ruines, / Et tous mes vieux aïeux; jeune et beau . . . / Moi, jeune
et beau!*), the alliterations (*Mon vieux donjon ducal, que je vous donnerais;
Et les vastes troupeaux qui tondent mes collines*), the insistent play on the
antithesis *jeune/vieux*—which impart a genuinely musical character to Ruy
Gomez's reflections on old age and death. Such a passage is far from being
an *hors-d'œuvre*; it expresses the very essence of the character's situation
throughout the play. It does this, however, not by means of the inward-
looking dialectic of "Cartesian" drama, but in the expansive, outward-
looking manner of Shakespeare. These are not gratuitous "lyrical"
embellishments, in other words, on the surface of a conventionally "dramatic" plot: the two elements are integrated into a new concept of "lyrical
drama," and the term fits Hugo's tragedies just as well as the opera to which
it is more often applied. George Steiner's comment on the "natural relationship" between romantic drama and opera—

In the French Romantic theatre, the core of drama is buried
beneath the mechanics of passionate presentation. The basic
quality of the work suffers no violence through the addition of
music. On the contrary, music rationalizes and completes the
elements of pure gesture and fantasy inherent in the material.
Melodic lines can safely carry a great burden of absurdity. Thus
it is in the operas of Donizetti, Meyerbeer and Verdi that Victor
Hugo's conception of dramatic form was most fully realized—

(The Death of Tragedy)

surely fails to do justice to the lyrical, or imaginative, quality of Hugo's
plays, and takes no account of the way in which "melodic lines" have
already been provided by the poet himself, fulfilling very much the function
that is here attributed to music.

Thus, the sustained duet of act 5, scene 3, lifts the emotional tone of the
finale on to a level that would be unattainable in the medium of prose: for
a brief moment, the hero's obsessive death-wish seems to have been exor-
cized, and he gives himself up to the lyrical celebration of his joy, with the
image of physical homecoming symbolizing a kind of spiritual rebirth:

> Que m'importe
> Les haillons qu'en entrant j'ai laissés à la porte!
> Voici que je reviens à mon palais en deuil.
> Un ange du Seigneur m'attendait sur le seuil.
> J'entre, et remets debout les colonnes brisées,
> Je rallume le feu, je rouvre les croisées,
> Je fais arracher l'herbe au pavé de la cour,
> Je ne suis plus que joie, enchantement, amour.
>
> (ll. 1927–34)

But we are not allowed to forget for long that this is only an interlude, and
it is Doña Sol who gives unwitting expression to the theme of the death-
wish; first in a figure of speech, charged with unconscious irony, at the
climax of her own lyrical response:

> Mon duc, rien qu'un moment!
> Le temps de respirer et de voir seulement.
> Tout s'est éteint, flambeaux et musique de fête.
> Rien que la nuit et nous. Félicité parfaite!
> Dis, ne le crois-tu pas? sur nous, tout en dormant,
> La nature à demi veille amoureusement.
> Pas un nuage au ciel. Tout, comme nous, repose.

Viens, respire avec moi l'air embaumé de rose!
Regarde. Plus de feux, plus de bruit. Tout se tait.
La lune tout à l'heure à l'horizon montait;
Tandis que tu parlais, sa lumière qui tremble
Et ta voix, toutes deux m'allaient au cœur ensemble,
Je me sentais joyeuse et calme, ô mon amant,
Et j'aurais bien voulu mourir en ce moment!
                                              (ll. 1949–62)

—and then in the flight of fancy which ironically heralds Ruy Gomez's summons on the horn:

—Ce silence est trop noir, ce calme est trop profond.
Dis, ne voudrais-tu pas voir une étoile au fond?
Ou qu'une voix des nuits, tendre et délicieuse,
S'élevant tout à coup, chantât?

                                              —Capricieuse!
Tout à l'heure on fuyait la lumière et les chants!

—Le bal! Mais un oiseau qui chanterait aux champs!
Un rossignol perdu dans l'ombre et dans la mousse,
Ou quelque flûte au loin! . . . Car la musique est douce,
Fait l'âme harmonieuse, et, comme un divin chœur,
Éveille mille voix qui chantent dans le cœur!
Ah! ce serait charmant!
      (*On entend le bruit lointain d'un cor dans l'ombre.*)
                  Dieu! je suis exaucée!
                                              (ll. 1969–79)

Judged by purely rational analysis, this moment of tragic irony may seem no more than a highly contrived example of Steiner's "absurdity"; but Hugo's poetry makes it so appropriate to its context, as the climactic point of a lyrical drama in which the themes of love, honour and death are inseparably interrelated, that his technique cannot be faulted.

   Not all the writing is of this quality, of course; nor is it intended that the same lyrical appeal should be expressed by every scene. Ruy Gomez's entry abruptly changes the tone: he is not meant to compete with the lovers for our sympathy at this point, and it is hard not to see him now, in melodramatic terms, as the *traître,* or villain of the piece. But once the necessary dramatic exchanges have taken place and the lovers have shared

the phial of poison, their final duet at once resumes the same fluent musi-
cality. The lyrical exaltation of the preceding passages is now muted into the
elegiac, as the imagery, proclaiming the identification of the lovers' "nuit de
noces" with their death-bed, nevertheless attenuates the harshness of death
by welcoming it as sleep:

> Oh! béni soit le ciel qui m'a fait une vie
> D'abîmes entourée et de spectres suivie,
> Mais qui permet que, las d'un si rude chemin,
> Je puisse m'endormir ma bouche sur ta main.
>
> (ll. 2155–58)

The supreme romantic myth of twin souls finding perfect communion
in a shared, unblemished love perhaps necessarily carries with it, in its most
sublime manifestations, an unconscious death-wish: there must be no harsh
awakening to the realities of life to follow the ideal happiness of the
wedding-night. If this is so, the last twenty lines of *Hernani*, seen as an
expression of romantic idealism, have an aesthetic rightness that makes
them as moving and as satisfying as those other magnificent embodiments of
this myth, the closing pages of Keller's *Romeo und Julia auf dem Dorfe* or
the finale of Verdi's *Aida*. . . .

LE ROI S'AMUSE

Hugo's *Le Roi s'amuse* was produced at the Théâtre-Français in November 1832: in spite of his uneasy relations with the company over *Hernani*,
he was determined to aim higher than the Porte-Saint-Martin. This time, he
had to contend both with the opposition of those who disapproved on
aesthetic grounds and with arbitrary political censorship. The play was
given a disastrous reception on the first night, and the following morning
Hugo was informed that the management of the theatre had been instructed
to suspend further performances—a suspension which was soon turned into
a definitive ban. According to Mme Hugo, the political ban was not
unconnected with professional jealousies:

> Le prétexte de la suspension était l'immoralité; la vérité était
> qu'un certain nombre d'auteurs classiques, dont plusieurs étaient
> députés, étaient allés trouver M. d'Argout et lui avaient dit qu'on
> ne pouvait tolérer une pièce dont le sujet était l'assassinat d'un
> roi, le lendemain du jour où le roi avait failli être assassiné; que
> *Le Roi s'amuse* etait l'apologie du régicide.
>
> (*Victor Hugo raconté par un témoin de sa vie*)

As for the author himself, although he was at pains, in the preface he wrote
for the publication of *Le Roi s'amuse* later in the same year, to thank his
literary opponents for the loyalty they had shown on this occasion:

> Le pouvoir s'est trompé. Son acte brutal a révolté les hommes
> honnêtes dans tous les camps. L'auteur a vu se rallier à lui, pour
> faire face à l'arbitraire et à l'injustice, ceux-là mêmes qui
> l'attaquaient le plus violemment la veille. Si par hasard quelques
> haines invétérées ont persisté, elles regrettent maintenant le
> secours momentané qu'elles ont apporté au pouvoir. Tout ce
> qu'il y a d'honorable et de loyal parmi les ennemis de l'auteur est
> venu lui tendre la main, quitte à recommencer le combat littéraire
> aussitôt que le combat politique sera fini.

—he made it quite clear elsewhere that he saw the ban on *Le Roi s'amuse*
as being "une persécution littéraire cachée sous une tracasserie politique":

> Le gouvernement prêtant main-forte à l'Académie en 1832!
> Aristote redevenu loi de l'État! une imperceptible contre-révol-
> ution littéraire manœuvrant à fleur d'eau au milieu de nos grandes
> révolutions politiques! des députés qui ont déposé Charles X
> travaillant dans un petit coin à restaurer Boileau! quelle pauvreté!

It seems likely that the persecution Hugo complains of here was not purely
imaginary, and that in attempting to impose his new kind of drama on the
public of the Théâtre-Français, he had to face determined opposition on
doctrinaire grounds that had little to do with the intrinsic merits of his
plays. At all events, whether the censor's ban on this occasion was imposed
for genuinely political reasons, or whether the machinery of government
was being used to promote the ends of literary rivalry and cultural preju-
dice, both the preface to the play and the speech Hugo made before the
Tribunal de Commerce in his unsuccessful appeal against the ban, are a
clear and courageous statement of the case against censorship. The former
in particular contains some excellent early examples—all the more effective
because dignified and restrained—of the satirical invective that he was to
use so devastatingly in *Les Châtiments*.

Even in 1832 there were those who suggested that the ban was mal-
adroit from the government's own point of view, and that it would have
been better to trust to the judgement of the public and wait for the play to
fail. By general agreement, *Le Roi s'amuse* is inferior to both *Hernani* and
Marion de Lorme, an obvious example of creation according to an a priori
formula. Ligier (who was cast as Triboulet) found the play extremely mov-

ing when it was read to the *comédiens,* especially the fifth act—but he also
testified to the exceptional difficulty of this same act from the point of view
of the actor playing the central role. It must indeed be a very demanding
part, both in its unusual length and in the emotional intensity called for:
from the end of act 2 onwards, when Triboulet discovers the abduction of
his daughter, there is a sustained intensity of feeling, with only a brief respite
in act 4. The whole of the last act is a series of impassioned, or frenzied,
soliloquies, with a minimum of contribution from other characters; and
although here the writing attains genuine imaginative power—for instance
where Triboulet's exultation over the prospective murder of the King turns
into *folie de grandeur*:

> Quel temps! nuit de mystère!
> Une tempête au ciel! un meurtre sur la terre!
> Que je suis grand ici! ma colère de feu
> Va de pair cette nuit avec celle de Dieu.
> Quel roi je tue!—Un roi dont vingt autres dépendent,
> Des mains de qui la paix ou la guerre s'épandent!
> Il porte maintenant le poids du monde entier.
> Quand il n'y sera plus, comme tout va plier!
> Quand j'aurai retiré ce pivot, la secousse
> Sera forte et terrible, et ma main qui la pousse
> Ébranlera longtemps toute l'Europe en pleurs,
> Contrainte de chercher son équilibre ailleurs!
> Songer que si demain Dieu disait à la terre:
> —O terre, quel volcan vient d'ouvrir son cratère?
> Qui donc, émeut ainsi le chrétien, l'ottoman,
> Clément-Sept, Doria, Charles-Quint, Soliman?
> Quel César, quel Jésus, quel guerrier, quel apôtre,
> Jette les nations ainsi l'une sur l'autre?
> Quel bras te fait trembler, terre, comme il lui plaît?
> La terre avec terreur répondrait: Triboulet!—
> Oh! jouis, vil bouffon, dans ta fierté profonde.
> La vengeance d'un fou fait osciller le monde!
> (5.1)

—the character never really recovers from the lack of cohesion of the first
two acts. For here we can see an example of characterization by the synthesis not only of antithetical, but even of apparently quite incompatible
elements. As we see him in act 1, Triboulet is the epitome of physical and
moral deformity, his misanthropy and cruelty symbolized by his hunched

back as he gloats over the misfortunes of the noblemen whose wives and daughters have been seduced by the King. This act closes with Saint-Vallier's curse on him; and the rest of the plot concerns the working-out of the curse, the retribution which awaits Triboulet. In the preface, Hugo refers to the ancient concept of Fatality underlying *Notre-Dame de Paris*:

> Au fond de l'un des autres ouvrages de l'auteur, il y a de la fatalité. Au fond de celui-ci il y a la providence.

—but another phrase from the preface provides an unconscious clue to the reason why this does not really work in *Le Roi s'amuse*:

> Cette malédiction, sur qui est-elle tombée? Sur Triboulet fou du roi? Non. Sur Triboulet qui est homme, qui est père, qui a un cœur, qui a une fille.

The dualism on which Triboulet's character is based is no longer discreet, as with Marion de Lorme, but a glaring juxtaposition of opposites. The devoted father of Blanche whom we see in act 2 is just as idealized as the perverted pander of act 1 is a caricature: both *sublime* and *grotesque* are too extreme, and since we scarcely see more than a flicker of the Triboulet of act 1 through the remainder of the play, we can hardly accept this as a viable synthesis. It really is almost as if retribution were falling on an innocent person—as if the sins of the court jester were being visited on a complete stranger in Blanche's father.

The historical aspect of the subject-matter is treated in a thoroughly cavalier fashion, and the effect is totally different from that produced by *Marion de Lorme*. The King is something of a travesty of the real François I, and local colour amounts to little more than the dropping of a few proper names; while for the character lent to Triboulet (who was a historical person), there is of course no justification at all. In addition, the mise en scène is that of melodrama. The setting of *Cromwell* and of *Marion de Lorme* had both been perfectly straightforward (a single, simple set for each act), and even that of *Hernani* had called for nothing more complicated than a conventional place of concealment (the cupboard in act 1, the hiding-place behind the portrait in act 3, Charlemagne's tomb in act 4); but *Le Roi s'amuse* calls for a complex set, such as had been developed in the popular boulevard theatres for Pixérécourt and other authors of melodrama. At one point in act 2, the action is carried on simultaneously by groups of characters both inside the garden of Triboulet's house and in the street outside; while in act 4, the set needs to show simultaneous action not only both inside and outside Saltabadil's hovel, but upstairs as well as downstairs indoors.

Altogether, it is easy to see that even without the censor's ban, *Le Roi s'amuse* could hardly have hoped for an easy passage at the Théâtre-Français; and it is somewhat ironical that of the three plays produced so far, the one which would almost certainly have given least offence to the purists at the Salle Richelieu was the one which had been staged elsewhere. For whereas *Hernani* and *Le Roi s'amuse* were both calculated to shock, by their stage effects as well as by their style, *Marion de Lorme* was much more sober in inspiration; as a version of a historical subject it was a great deal more responsible; and it is likely, moreover, that it would have been given a more accomplished production at the Théâtre-Français than it received at the Porte-Saint-Martin. A performance of *Marion de Lorme* at the Théâtre-Français in 1831 would probably have given Hugo the best possible chance of imposing himself on the audience that he made repeated, but unsuccessful, attempts to conquer; and this might well have made a significant difference to the future history of romanticism in the theatre.

More than any other of Hugo's verse plays, *Le Roi s'amuse* justifies the description, often applied indiscriminately to them all, of "versified melodrama." Yet the epithet here is by no means lightly to be disregarded: the fact that Hugo chose the medium of verse is all-important. Once again, as with *Hernani,* the most impressive passages are set pieces whose effect depends only to a limited extent on context. Indeed, here it is perhaps not merely, as with *Hernani,* a question of independence of dramatic context: the *morceaux de bravoure* which go some way towards redeeming *Le Roi s'amuse* also stand independent of Triboulet's tirade in act 3, and from the final soliloquy over his daughter's body, Berret comments:

> Sans doute ces sentiments perdent-ils à être exprimés contre toute vérité historique, ou quelquefois même contre toute vraisemblance psychologique: qu'importe, ils nous émeuvent, hors du personnage. Je ne crois pas qu'ils gagnent quelque chose à être sentis et exprimés par un monstre difforme et par ailleurs de cœur méchant, mais je ne sais pas non plus s'ils seraient plus émouvants dits par un personnage dont toute l'âme serait en harmonie avec eux. Ils portent en euxmêmes, et grâce au miracle de l'expression, leur vertu émotive.
>
> (*Victor Hugo*)

One could hardly ask for a more telling characterization of the "operatic" quality of Hugo's writing. And it is perhaps no coincidence that out of this play was to be produced the most successful of all the operas based on any of Hugo's plays: the brightest future of *Le Roi s'amuse*, in fact, lay ahead of it as *Rigoletto*.

RUY BLAS

If the characterization of Triboulet constitutes a major obstacle to the spectator's, or reader's, ready acceptance of *Le Roi s'amuse*, at first sight the role of the central character of *Ruy Blas* presents a similar difficulty. Morally, and in dramatic terms, the character of Ruy Blas is plausible and consistent: the internal psychological aspect of the *grotesque/sublime* antithesis has been handled here with a good deal more discretion than in the case of Triboulet. But socially and historically, the character seems thoroughly absurd, and we find it difficult to take seriously, particularly in a seventeenth-century Spanish setting, the notion of a lackey who becomes prime minister and who loves, and is loved by, a queen. In other words, within the dramatic context established by the playwright, Ruy Blas is plausible enough, but the acceptance of that particular contextual framework requires a considerable suspension of disbelief.

More attention has been given to the sources of *Ruy Blas* than is the case with any other of Hugo's plays. For the theme of revenge by means of a valet disguised as a nobleman in love, Molière's *Précieuses ridicules*, Edward Bulwer Lytton's romantic comedy *The Lady of Lyons* (1838), and L. de Wailly's novel *Angelica Kaufmann* (1838) have been cited; for the Spanish background and intrigues at the court of Charles II, the anecdotal memoirs of Mme d'Aulnoy, *Mémoires de la cour d'Espagne* (1690) and *Voyage d'Espagne* (1692), and the play *La Reine d'Espagne* by Hippolyte de Latouche (1831); Lemercier's *Pinto* (1800) for the characters of Don Salluste and Don César, as well as, for the latter, Maurin de Pompigny's comedy *Le Ramoneur-Prince* (1784); and for the rise of a man of humble birth to a position of supreme political power (coupled with the favours of a queen) Gaillardet's play *Struensée* (1833). The hunt for sources *qua* sources has very little to do with appreciation of the intrinsic qualities of Hugo's play; what the more interesting of these comparisons do show, however (leaving aside such fortuitous coincidence of plot as that with *Les Précieuses ridicules*), is that the twin themes of *Ruy Blas* were justified not only by analogues within the romanesque literature of the period, but also by historically authenticated parallels. The marriage of Angelica Kaufmann, the Swiss painter, to a valet posing as a Swedish nobleman—possibly engineered by a disappointed lover—had actually taken place in 1767; and as

for examples of a sudden rise from obscurity to a position of political
power, in the second of Mme d'Aulnoy's volumes Hugo could have found
an account of the career of Fernando de Valenzuela (1630–92), the son of
an impoverished nobleman, who began life as a humble page in a duke's
household, and not only rapidly rose to be prime minister, but was made a
grandee of Spain and generally supposed to be the lover of the Queen
Regent, while the meteoric career of Johann Struensee (1731–72) followed
a similar pattern: a German physician who knew no Danish, he nevertheless
became prime minister and dictator of Denmark, and lover of Queen Caro-
lina Matilda.

   It is evident, then, that Hugo could have defended himself against
charges of improbability by invoking the sort of argument used by Corneille,
for whom the "possible improbable" was always preferable to the Aristo-
telian "probable," and who declared that "le sujet d'une belle tragédie doit
n'être pas vraisemblable." Like Corneille in *Héraclius* or *Pertharite,* he
chose a subject which, however unlikely, could be justified by an appeal to
analogous cases from real life. But of course it is not only the choice of
general theme in *Ruy Blas* which makes it difficult to take the play seriously;
it is also the trivialization of a "serious" subject by an excessive reliance on
material accessories, and the fact that the final catastrophe depends less on
character or on tragic fate than on chance (the roles of Don César, Don
Guritan). It is not even as if Hugo set out deliberately, like Scribe in *Le Verre
d'eau,* to illustrate the role of chance in determining the course of history;
there seems little doubt that he intended *Ruy Blas* to be every bit as serious
a contribution to historical drama as *Marion de Lorme,* for instance, had
been: we have only to look at the passage in the preface where he refers to:

> l'impression particulière que pourrait laisser ce drame, s'il valait
> la peine d'être étudié, à l'esprit grave et consciencieux qui
> l'examinerait, par exemple, du point de vue de la philosophie de
> l'histoire.

Although Hugo went out of his way to claim fidelity to historical details, the
only kind of historical truth the play possesses is that broad epic conception
of "la couleur des temps," that intuitive grasp of the moral character of an
age, that was later to be so characteristic of the *Légende des siècles.* From
a strictly dramatic point of view, in terms of character and plot, *Ruy Blas* is
the least "historical" of Hugo's plays so far.

   In fact it is another case, like *Hernani,* of the historical setting being
chosen after the event, in order to provide a framework for an abstract, a
priori theme, which constitutes the raison d'être of the play. This is the

attitude to history of Corneille or of Voltaire—very different from the method of the authors of the "scènes historiques," which Hugo himself had approached much more closely in *Cromwell* and *Marion de Lorme.*

The plot of *Ruy Blas*—more obviously melodramatic than that of *Hernani* or *Le Roi s'amuse*—serves as a vehicle, once more, for a highly operatic treatment of the principal theme—the incompatibility of an ideal love with the demands of the real world—together with the subsidiary themes of political ambition, honour and revenge. Again, the lyrical quality of its "arias" and "duets" is the play's most attractive feature, and it is this which has led many commentators to prefer *Ruy Blas* to all the rest of Hugo's theatre. But alongside its romantic *pathétique* and its lyrical élan, this play possesses a much stronger comic element than any of the other plays since *Cromwell*; and the role of Don César de Bazan probably represents Hugo's masterpiece as a creator of comedy. This is no dramatic *hors-d'œuvre,* for Hugo is quite right in claiming that *Ruy Blas* exemplifies more fully than preceding plays the conception of "le drame romantique" as a synthesis of the recognized dramatic genres:

> Les trois formes souveraines de l'art pourraient y paraître personnifiées et résumées. Don Salluste serait le drame, don César la comédie, Ruy Blas la tragédie. Le drame noue l'action, la comédie l'embrouille, la tragédie la tranche.
>
> (Preface to *Ruy Blas*)

Nor, despite César's celebrated entry via the chimney, is his role merely to be regarded as a concession to the popular taste for farce; and Sarcey has left a very shrewd analysis of the nature of the comedy created by this character:

> C'est que, dans ce quatrième acte, le comique n'est ni dans la situation, ni même dans l'esprit du dialogue. C'est un comique tout particulier qui résulte tout entier de la sonorité de l'alexandrin et du contraste de cette sonorité avec l'idée exprimée par le vers ou les mots employés par lui. Il y a là, comme dans tout contraste, une source de comique qui n'est à l'usage que des excellents ouvriers en vers, et Victor Hugo est le premier de tous. Gautier s'en est servi également dans le *Tricorne enchanté,* et Banville en a repris la tradition dans ses *Odes funambulesques.* Ce dernier a fait en ce genre des chefs-d'œuvre d'excellente bouffonnerie. Aucun n'approche du quatrième acte de Victor Hugo.

Sarcey's paragraph was written before Rostand's *Cyrano de Bergerac*, which perhaps illustrates an even more striking development of this particular manner; but César is a very worthy predecessor of Cyrano, and none, apart from Hugo's conservative contemporaries, have doubted the contribution this character makes to the overall success of *Ruy Blas*.

For the staging of *Ruy Blas* in 1838—it followed the series of three plays in prose which will be discussed [elsewhere]—Hugo chose neither the Théâtre-Français nor the Odéon, but the Théâtre de la Renaissance. The former Salle Ventadour had recently been acquired by the manager Anténor Joly, and was refitted and decorated for its opening in November 1838 with Hugo's play. For Ruy Blas, Hugo and Joly chose Frédérick Lemaître, whose reputation had been made on the "boulevard du crime," but who had already by this time acted with success in Hugo's *Lucrèce Borgia* and in Dumas's *Kean*. The role of the Queen had been written with Hugo's mistress Juliette Drouet in mind (she had already played a small part in *Lucrèce Borgia* [1833], and had failed completely in the role of Jane in *Marie Tudor* in the same year). But Mme Hugo took advantage of a short absence on her husband's part to write to Joly expressing her doubts about Juliette's talent; the letter had the desired effect, and the part was given to Atala Beauchêne, Frédérick's own current mistress. Despite the by now familiar opposition of the critics, the reception given to the play was very favourable; it ran for fifty performances before being taken off to please Villeneuve, Joly's business associate in the Renaissance, who was a partisan of musical comedy and had had a clause inserted in their agreement providing for equally favourable treatment of this genre. Once again, therefore, a play by Hugo was denied the complete success it might have had, through factors which had nothing to do with its intrinsic merits.

Frédérick toured the provinces with *Ruy Blas* in 1839, and when the play was revived at the Porte-Saint-Martin in 1841 he again played the lead; he regarded it as one of his finest parts, and the impression he made on audiences as Ruy Blas was sensational. In terms of its impact on the contemporary public, this must count as the greatest success in the history of romantic drama; moreover, *Ruy Blas* is of all the works of the romantic dramatists the one which really proved an unqualified success when taken into the repertory of the national theatres. This happened in very favourable circumstances, for both at the Odéon in 1872 and at the Théâtre-Français in 1879 the part of the Queen was played by Sarah Bernhardt. On the latter occasion, with Mounet-Sully as Ruy Blas and Coquelin as César, the play obtained from Sarcey the sort of enthusiastic review which consecrated it as a classic of the French theatre, and compensated in large measure for the scorn, or animosity, of the critics of Hugo's own generation:

> Il a suffi d'un demi-siècle pour balayer toute cette poussière de critiques, et *Ruy Blas* est entré glorieusement dans cette région sereine où planent les véritables chefs-d'œuvre. Personne ne s'inquiète plus de marquer les invraisemblances ni les absurdités de ce conte de fées étrange sur lequel Victor Hugo s'est plu à jeter la pourpre de sa poésie. . . . On a passé condamnation sur tout cela; on n'y fait plus attention. On prend même en pitié les retardataires qui s'amusent à ces objections inutiles. On est tout entier et sans partage aux beautés qui ont fait, avec l'aide du temps, de l'œuvre du poète un éternel chef-d'œuvre.

Whatever the significance of such a passage may be from a historical point of view, and despite the perception shown in Sarcey's analysis of Hugo's poetic style, it is important to remember that this critic's standpoint was in its way as biased as that of Gustave Planche or any other antiromantic of the 1830s. Sarcey's criterion was above all theatrical effectiveness; he prized the neat, logical construction of the best examples of romantic drama, but was much less concerned with the subtler aesthetic of romantic tragedy.

For in two plays at least, Hugo had brought "le drame romantique" to a higher and more ambitious artistic level, where it could challenge the greatest classical tragedies on their own ground of a pure, refined *sublime*. If *Hernani* and *Marion de Lorme* had not quite succeeded in achieving this, they had been magnificent failures: plays in which, as in Shakespeare, the grotesque element serves merely to enhance the sublime, and in which any subsidiary, discordant reactions on the audience's part are subsumed in an overall response that can be compared without any doubt to the response we make to genuine tragedy. *Ruy Blas* is perhaps the best of the plays in which the dramatist—consciously or unconsciously—aimed less high: the plays in which the mixture of sublime and grotesque is more blatant, the juxtaposition of comic and serious elements more obtrusive. Dr Ubersfeld, in her "Notes pour une étude littéraire," examines Hugo's notion of an "esthétique de la totalité," adumbrated in the preface to *Ruy Blas*, and suggests that the effect of diffuseness or dispersion we experience here is one we normally associate with nondramatic fiction: "l'esthétique de *Ruy Blas* se rapproche de l'esthétique du roman." There are, indeed, first-class scenes of suspense, or of pathos; there are magnificent virtuoso passages such as Ruy Blas's hundred-line tirade of act 3:

Bon appétit, messieurs! O ministres intègres!
Conseillers vertueux! voilà votre façon
De servir, serviteurs qui pillez la maison!
Donc vous n'avez pas honte et vous choisissez l'heure,
L'heure sombre où l'Espagne agonisante pleure!

(ll. 1058ff.)

The whole, in fact, may be superb theatrical entertainment; but in the final analysis, *Ruy Blas* is completely lacking in the cathartic power of real tragedy. We have no difficulty in identifying ourselves with Hernani and Doña Sol, with Marion de Lorme and Didier—but such an identification, so essential to the tragic process, is as impossible with Ruy Blas and his Queen as it is with Triboulet. In the latter case I have suggested that it is the internal cohesion of the character that is at fault, but with the central characters of *Ruy Blas* the fault seems rather to be that the dramatic framework which surrounds them fails to carry conviction. It is interesting to see that both Sarcey and Dr Ubersfeld use the same term to describe the "unreality" of *Ruy Blas,* the latter echoing Sarcey when she talks of "un canevas de conte de fée." There is indeed something "onirique," as she says, in this fable in which "le héros délivre la reine prisonnière du méchant enchanteur, extermine les forces du mal et meurt." The robust nature of Hugo's creative imagination did not, of course, allow him to leave his characters in the diaphanous dreamworld of a Novalis or a Maeterlinck, where a myth of such universal appeal might have been able to achieve a very different sort of tragic effect, no less genuine; but the transposition to the real world has been only imperfectly realized, so that instead of being moved by a poetically valid re-creation of the world of reality, we must resign ourselves to being intrigued by the gratuitous extravagance of a dreamer's fancy.

PATRICIA A. WARD

La Légende des siècles

Charles Baudelaire paid tribute to the originality of Hugo's epic when he said of *La Légende des siècles* that "Victor Hugo a créé le seul poème épique qui pût être créé par un homme de son temps pour les lecteurs de son temps." Both the "primary" and "secondary" epic forms had aroused interest earlier in the period. The neoclassical epic had retained its popularity and the desire to write a long, narrative poem was strong among the romantics, particularly Lamartine. As Herbert J. Hunt has indicated, writers such as Ballanche, Quinet, and Soumet also tried to put their metaphysical systems into epic form.

On the other hand, romanticism had brought "popular" poetry (or the "primary" epic) to the attention of the public. When the ideas of Herder were being disseminated in France, Abel Hugo edited and translated the *Romancero*. The Baron von Eckstein lectured on Eastern and Western epic poetry at the Société des Bonnes Lettres and published extracts of "popular" poetry in the *Annales* and the *Catholique*. Hugo himself repeats romantic theory about the "primary" epic as late as the 1860s when he comments that "ces puissantes légendes épiques, testaments des âges, tatouages imprimés par les races sur l'histoire, n'ont pas d'autre unité que l'unité même du peuple. Le collectif et le successif, en se combinant, font un. *Turba fit mens.*" The original scheme for the *Légende,* a series of "petites épopées," also reveals Hugo's interest in popular poetry. The two earliest medieval poems in the work, "Le Mariage de Roland" and "Aymerillot," are based

From *The Medievalism of Victor Hugo.* © 1975 by Pennsylvania State University. Pennsylvania State University Press, 1975.

on Jubinal's faulty popularization of contemporary scholarship on the *chanson de geste,* but they indicate that Hugo's original intention was to create a number of short narrative poems with a basis in history.

Eventually, Hugo extended the meaning of the term epic far beyond its narrow, generic definition. The 1859 preface indicates that the *Légende* is epic because of the magnitude and scope of its conception—just as *Notre-Dame de Paris* and *Les Burgraves* were characterized by epic dimensions. Hugo says that his ambition was "exprimer l'humanité dans une espèce d'oeuvre cyclique; la peindre successivement et simultanément sous tous ces aspects." Hugo is concerned less with an accurate portrayal of the historical details of each successive century than with the collective movement of humanity. Although there is a plethora of historical detail in the *Légende,* Hugo is not concerned with accuracy; he mixes legend and history for a special local color. The legendary was as valid as historical fact in a literary reconstruction of an era.

In the *Légende,* the most important poems (those pointing to man's progress, particularly "Le Satyre," "Pleine mer," and "Plein ciel") bypass the restrictive limits of time by their mythic and visionary qualities. Published in the 1859 *recueil,* these poems are written more in the vein of *La Fin de Satan* and *Dieu.* They are doors permitting us to pass from one historical period to another, ending with an apocalyptic future. The *Légende* is only the first work of a proposed trilogy so that the epic scope of Hugo's creative ambitions is not restricted by recorded history, and the past is of less importance than the future.

> C'est l'avenir,—du moins tel qu'on le voit en songe,—
> Quand le monde atteindra son but, quand les instants,
> Les jours, les mois, les ans, auront rempli le temps.
>
> ("La Trompette du jugement")

> Le beau Progrès vermeil, l'oeil sur l'azur fixé,
> Marche, et tout en marchant dévore le passé.
>
> ("Abîme")

Hugo shared with others of his century the obsession with discovering the laws of historical development. But much of this interest in finding the end of history stemmed from the personal conviction that the future must justify his own political choices. In 1855, he wrote about this end in a letter. "Je ne suis pas pressé, moi, car je suis beaucoup plus occupé du lendemain que de l'aujourd'hui. Le lendemain devra être formidable, destructeur, réparateur et toujours juste." In working out his belief in both social and cosmic progress, Hugo formulated a vision of history, evident in his poetry, but never explicitly stated as a philosophy of history.

Again, there are striking parallels between Michelet and Hugo. Both interpreted history as the progress of man toward liberty, although not as a continuous movement without setbacks. Both saw in history a sequence of symbolic actions as "l'humanité se crée." And both recognized that the nature of human progress derived from the double nature of man, "homo duplex" with his capacity for good and evil. Michelet had absorbed Vico and the German historians, but in the *Légende,* belief in progress is expressed through images, particularly of ascent into light, and by the theme of love. Nevertheless, the orientation of the epic is toward the metaphysical beliefs of the exile years, not toward nineteenth-century historicism.

> L'air est plein de senteurs douces,
> Un ensemencement de fleurs couvre les mousses,
> L'homme est ombre; on ne peut guère dire pourquoi
> Nous sommes sur la terre. Et bien, je le dis, moi,
> C'est pour aimer.
>
> ("L'Amour")

Of revolutions, however, Hugo has little to say, for love is the liberating force of the spirit. "Les révolutions, archanges de clarté, / N'ont mis que la moitié de l'homme en liberté! / L'autre est encore aux fers, et c'est la plus divine."

This idea of progress affects both the form of the work and the interpretation of history; it displaces the largely anecdotal quality of the original conception. History is also a series of symbolic actions which have either promoted or hindered human progress. Few qualifications or refinements of historical vision are possible in this "grand ensemble blanc-noir du monde." The characters in the drama of recorded history are as symbolic as those of *Les Burgraves.* If Hugo shows any concern for detailed historical interpretation, it is to illustrate the pattern of tyranny and oppression against which man must fight. A number of symbolic tyrants and heroes thus emerge, and the implications of their struggles would have been clear to the reader living under the rule of Napoleon III. Charles Baudouin has seen the theme of the hero and the villain in terms of the archetypal myth of the combat between man and a monster or dragon: "l'Homme, qui se dresse contre *les rois* et *les dieux,* ses maîtres de toujours, à la manière du héros provoquant le monstre."

In the spectrum of history, Hugo was still drawn toward the European Middle Ages, toward the era of *chevaliers* and usurping tyrants, heroes and monster figures. The organization of the first series of poems of the *Légende*

(1859) indicates how completely the opposition between progress and political oppression dominates Hugo's interpretation of the medieval period. After the key poem "Conscience," symbolizing the remorse of fallen man in the section entitled "D'Eve à Jésus," we pass quickly from Rome and Islam to the Middle Ages, which provide the setting for more poems than any other era. This series ("Le Cycle héroïque chrétien," "Les Chevaliers errants," "Les Trônes d'Orient," "L'Italie—Ratbert") characterizes the repression that results from rule by the unjust. There is a succession of malicious rulers such as the Spanish kings of "Le Jour des rois," the "infants d'Asturie," Joss and Zéno of "Eviradnus," Ratbert, and Gaïffer-Jorge. Hugo even defends himself on this point in the preface. He says that the disproportionate thematic emphasis on oppression in the medieval section of *La Légende des siècles* will be counterbalanced by the completed poem, with its movement toward freedom. The sections added in 1877, "Après les dieux, les rois," "Avertissements et châtiments," and "Le Cycle pyrénéen," reinforce this picture of an age of oppression; fixed republicanism and opposition to the rule of Napoleon III are the determining factors in this pessimistic portrayal of the Middle Ages.

In the collection of 1859, the series describing the despotic and corrupt Ratbert is followed immediately by "Le Satyre," the Renaissance myth which is the pivotal poem of the work. The contrast between the two eras appears complete; the Middle Ages become "la prison qu'on brise." In both *Notre-Dame de Paris* and *Le Rhin*, Hugo had juxtaposed the fifteenth and sixteenth centuries, describing the Renaissance as a revolution of the human spirit, illustrated best by the influence of the printed word. The "Satyre" embodies these opinions in his Promethean defiance of the gods, and his transformation into Pan as he sings of man's slow ascent toward freedom. This mythic pattern indicates the importance Hugo attached to the Renaissance as does the fact that he defined the era in terms of the creativity of the human spirit. The myth also describes Hugo's all-embracing poetic experience and consequently takes precedence over the narratives of the monster kings of the Middle Ages. The short poem "L'Hydre" of the second series suggests the mythic pattern of the epic's medieval poems. A knight approaches the monster who asks why he has come. "Est-ce pour moi, réponds, ou pour le roi Ramire? / —C'est pour le monstre.—Allors, c'est pour le roi, beau sir, / Et l'hydre, reployant ses noeuds, se recoucha."

Another facet to Hugo's portrayal of the Middle Ages is the extension of his interest in chivalry. Although darkness and despotism mark the medieval world, the knight represents the light of progress—the individual with colossal strength and penetrating vision who rises above his century, if only for a brief period. "C'est une période de ténèbres où ne surgit ici ou là, comme une trouée de jour, qu'un être de fraîcheur et de force en qui s'épanouit un printemps d'héroïsme" (P. Zumthor, *Victor Hugo poète de Satan*).

As I have already indicated [elsewhere], "La terre a vu jadis errer des paladins," the introductory poem to the cycle "Les Chevaliers errants," is one of the most effective presentations of the knight.

> La terre a vu jadis errer des paladins;
> Ils flamboyaient ainsi que des éclairs soudains,
> Puis s'évanouissaient, laissant sur les visages
> La crainte, et la lueur de leurs brusques passages;
> Ils étaient, dans des temps d'oppression, de deuil,
> De honte, où l'infamie étalait son orgueil,
> Les spectres de l'honneur, du droit, de la justice.

The imagery conveys the great gulf separating these individuals from the masses. The knights are a sudden, evanescent gleam in the night, leaving behind a reflection of themselves. They inspire fear, and their bellicose nature is suggested by the adjective "brusque." Hugo calls them "éclairs soudains," an image denoting action, and "spectres" of honor, right, and justice, indicating the visionary powers of these figures who remind a depraved era of vanished moral good.

Subsequent lines reinforce these images, but in the final stanzas the chivalric quest is conveyed by geographical, historical, and legendary allusions denoting voyage. Dürer's knight from the Rhine and the mysterious, shadowy *paladin* supersede the imagery of light which begins the poem. "O les noirs chevaucheurs! ô les marcheurs sans trêve!"

> Partout où surgissait leur ombre colossale,
> On sentait la terreur des pays inconnus;
> Celui-ci vient du Rhin; celui-là du Cydnus;
> Derrière eux cheminait la Mort, squelette chauve.

In naming typical paladins, Hugo mentions in order historical, legendary, and imaginary knights: Bernard, Lahire, and Eviradnus, making no distinction between the three categories. The final lines, "Et ces grands chevaliers mêlaient à leurs blasons / Toute l'immensité des sombres horizons," suggest a "voyage éternel," a voyage of the spirit beyond the geographical limits which are specified: *L'Albe, la Bretagne, le Nil, l'Afrique, l'Inde, Tyr, Héliopolis, Solyme, Césarée.*

This is one of the few poems in the *Légende* that give a *general* image of a single aspect of the Middle Ages, and it is distinct from poems like "Les Quatre Jours d'Elciis" which contain rhetorical indictments. The symbolic heroic figure introduces the medieval cycles that define history in terms of the conflicts of extraordinary men, both good and bad. Paradoxically, these unusual characters symbolize Humanity and the progressive and regressive forces within civilization. "Le siècle de l'individu est le siècle des masses." As in *Notre-Dame de Paris,* the masses are not capable of the individuality or total free will they will reveal later in their revolutionary actions. Nevertheless, in "Les Quatre Jours d'Elciis," the old man warns the kings and clergy that an uprising will come.

> Non, je vous le redis, sire, le grand dormant
> S'éveillera; non, non, Dieu n'est pas mort. O princes,
> Ce peuple, ramassant ses tronçons, ses provinces,
> Tous ses morceaux coupés par vous, pâle, effrayant,
> Se dressera, le front dans la nuée, ayant
> Des jaillissements d'aube aux cils de ses paupières.

In his exhaustive study of the sources of the medieval poems in the *Légende* [*La Philosophie de Victor Hugo en 1854–1859*], Paul Berret concludes that this is not an "objective" epic, for, in large part, it is a continuation of the social satire of *Les Châtiments.* Placed in the context of nineteenth-century politics, the Middle Ages become, more than ever, an allegory of the contemporary scene with a fixed pattern of reference between the symbolism of particular poems and the general evil which is being attacked. Ratbert is closely linked with Napoleon III, and the murder of Isora should be read in the context of "L'Enfant de la nuit du quatre." Events in "L'Italie—Ratbert," "d'Elciis," and "Le Comte Félibien" are rooted in the actions of Austria toward Italy.

If the allegory is extended to include the chivalric heroes, we find that they represent Hugo himself. He is the Cid in exile, refusing amnesty, and the isolated Welf or Masferrer, splendid in this defiance. Modifications in the imagery and poetic form of the *Légende* correspond to the increasing personalization within Hugo's concept of chivalry and of the defiant hero. The ideal is represented by "La terre a vu jadis," a symbolic statement of the function of the knight. The specific characters in the *Légende* fall into two general categories, those drawn from historical precedents and those imaginary heroes designated by Hugo himself as medieval. Chronologically, Hugo turned first to the figures of Roland, Charlemagne, Aymeri, and the Cid.

In both "Le Mariage de Roland" and "Aymerillot," heroism is suggested by the action of the poem. Although in the opening stanza of "Le

Mariage" the battle between Roland and Olivier is described by imagery which occurs also in "La terre a vu jadis," elsewhere in the poem the two are simply "les héros." "C'est le duel effrayant de deux spectres d'airain, / Deux fantômes auxquels le démon prête une âme, / Deux masques dont les trous laissent voir de la flamme." Hugo creates the illusion of furious action through onomatopoeia: "O chocs affreux! terreur! tumulte étincelant!" The opening of the poem leads the reader to believe that the narrative will depict the physical bravery of two ferocious young warriors, but the actual focus is on the pauses in the action. In emphasizing that heroism depends on the naïve determination of each man to "play fair" and that physical bravery is relative between equally matched opponents, Hugo ironically undercuts the popular concept of heroic action in the *chanson de geste*. For example, when Olivier's sword is broken, Roland does not take advantage. "Çà, dit Roland, je suis neveu du roi de France, / Je dois me comporter en franc neveu de roi / Quand j'ai mon ennemi désarmé devant moi, / Je m'arrête." The irony of the final lines brings this battle (which would otherwise carry on interminably) to a perfect conclusion. Olivier suggests that he and Roland should become brothers and that Roland marry his sister. "C'est ainsi que Roland épousa la belle Aude."

The effect of Hugo's poem is entirely different from that of its source, the thirteenth-century epic *Girart de Vienne*. The narrative framework is undoubtedly the form of the medieval poem, even though Hugo got his material secondhand from Jubinal. In the medieval narrative the combat of Olivier and Roland climaxes the long feud between Charlemagne and Girart over the Duchess of Bourgogne, and an angel from God brings the fight to a close by demanding that the two make peace and fight the pagans instead of each other. As part of the agreement, Aude is given to Roland. Hugo uses just this single incident, removes the psychological study and divine intervention, and adds the brief dénouement. Berret claims that this elimination of the supernatural highlights the heroism of the two combatants in the Hugo poem. However, there is a complete contrast between Olivier and Roland in action and in conversation; Hugo's irony underlines this contrast and the adolescent nature of their heroism.

"Aymerillot" provides another interpretation of the hero's role by means of an adaptation of a *chanson de geste*. Relying on Jubinal's version of *Aymeri de Narbonne*, Hugo relates only the first incident of the epic. Charlemagne, returning from Roncevaux, finds all his barons except the youthful Aymeri unwilling to take Narbonne; Aymeri conquers the town and receives it as a fief from the emperor. Once again, the poem extends the interpretation of heroism given in the medieval epic. The central portion of

"Aymerillot" does not treat the capture of Narbonne or Aymeri's heroism, but rather the excuses of the barons whom Charlemagne asks to take the town. By means of dialogue and discourse, Hugo suggests that daring heroism is synonymous with youth; however, he makes his point by emphasizing the attitudes of those who are older. "Nous voulons nos foyers, nos logis, nos amours. / C'est ne jouir jamais que conquérir toujours."

In the course of the poem, Charlemagne gains in stature as he asserts his leadership. When he is first introduced before he sees Narbonne and decides it must be won from the Saracens, he is overcome with grief at the death of Roland at Roncevaux. The poem becomes more solemn when Charlemagne, like Barbarossa chastising the Burgraves, berates the cowardice of the barons and laments the deaths of Olivier and Roland.

> Pâle, effrayant, pareil à l'aigle des nuées,
> Terrassant du regard son camp épouvanté,
> L'invincible empereur s'écria: "Lâcheté!
> O comtes palatins tombés dans ces vallées,
> O géants qu'on voyait debout dans les mêlées,
> Devant qui Satan même aurait crié merci,
> Olivier et Roland, que n'êtes-vous ici!
> Si vous étiez vivants, vous prendriez Narbonne."

The next episode is not unexpected as Aymeri, who is compared to David of the Old Testament, steps forward—despite the skepticism about his youth—and volunteers to take Narbonne. The dénouement follows abruptly and is in direct contrast to the foregoing dialogue between Charlemagne and his inactive lords. "Le lendemain Aymery prit la ville."

In choosing the Cid as the central character for "Le Romancero du Cid" (1856), Hugo follows the dictates of his Juvenal-Dante role. Both the characterization of the hero and the poetic form reflect Hugo's extra-literary goal of attacking Napoleon III. A verse form of seven-syllable lines and quatrains suggests the oral *romancero*, but irony is created by discrepancies between the title, which indicates a recounting of heroic action, and the content, a catalog of unheroic actions and attitudes leveled by the Cid against the king.

An older, solitary Cid defines his personal heroism in this bitter monologue addressed to the king Don Sanche, a figure representing all the monarchs whom the historical Cid had served. Rhetoric accentuates the parallel between the isolated, virtuous campeador and Hugo in exile as in the direct address and repetitions of the following passage.

Roi, le Cid que l'âge gagne,
S'aime mieux, en vérité,
Montagnard dans sa montagne
Que roi dans ta royauté.

A short poem from the same period makes the same identification between Hugo and the Cid. Published in the "livre satirique" of *Les Quatre Vents de l'esprit,* "Lorsque j'étais un tout jeune homme pâle" compares the young poet to the Cid armed for battle. When the Muse asks about the youth's armor, he replies that his weapons are "la haine du mal"and "l'amour du juste" and that his shield is "mépris et dédain."

The vituperative progression of language within the "Romancero du Cid" depends on the egocentricity of the Cid who continuously contrasts himself and the king.

Roi, c'est moi qui suis ma cage
Et c'est moi qui suis ma clé;

C'est moi qui ferme mon antre;
Mes rocs sont mes seuls trésors;
Et c'est moi qui me dis: rentre!
Et c'est moi qui me dis: sors!

As the use of the metaphor of the free, savage animal in this citation implies, the Cid sees himself as justly self-righteous because of the moral qualities of the king who is "jaloux, ingrat, défiant, abject, fourbe, voleur, soudard, couard, moqueur, méchant." For the Cid, as well as for Hugo, the basic attribute of the political hero is personal honor—"cet astre de la nuit noire." The final wish of the Cid is that, when he dies, "On allume à cette étoile / Le cierge de mon cercueil."

The portrayal of the Spanish hero in "Le Cid exilé" also owes little to the Middle Ages. The poem falls neatly into two parts, each reflecting a different aspect of Hugo's personal experience. Berret believes that Hugo wrote this piece after having refused Napoleon III's offer of amnesty in August of 1859 (despite the manuscript date of February 11, 1859). In any case, the dominant theme, enunciated in the first part of the poem, is that history justifies the exiled hero, although he may be consigned to oblivion by political decree: "L'exil, est-ce l'oubli vraiment? Une mémoire / Qu'un prince étouffe est-elle éteinte pour la gloire?" Hugo answers this question with a myth, indicating his faith that history ultimately grants recognition to the exile. A traveler, in search of the "Pic du Midi," travels for three days

("Le genre human dirait trois siècles") and suddenly catches sight of the
terrifying mountain.

> Un pignon de l'abîme, un bloc prodigieux
> Se dresse, aux lieux profonds mêlant les lieux sublimes;
> Sombre apparition de gouffres et de cimes,
> Il est là; le regard croit, sous son porche obscur,
> Voir le noeud monstrueux de l'ombre et de l'azur,
> Et son faîte est un toit sans brouillard et sans voile
> Où ne peut se poser d'autre oiseau que l'étoile;
> C'est le Pic du Midi.
>
> > L'Histoire voit le Cid.

One might interpret the final hemistich as "L'Histoire voit Hugo."

The second part of the poem presents in a narrative form the king's
decision to recall the Cid, the embassy of Don Santos, and the exile's rejection of the invitation to return. Once more, irony is basic to the
dénouement of the anecdote. Alphonse's decision to recall the Cid is treated
as a mere whim. " 'Ruy Diaz de Bivar revient. Je le rappelle. / Je le veux.' "
The ambassador explains the king's anger that the Cid has not shown
proper respect to his lord; no vassal has ever greeted his lord "avec un
respect plus semblable au mépris." After Don Santos requests that the Cid
show more respect to the king, Ruy Diaz de Bivar speaks for the first time,
concluding the poem. "—Sire, il faudrait d'abord que vous fissiez en sorte /
Que j'eusse de l'estime en vous parlant à vous."

In the second half of "Le Cid exilé," description is as important as
narrative, for Hugo depicts the plains of Spain and the independent men
who inhabit them. He draws upon impressions from his 1843 trip to the
Pyrenees and creates a counterpart for the myth of the traveler which he
uses earlier in the poem.

> Peu d'herbe; les brebis paissent exténuées;
> Le pâtre a tout l'hiver sur son toit de roseaux
> Le bouleversement farouche des nuées
> Quand les hydres de pluie ouvrent leurs noirs naseaux.
> Ces hommes sont vaillants.

The Cid finds complete acceptance among such people who live freely and
without sham; he in turn is their protector. Like Hugo, he is the champion
of social justice, seeing between himself and the inhabitants of the territory
of his exile the bond of independent spirits.

> Les rayons du grand Cid sur leurs toits se répandent;
> Il est l'auguste ami du chaume et du grabat;
> Car avec les héros les laboureurs s'entendent;
> L'épée a sa moisson, le soc a son combat.

Both of these poems on the Cid were not published until the second series of the *Légende*, and, in the final organization of the epic, they are more closely associated with the attack on the monarchy as an institution than with the glorification of the chivalric ideal. On the other hand, "Le Petit Roi de Galice" and "Eviradnus," written in December 1858 and January 1859, are placed immediately following "La terre a vu jadis," and the poems are directly related to one another. Thematically, they treat the hero's rescue of a helpless heir from the hands of usurpers (the "infants d'Asturie" and "Joss" and "Zéno"). Hugo reserves harsh condemnation for the villains of these pieces, describing the would-be destroyers of Mahaud in "Eviradnus" as sterile and rotten. But the heroes dominate these narratives and exemplify that rough, ferocious gleam of light shed by the chivalric ideal. Roland, the last "historical" figure in the medieval poems of the *Légende*, embodies righteous indignation as he attacks the kidnappers of the "petit roi." "J'ai la Colère pour nom," he cries. Eviradnus achieves mythic grandeur beyond even that of the initial phrase—"le Samson chrétien"—which Hugo uses to introduce him.

Hugo's travels in Spain and Germany were a major inspiration for both poems. As a result, décor becomes more than a picturesque setting; the essence of each heroic action is reinforced and amplified by the external atmosphere. The narrative form of "Le Petit Roi" is one of the few heroic *récits* in which Hugo handles the narrative with considerable economy. Unconsciously, he may have been following the model of the *chanson de geste,* for Roland's abrupt appearance and his defeat of the Infants suggests a heroism of action. The story of usurpation is a synthesis of Spanish politics at the end of the eighth and beginning of the ninth centuries; the rescue of the adolescent king is also symbolic of individualistic attempts to combat the decline of order in medieval society.

The outstanding feature of "Le Petit Roi" is the complete accord between the harsh setting, the portrayal of the angry hero, and the ferocious combat. The rough verbal texture underlines this heroism of action and the nature of the countryside.

> On entend dans les pins que l'âge use et mutile
> Lutter le rocher hydre et le torrent reptile;
> Près du petit pré vert pour la halte choisi,

> Un précipice obscur, sans pitié, sans merci,
> Aveugle, ouvre son flanc, plein d'une pâle brume
> Où l'Ybaïchalval, épouvantable, écume.
> De vrais brigands n'auraient pas mieux trouvé l'endroit.

Roland speaks in a surprisingly sharp, down-to-earth fashion, emphasizing the hardships of the life of active heroism. "Ah! pardieu, s'il est beau d'être prince, c'est rude." And the combat is harsh—"un choc hideux de javelines"—as the single hero is pitted against the ursurpers. "Tous d'un côté; de l'autre, un seul; tragique duel! / Lutte énorme! combat de l'Hydre et de Michel!"

"Eviradnus" ushers in an entirely different world. The poem contains most of the elements of a Gothic romance, set in a Black Forest. Hugo creates a mood of mounting terror in the penetration of the sinister woods, the manor of Corbus, and the banquet hall where Mahaud is to spend the night before she becomes the marquise. "Rien ne parle en ce lieu d'où tout homme s'enfuit. / La terreur, dans les coins accroupie, attend l'hote." The narrative presents that combination of legend and history expected from a *Castle of Otranto*. According to a legend cited in the poem, each new lord of the manor of Corbus dines alone one evening in the formidable castle; the custom has been in effect for centuries; thus an additional layer of time is added to the already distant medieval past of the *récit*. There is an element of the sensational in Eviradnus's rescue of the capricious Mahaud from her rivals, the German emperor and the Polish king, who plot an ambush in the castle and suffer the catastrophe of death in the gaping abyss beneath the banquet hall. The fact that Eviradnus appears as a specter from among the rows of crested armor in the hall gives the tale an appropriate "supernatural" turn while the attention Hugo gives to describing details of the décor and costumes in the banquet hall also adds to the parallels between the poem and the Gothic romance of the *roman terrifiant*.

Eviradnus assumes heroic proportions beyond even Roland. He is a figure of *démesure* before he even acts.

> Quand il songe et s'accoude, on dirait Charlemagne;
> Rôdant, tout hérissé, du bois à la montagne,
> Velu, fauve, il a l'air d'un loup qui serait bon;
> Il a sept pieds de haut comme Jean de Bourbon.

When Eviradnus eventually raises the visor of his helmet and surprises the plotters, Hugo uses a Homeric simile to describe him. It is almost the last verbal device left to indicate the heroic proportions of this figure.

> Comme sort de la brume
> Un sévère sapin, vieilli dans l'Appenzell,
> A l'heure où le matin au souffle universel
> Passe, des bois profonds balayant la lisière,
> Le preux ouvre son casque, et hors de la visière
> Sa longue barbe blanche et tranquille apparaît.

In contrast to the economy of the narration of "Le Petit Roi," each element of the adventure in "Eviradnus" is introduced by clusters of images. This expansive technique creates a reverberating effect, a sonority and dense verbal texture, perfectly suited to the nature of this grotesque adventure. Hugo reproduces, for instance, the guttural sounds of German in drawing upon his memories of his Rhine trip for the description of the castle in its forest setting. His treatment of the empty suits of armor in the banquet hall represents the most protracted elaboration in the poem. The armor, a symbolic and sinister echo of the past, is described by slow-moving lines of echoing vowels and sibilants.

> Ces sphinx ont l'air, au seuil du gouffre où rien ne luit,
> De regarder l'énigme en face dans la nuit,
> Comme si, prêts à faire, entre les bleus pilastres,
> Sous leurs sabots d'acier étinceler les astres,
> Voulant pour cirque l'ombre, ils provoquaient d'en bas,
> Pour on ne sait quels fiers et funèbres combats,
> Dans le champ sombre où n'ose aborder la pensée,
> La sinistre visière au fond des cieux baissée.

The insertion into the narrative of the light *chanson,* "Si tu veux, faisons un rêve," underlines the resonance of the rest of the poem.

Other heroic figures in the medieval poems of the *Légende* are not active characters in a symbolic adventure. Their heroism, unlike that of Eviradnus, is not related to the chivalric ideal of the *paladin*. Growing out of Hugo's realization that his political exile and isolation were becoming more or less permanent, each figure is a defiant opponent of tyranny. This fixed symbolic role indicates the sharp tone of the second series of the *Légende* in which most of these figures appear. Their defiance may be verbal and often takes the form of raging discourse. Without fail, the courageous prophet of truth is an old man, representative of the heroes of another age. Elciis, in "Les Quatre Jours d'Elciis" (1857), enunciates the theme of the decline of greatness. "Quelle nuit! N'est-ce pas le plus dur des affronts / Que nous les preux ayons pour fils eux, les poltrons!" Similarly, Onfroy is called

"ce héros d'un autre âge" after he has defied Ratbert, and the theme reoc-
curs much later in "La Paternité" (1875). "On n'est plus à présent les
hommes d'autrefois." A striking example of this verbal defiance is found in
"Le Comte Félibien" (1876); as the old man appears, he is acclaimed first as
Dante.

> L'un crie: Alighieri! c'est lui! c'est l'homme-fée
> Qui revient des enfers comme en revint Orphée;
> Orphée a vu Pluton, et Dante a vu Satan,
> Il arrive de chez les morts; Dante, va-t'en!

Félibien condemns the murderous atrocities of the sixteenth century and
accuses the killers of suppressing the "promesse obscure du destin!"

Masferrer and Welf are heroes of a slightly different coloring; although
one is Spanish and the other Scandinavian, both are derived from Job of *Les
Burgraves*. Symbolic, too, of defiance, they denounce the present generation
by their isolation in an impregnable fortress. Masferrer (1859) is described
as a man of solitude, a bandit, who has a strange communication with the
savage world of nature. "Calme et formidable," he has "Avec la ronce et
l'ombre et l'éclair flamboyant / Et la trombe et l'hiver de farouches
concordes." He rejects with a wave of his hand the offer of the kingship by
the cruel lords of northern Spain, "ces noirs seigneurs," who cause misery
among the people.

Similarly, Welf (1869) is portrayed as the "protecteur d'un pays
inconnu." He rejects all authority, clerical and civil, for he is "un spectre en
liberté songeant au fond des nuits." "Rois, l'honneur exista jadis. J'en suis
le reste. / C'est bien. Partez. S'il est un bruit que je déteste. / C'est le
bourdonnement inutile des voix." In the climax to this poetic drama, Welf
is captured as he offers aid to a beggar who seeks shelter. His demise is a
fitting commentary on the fate of this second group of prophetic heroes in
the *Légende*. Representatives of the Titans of the past, they have little
authority among a generation of lesser men, but they symbolize the type of
man who will reappear in the future.

Although on the highest level the conflict in the Middle Ages was
symbolic of man's struggles for moral and spiritual progress, Hugo's personal involvement usually caused him to define the struggle in political
terms. Further, his sense of having an all-embracing poetic vision resulted in
the epic *démesure* evident in both the conception of characters and the form
of his poems. When Hugo is at his best, his grand vision and verbal sonority
achieve the proportions of myth; irony and bitter satire are used to good
effect. His weakest poetry seems contrived. In "La Confiance du marquis

Fabrice," for instance, there is a narrative comparable to that of "Eviradnus."
The principal characters are the same: Ratbert, the evil usurper, Fabrice, the
aged hero, and Isora, the heiress, but the roles have a different import.
Fabrice is described as a star, now extinct "dans un morne brouillard," and
he becomes the victim of the unscrupulous machinations of Ratbert who
murders Isora. Poetic justice is arbitrarily administered when, as Ratbert
watches the decapitation of Fabrice, his own head rolls to the ground.

In order to make clear the ruthlessness of the tyrant, Hugo emphasizes
the sentiment and melodrama of the relationship between the grandfather
and granddaughter, which is like that of Jean Valjean and Cosette. "Ce
vieillard, c'est un chêne adorant une fleur." In "Eviradnus," on the other
hand, he creates an atmosphere of visual and verbal terror and grandeur
which reinforces the positive heroic act. But "La Confiance du marquis
Fabrice" juxtaposes the malicious joy of the king and his underlings with
the sentiment surrounding Fabrice and Isora, and the reader becomes pain-
fully aware that the grotesque has been carried too far.

> Il semble qu'on pourrait à peine distinguer
> De ces hommes les loups, les chiennes de ces femmes;
> À travers l'ombre on voit toutes les soifs infâmes,
> Le désir, l'instinct vil, l'ivresse aux cris hagards,
> Flamboyer dans l'étoile horrible des regards.

"L'Aigle du casque" (1876), almost the last medieval poem Hugo wrote
for the *Légende*, is an interesting exception to the series of heroic conflicts
he envisioned. Tiphaine is a part of the chivalric world but he deviates from
the ideal because he is without mercy. Hugo does not indict the ferocious
warrior on political grounds but portrays the moral "flaw" of Tiphaine who
persists in the pursuit of a youth who is by no means his equal. Following
a pledge made to his dying grandfather, Jacques at the age of sixteen challenges Tiphaine to fight. When the meeting occurs, Jacques runs away, and
the older man refuses three pleas for mercy as he pursues and kills his
opponent.

One source for the tale was Jubinal's adaptation of Raoul's chase after
Ernaut from *Raoul de Cambrai,* published thirty years earlier, but the more
influential source was probably the translation of Bürger's ballad "Le Féroce
Chasseur." In this poem the huntsman refuses three times to show mercy; he
engages in a relentless pursuit of his victim until he suddenly finds he is
being chased by satanic forces, and the narrative comes to a supernatural
conclusion. The influence of the rhythmic ballad form on "L'Aigle du

casque" places it apart from most of the other medieval poems of the
Légende.

The opening lines of "L'Aigle du casque" set the stage for the tragic
adventure to follow. "O sinistres forêts, vous avez vu ces ombres / Passer,
l'une après l'autre." The setting in Scotland is vague, perhaps because Hugo
had not been there, but he returns to the general descriptive *topoi* used in
the *Odes et ballades*. He depicts the old chiefs of Scotland as having the
same characteristics as the countryside and then adds a few authoritative
names from Moréri's historical dictionary. He emphasizes again the historical distance between the era of the adventure and the time of its poetic
recreation. "Ainsi les anciens chefs d'Ecosse et de Northumbre / Ne sont
guère pour nous que du vent et de l'ombre." Then, after setting the stage for
the action, Hugo begins it with a single hemistich: "Fanfares. C'est Angus."

Since the conflict is tinged with tragedy, Hugo cites Greek and Ossianic
mythology to make the most of the unequal match: the pairs Hercules and
Hylas, Polyphemus and Acis are unequal as opposed to Ajax and his equal
Mars or Fergus and Fingal. Angus (Jacques) comes nonchalantly to the
battle, totally unprepared for the violence which awaits him. Both the rhythm
and the imagery change when Tiphaine appears on the scene.

> On lit sur son écu, pur comme le matin,
> La devise des rois d'Angus: *Christ et Lumière.*
> La Jeunesse toujours arrive la première;
> Il approche joyeux, fragile, triomphant.

The trumpet sounds and Tiphaine comes into view.

> Et brusquement on sent de l'ombre autour de soi;
> Bien qu'on soit sous le ciel, on se croit dans un antre.
> Un homme vient du fond de la forêt. Il entre.
> C'est Tiphaine.
>   C'est lui.

Once the chase is under way, the key moment in the action is introduced by
a Homeric simile, as in "Eviradnus." Angus's sense of being pursued is
compared to a dream or nightmare experience. Then the rhythm of the
poem increases measurably.

> O terreur! et l'enfant, blême, égaré, sans voix,
> Court et voudrait se fondre avec l'ombre des bois.
> L'un fuit, l'autre poursuit. Archarnement lugubre!
> Rien, ni le roc debout, ni l'étang insalubre,

> Ni le houx épineux, ni le torrent profond,
> Rien n'arrête leur course; ils vont, ils vont, ils vont!

The chase and the dénouement are handled well. Even Hugo could not hope to maintain the momentum of an infernal chase for long, so he concludes the poem with three successive incidents which flash by and are experienced as though from Tiphaine's horse as Tiphaine rejects all pleas for clemency. He is merciless as he kills Angus, but poetic justice administers a severe punishment to him in return; the eagle on his helmet comes to life and attacks Tiphaine.

The appearance of the "Aigle du casque" among the final poems of the *Légende* indicates the continuity of Hugo's medievalism, despite the variety of poetic forms that suggest the diverse sources of these "medieval" pieces. None of the short poems of the *Odes et ballades* can equal the conception of "L'Aigle du casque," but the later poem stems from an interest in narrative poetry dating back to the early years of Hugo's career. The central figure within this particular narrative exists, not simply as a political example, but as a symbol from the medieval past in the poet's evolving vision of a humane world.

RICHARD B. GRANT

Les Travailleurs de la mer:
Towards an Epic Synthesis

For many years after its publication in 1866 *Les Travailleurs de la mer* was ignored by critics of nineteenth-century French fiction.

Reasons for this neglect are not hard to find. In an age dominated by the concept of social realism and its portrayal of the average person, nonrealistic fiction was by and large not taken very seriously. In the case of *Les Travailleurs de la mer* it cannot be denied that on the whole the characters give the impression of being two-dimensional, and Gilliatt's heroics on the Rochers Douvres as he single-handedly removes the engine of a wrecked steamship and brings it back to shore in an effort to win the hand of the girl he loves were simply unacceptable by the canons of realism and naturalism. Popular taste, on the other hand, usually cares little for the drab gray tones of novelistic sociology. *Les Misérables* became a steady bestseller after its publication, despite the derogatory reactions of aesthetes like Baudelaire and the Goncourts, and *Les Travailleurs de la mer* to a lesser degree has also penetrated popular consciousness. After all, it does tell an exciting story, and Jacques Cousteau is still trying to correct popular misconceptions about the octopus.

Yet even popular taste has a problem with *Les Travailleurs de la mer,* because the work is not limited to Gilliatt's heroics. It is accompanied first by an encyclopedic and documentary preface ("L'Archipel de la Manche") that the editor Lacroix feared might be uninteresting enough to hurt the sale of the book to the general public, with the result that it was omitted from the first edition. As if this were not enough, entire sections within the fiction

From *L'Esprit Createur* 16, no. 3 (Fall 1976). © 1976 by *L'Esprit Createur*.

proper are devoted to matters extraneous to the plot. One entire chapter entitled "La Vieille Langue de mer" is a catalogue of old and new sailing terms. In part 2 the chapters "Sub re" and "Sub umbra" are primarily metaphysical speculations, and there are throughout constant digressions developed on many subjects at almost unendurable length. These range from listing local superstitions on the Channel Islands off the Norman coast to naming most of the parts of a steamship in language so technical that the average reader can hardly understand it. It is not surprising, therefore, than when today's *Classic Comics* retells the story, it omits anything documentary or metaphysical.

In recent years, however, critics have been taking a new look at *Les Travailleurs de la mer*. Charles Baudouin recognized in it a psychoanalytical treasure, interpreting the octopus as a projection of Hugo's own personal obsessions. Pierre Albouy saw behind the personal struggles of Mess Lethierry to make a commercial success of his steamship, the *Durande*, Hugo's hope for the social progress that he was sure would eventually result from the French Revolution. Elsewhere, I have myself studied Gilliatt's act of saving the wrecked *Durande* as fitting into an archetypal quest motif. But in each case, these (and other) critics have concentrated on one aspect of the fiction only and have ignored the rest. What remains to be decided is whether the text makes sense *as a whole,* whether the apparently disparate elements can be viewed as an organic totality.

If these parts are to be seen as forming a coherent whole, it will be possible to do so only by considering the text as an epic. Many critics have used the word "epic" in reference to *Les Travailleurs de la mer,* but they have used it only in passing and have made no effort to define it. As if cognizant of this fact, Raouf Simaïka has attempted to develop the concept more fully in his *L'Inspiration épique dans les romans de Victor Hugo.* But his effort is far from satisfactory. He defines the epic in such vague terms as to be almost meaningless. He does sense its central concept of totality, but when dealing with *Les Travailleurs de la mer* he can do no better than list under the heading "epic" such banalities as "le grandiose," "l'horrible," and "le pathétique," designations which could easily fit melodrama or myth. Clearly we must begin again.

In his *Anatomy of Criticism* Northrop Frye, cognizant of the fact that all epics are not alike, breaks them down into numerous subtypes (e.g., epics of return, conquest epics, national epics, etc.), but nonetheless he sees them all, whether classical or Christian, as tending toward a similar goal. All epics, he believes, represent the coming into possession of one's own under the benevolent eyes of the gods. The goal is the establishment on earth of a

divinely inspired society, and even beyond that, we have the ultimate apocalyptic vision in which all reality is assimilated into the godhead, in which
"God again is 'all in all.' " This basic pattern finds a simple human expression in a return epic like the *Odyssey;* it stresses military conquest in the
Iliad; we find the theme of the creation of a new city in the *Aeneid.* When
we move from the classical to the Christian epic, we find the same patterns
with a "progressive completeness of theme." In *La Chanson de Roland* the
Christian epic is blended with the national epic, and it is the nation chosen
by God (France) that will spread truth and light to every other culture.
Roland and Charlemagne, its heroes, incarnate the qualities of the divinely
inspired culture, representing the nation's religious faith (in this case Christianity) and its social structure (feudalism). These heroes are larger than life
because they stand for the nation itself. In Dante and Milton we move
beyond the single nation to a universal vision of salvation. It is not surprising, then, that the epic tends to have "an encyclopedic range of . . . theme,
from heaven to underworld, and over an enormous mass of traditional
knowledge." For Frye the Bible is the ultimate epic of our culture, "a gigantic cycle from creation to apocalypse," whose central core is the giving
of the law to the establishment of the kingdom of the law (Old Testament)
and the ushering in of the millennium (New Testament).

Where Northrop Frye concentrates largely on the content of epic, Robert
Scholes and Robert Kellogg are particularly concerned with its historical
evolution. They begin with Homer, positing that there was in his work an
"epic synthesis," that is, that in the *Iliad* "materials drawn from myth and
history, from experience and imagination are combined," that "behind the
epic lies a variety of narrative forms . . . which coalesced into a traditional
narrative [Homer's], which is an amalgam of myth, history, and fiction"
(*The Nature of Narrative*); in short, that every literary form and every
literary tone fuse together in Homer. These critics then go on to develop the
thesis that this early synthesis broke down with the development of Western
culture during the next two millennia, creating all the established genres of
Western narrative literature, whose dominant modes range (although often
in combination) from idealizing romances or didactic moralizing at one
extreme to historical, sociological, or psychological empiricism at the other.

Scholes and Kellogg then go on to postulate that with the Renaissance
and Boccaccio the strands of narrative began little by little to recombine,
culminating in the early twentieth century with the fiction of Joyce, Proust,
Mann, and Faulkner. The total validity of their hypothesis may be open to
some question (Virgil and Dante are conveniently overlooked), but there
can be no doubt that in France this hypothesis does describe the general

movement of literature from Racine to Proust. Boileau's *Art poétique* preached the separation (and hierarchy) of genres in the high classical period, but by 1827 Hugo's *Préface de Cromwell* was calling for their recombination. In fact it was the nineteenth century which gave the greatest impetus to the movement toward the "total" fiction of the first half of our own century, because it was itself striving to achieve a vision of organic totality.

The quest for wholeness in the nineteenth century was caused first of all by the destruction of the *ancien régime* and its theories of carefully structured hierarchies—man separate from and superior to beasts, noblemen distinct from commoners, and tragedy "higher" than farce. The French Revolution brought with it the need for a national economy and a national army, and progressively throughout the nineteenth century changes took place in philosophy, science, history, politics, and psychology. One can hardly go into detail in an article, but at the heart of it all was the concept of dynamic progress towards a perfectly integrated scheme of things. In abstract philosophical and metaphysical thinking we find a resurgence of interest in Illuminism and in the old idea of the Great Chain of Being, which abolished absolute barriers between God and man. In science Geoffroy Saint-Hilaire propounded the ultimate unity of composition and Lamarck (after Buffon) proposed its organic evolution. This thinking led directly to Darwin. As far as the philosophy of history is concerned, Michelet adopted Vico's principle of the living force of humanity in the process of creating itself. Marx's vision of a classless state is only one concrete application of this historical view in a century when Utopian thinking abounded. In such an intellectual climate it would have been surprising indeed had literature not felt the influence. Balzac and Goethe were both passionately interested in Saint-Hilaire's debate with Cuvier at the Collège de France in 1830, and the sense of organic unity is visible behind the very structure of Balzac's *La Comédie humaine* and a generation later Zola's *Rougon-Macquart*. To move outside of France, it is no coincidence that Wagner, with his ideas of total art (music, drama, décor), was a nineteenth-century composer.

Victor Hugo, the "écho sonore" of his century, was keenly aware of this thrust towards organic unity. Although he was repelled by Darwin and Marx, his interest in universal freedom on the social scale (*La Légende des siècles*) and individual salvation for all (*La Fin de Satan*) marks him as a man of his era. *Les Travailleurs de la mer*, too, should be studied as an attempt at total art, as an effort to recreate both in content and in form an epic synthesis. The epic, we indicated above, tells of the struggle of a man (the *Odyssey*), of a state (the *Iliad, La Chanson de Roland*), or of the world

(Hugo's own *La Légende des siècles*) to come into possession of its own in conformity with the will of God. When there is resistance to the chosen ones (in the examples given, Penelope's suitors, the Trojans and the Sarracens, and the forces of reaction incarnated in kings and priests), the battle is joined. In *Les Travailleurs de la mer* the enemy is the sea, Hugo's symbol of the wild, destructive powers of nature on the realistic level, and of the equally dangerous and chaotic power of the unconscious at a more metaphorical level. And in Hugo's mind the sea is malevolent: "La vague est hypocrite; elle tue, vole, recèle, ignore et sourit." In Hugo's universe evil cannot create either total beauty or meaningful order. So in *Les Travailleurs de la mer,* when the sea does create, the result is often monstrous. An ocean reef, in this case the Rochers Douvres, is "hideux, traître, obscur, plein de caves." Under the surface "de vagues linéaments, de gueules, d'antennes, de tentacules, de nageoires ... y flottent, y tremblent, y grossissent, s'y décomposent et s'y effacent." Above the sea, too, in winds and hurricanes, all is "furie et pêle-mêle." Like the sea, these winds also create monsters: "Des têtes monstrueuses s'ébauchent," and the monsters of both wind and sea are eager to destroy anything that resists their fury. Hugo makes explicit the concept of evil present in the forces of nature: "Le mal ... est ouragan, et il tourmente la marche d'un navire; il est chaos, et il entrave l'éclosion d'un monde." At best the energy of the sea is useless—even when it creates the beauty of the octopus's cave, it seems incomplete to Hugo who suggests that a Michelangelo is needed to finish it. So powerful is the ocean and so malevolent that Hugo almost abandons his optimism as he ponders "le prodigieux travail inutile de la mer, ... toute cette peine pour rien!" It is true that he adds: "Pour rien, non. Mais ô Inconnu, toi seul sais pourquoi." There is a note of despair in such an utterance, however. Pondering the grotesque monsters of the deep, like the octopus, he confesses: "L'optimisme, qui est le vrai pourtant, perd presque contenance devant eux." It is clear that his faith has been shaken. To recapitulate: Hugo sees nature in constant transformation, but even at best it achieves nothing meaningful; at worst, it is man's enemy and a region of horror.

Part of the sense of horror is to be found in the idea that for Hugo these forces of evil limit man's freedom by seizing and imprisoning him. Speaking of the steamship, the *Durande,* stuck in the Rochers Douvres, Hugo remarks: "Cet écueil, tenant ainsi sa proie et la faisant voir, était terrible." Nature imprisons not only objects but men. When Gilliatt moves out to the reef, "la mer, geôlière, le surveillait," and later the octopus, at one level a concretization of the sea's formlessness, seizes the hero in its tentacles.

But the sea also represents that area of the world that has not come under man's civilizing influence, his enlightened progress toward the good. Hence the vital importance of the steamship, which can subdue the elements and bring freedom and prosperity. It is a weapon in the combat against darkness just as much as Roland's sword Durendal. In fact it would not be difficult to establish parallels between the nationalism of *La Chanson de Roland* and Hugo's belief that France has a special role to play in the divine scheme of things. Hugo usually sees France as the nation destined to overcome the stifling and imprisoning institutions of church and monarchy and bring liberty and prosperity to the world. In one of the poems of *La Légende des siècles,* entitled "1453," he puts it succinctly. A giant is speaking to the Turks before Constantinople:

> Mon nom sous le soleil est France.
> Je reviendrai dans la clarté,
> J'apporterai la délivrance,
> J'amènerai la liberté.
>
> . . . .
>
> Derrière moi l'ombre est ouverte;
> Le lion qui me suit, c'est Dieu.

In *Les Travailleurs de la mer* Hugo is less blatantly nationalistic, seeing rather in the mixture of the Anglo-French culture of the Channel Islands a happy combination of races that can bring light to the world. But these Islands had had to overcome their own darkness. Once inhabited by pirates and controlled by feudalism, they had had to free themselves and become "une république de fait," and although a few superficial vestiges of feudalism remain, the old tyrannies of repression and even war "disparaissent . . . au frottement du progrès." Now the Islanders have civilized the land on which they live and have become peaceful explorers and commercial shippers. In fact, they have become enlightened thanks to their "incorruptible aptitude au progrès" even more rapidly than the other nations of Europe. As a result they can now turn outward and help others to attain the same prosperity and freedom that they themselves enjoy. "Ces pauvres pêcheurs sont dans l'occasion magnifiques; dans les souscriptions pour les inondés de Lyon et les affamés de Manchester, Jersey et Guernesey ont plus donné, proportion gardée, que la France et l'Angleterre. . . . Ils vont partout. Ils essaiment. L'archipel normand colonise aujourd'hui, comme jadis l'archipel grec. C'est là une gloire," and Hugo concludes that "la civilisation de l'archipel normand est en marche et ne s'arrêtera pas."

Yet if the inhabitants of the Channel Islands are destined to bring light to the world in one sense, in another they are merely representative of a certain type of people: "Au surplus, tous les archipels sont des pays libres. Mystérieux travail de la mer et du vent." Hugo explains why: "La cohabitation avec les phénomènes peu maniables [i.e., the ocean] produit une rude race d'hommes qu'il faut aimer, les marins. Il n'y a pas d'autres conquérants qu'eux." Why are sailors so special? Because these people live on the frontier between order and chaos, that is, between land and sea. They have already conquered the land, establishing order with roads, houses, walls, but the ever-beckoning sea represents a greater challenge. Even more, anyone who lives—like Hugo—on the edge of the abyss must become special, if not a "pensif" or a "songeur," at least a hero of some kind.

In *Les Travailleurs de la mer* the character who represents, not the "songeur" or the "mage," but merely the active hero who epitomizes the forces of social progress is Mess Lethierry. For years he had fought the sea and now, semi-retired, he has invented a steamship to conquer it. The sea is not his only enemy. He is hostile to all forces of reaction. Like Hugo himself, he is extremely anticlerical, especially since the clergy had fought progress on the Channel Islands by claiming that a steamship was against God's will, because what God had separated (fire and water) man should not join. Hugo carefully links Lethierry to the French Revolution. The old sailor declares: "J'ai tété '89," and at one point in his planning for the story Hugo had intended Lethierry to be one of the crowd that had stormed the Bastille. Hence it is not surprising that he is called "l'homme révolution" and that his ship, the embodiment of progress, was launched on July 14. As long as Lethierry stays close to the sea he remains a superior man ("Un être qu'un suroît transfigure et qu'une redingote abrutit"), capable of bringing the timid into the full bounty of nineteenth-century progress. He is fully aware of the civilizing mission of the modern, nonmilitary hero: "On fait des gravures de Napoléon; moi, j'aime mieux ça [i.e., saving the ship] que la bataille d'Austerlitz."

In generalizing about the achievements of the modern hero Hugo remarks: "Ne pas laisser discuter sa conscience ni désarmer sa volonté, c'est ainsi qu'on obtient . . . le triomphe," and "Croire n'est que la deuxième puissance; vouloir est la première." Thanks to conscience and will, human labor becomes "une force . . . transfiguratrice," and "grâce au progrès, grâce à l'admirable esprit d'initiative de ce vaillant petit peuple insulaire, tout s'est transformé depuis quarante ans dans l'Archipel de la Manche. Où il y avait l'ombre, il y a la lumière." Hugo has given us in *Les Travailleurs de la mer* a bourgeois liberal version of a social conquest epic.

But Lethierry, a man of reason, has his limitations, as does reason itself.

He is helpless against the ultimate fatality that lies behind "l'anankè des dogmes, l'anankè des lois, l'anankè des choses." These are not absolute fatalities, however, and can be overcome. It is "l'anankè suprême, le cœur humain," that defeats him. He has not reckoned on Sieur Clubin's treachery, and with the loss of the *Durande* on the reefs, Lethierry, the proponent of freedom, collapses and withdraws into a perpetual stupor, a prisoner of his grief.

It is at this point that Gilliatt, Hugo's other hero, takes command of the action. This doubling of the hero is not unique in the tradition of the epic (one thinks, e.g., of Roland and Charlemagne). Nor is it the only example in Hugo's work. In *Les Misérables* Mgr. Myriel, while admirable in every way, is nonetheless limited by his administrative responsibilities, and it is Jean Valjean who must go beyond ordinary human limits in order to save others. In *La Fin de Satan* Jesus dies, and it is Barabbas who prefigures a new humanity that leads directly to the French Revolution and beyond. Gilliatt is of this second tradition. He goes beyond the ordinary and saves the ship (symbolically saving progress) when Lethierry cannot. He can do so because he is a hero of a different kind, one of those "songeurs" so dear to Hugo who can penetrate the unknown.

For Lethierry the ocean is a dangerous place that needs to be subdued, but for Hugo and Gilliatt it is much more. It is an opening onto the infinite. When Gilliatt goes out onto the reef miles from shore, he sees the Durande stuck, like a great crosspiece between two vertical rocks: "Cela ressemblait à une porte. A quoi bon une porte dans cette ouverture de toutes parts qui est la mer? . . . Cette silhouette farouche se dressait sur le clair du ciel." Hugo adds the sinister comment: "Cela semblait attendre." It is waiting for someone who will dare, not only to leave solid land and go out to the very edge of the unknown, but to go through the door to the unexplored and the infinite. It is at this point that Hugo's narrative modulates from the social to the personal, when what Hugo calls "cette Iliade à un" puts its stress on the individual psychological quest.

Gilliatt is a solitary young man, attached only to a mother figure, and he has difficulty achieving normal sexual development. Observing girls bathing in a remote inlet, he notes that the sight of a naked woman horrifies him. This attraction-repulsion was not unlike Hugo's own attitude, of course. Hugo, too, was a voyeur and attracted but yet fearful of sex. As he comments in *Les Travailleurs de la mer:* "Quand la femme se fait, l'ange s'en va." Gilliatt is eager for love nevertheless, and it is to win Déruchette that he goes out to save the engine of the *Durande*. Hugo makes it clear that Déruchette and *Durande* are varieties of the same name and that the ship *is* (metaphorically) the girl. Gilliatt is unaware of his contribution to the march of progress, however. It is only the personal conquest of the ship's engine, a symbol of Déruchette's sexuality, that interests him.

A more formidable encounter awaits him in the octopus's cave, for the octopus is aggressive, not passive like the ship stuck between the rocks. In this part of the fiction, sexuality becomes open and insistent. Even the cave itself is described with the ambivalence that is always present when Hugo deals with sex. It is beautiful in a feminine way but deadly: "Toute la coquetterie possible à une caverne était là. La surprenante lumière édenique qui venait de dessous l'eau . . . estompait tous les linéaments dans une sorte de diffusion visionnaire. Chaque vague était un prisme," but "cette cave figurait le dedans d'une tête de mort énorme et splendide; la voûte était le crâne, et l'arche était la bouche; les trous des yeux manquaient." Hugo concludes: "C'était on ne sait quel palais de la Mort, contente."

The inhabitant of the grotto is equally feminine and equally ambivalent: "A l'extrémité de la cave . . . derrière une nappe de clarté verte interposée comme un voile de temple, on apercevait hors du flot une pierre à pans carrés ayant une ressemblance d'autel. . . . Il semblait qu'une déesse vînt d'en descendre." But beauty gives way to a less idealized vision. The cave has a "végétation hideuse," and in its "magnificence affreuse" the female sea "y développe à l'aise son côté inaccessible à l'homme," and "elle y dépose ses secrétions vivantes et horribles." To enter this deadly womb, Gilliatt "à ses risques et périls" has to squeeze his way in: "la fissure était resserrée et le passage presque impossible." Then the truly horrible side of nature (and of feminine sexuality) is revealed as the octopus seizes Gilliatt, who will be "vidé dans cet épouvantable sac." Gilliatt's phallic knife is his only recourse. He manages to stab the monster, cut out its eyes, and kill it.

The psychological meaning of this scene is not hard to discern. The "goddess" of the cave is called a "Diane pouvant aimer," and we remember that Diana had Acteon destroyed for his voyeurism. Baudouin sees in this threatening female figure the "Terrible Mother," against whom aggressive fantasies are directed and from whom counteraggression is feared. Small wonder, then, that the battle in the cave is so desperate. By killing the monster, Gilliatt is transformed; he has symbolically overcome the terrors of sexuality and freed himself from their grip on him. Henceforth he will be free to serve others. And he does. He returns to land only to discover Déruchette in love with the local minister and to watch her faint in horror at seeing him reappear, because he is just as he came from the reef, hairy, brutish, bleeding, dressed in rags. Transformed beyond the limits of humanity, having become almost a mythic figure (Hugo calls him a Titan), he could hardly accommodate himself to daily reality. A hero of this stature, almost a godlike figure, has a different function. His task is to save others and then move on. Gilliatt almost magically arranges the marriage of Déruchette and the young minister (bypassing the anticlerical Lethierry, who would never have given his permission) and then returns to the sea in death. His death in one sense is not failure but a culminating act of completion. His heroic quest is completed; his psyche is integrated.

Normally, of course, psychology with its stress on the individual is at opposite poles from the global vision that we associate with the epic. Of course there can be psychological characterization in an epic (from Achilles to Roland and Ganelon), but in *Les Travailleurs de la mer* psychology is handled differently. Just as the octopus's cave seems like the interior of a skull, so the entire seascape is in a real sense a projection of Gilliatt's inner psyche. All the unknown, all the storms, all the submarine horrors that are "real" at the narrative level, also are aspects of Gilliatt's inner being, of his uncertainties, his turmoil, and his inner fears and desires. Thus individual psychology fuses with the epic scene, becoming as vast as the elements themselves and forming, paradoxically, the second aspect of the total epic of Hugo's fiction.

The third major aspect of *Les Travailleurs de la mer,* the one most often neglected by critics, is neither social nor psychological, but enumerative. As I indicated at the outset, Hugo constantly intervenes in his narration to give the reader almost endless lists ranging over an enormous mass of material. This seemingly gratuitous cataloguing crops up now and again in literature. It is very visible in Rabelais and forms the basis of Flaubert's *Bouvard et Pécuchet.* Northrop Frye has associated these examples with the old tradition of the "anatomy," as used in Burton's *Anatomy of Melancholy.* While Scholes and Kellogg might see in this encyclopedic cataloguing a combination of the didactic and the empirical, to Frye this subgenre of fiction constitutes a kind of maddened pedantry that can be used for satirical purposes, but when used in an epic context it can also contribute to that "enormous mass of traditional knowledge" associated with the epic itself.

In developing this aspect of his fiction, Hugo begins with the natural order. In "L'archipel de la Manche" Hugo lists all the flowers that grow on Guernsey (chap. 2). In the following chapters he names all the different grasses that grow there. Nothing could be more pedantic than the following taxonomic listing from chapter 4: "Vous y trouvez des fétuques et des paturins, comme dans la première herbe venue, plus le cynodon pied-de-poule et la glycérie flottante, plus le brome mollet aux épillets en fuseau, plus le phalaris des Canaries, l'agrostide qui donne une teinture verte, l'ivraie

raygrass, le lupin jaune. . . . Est-ce tout? Non, il y a encore"; and the bo-
tanical lists continue not only in this paragraph but in some of the following
chapters.

In chapter 5 of this prefatory section Hugo begins to catalogue the
ocean and its dangers, its storms, winds, and currents. In the fiction proper
we are treated to an explanation of storm patterns around the world, list-
ings of the dangerous reefs in the area, and when Gilliatt goes out in his little
boat to the Rochers Douvres, the encyclopedism takes on an even more
insistent note. Hugo gives us almost a treatise on the winds and the natural
electric phenomena of coastal regions. This is followed by other lists, this
time of underwater treasures: "Sous ces végétations se dérobaient et se
montraient en même temps les plus rares bijoux de l'écrin de l'océan, des
éburnes, des strombes, des mitres, des casques, des pourpres, des buccins,
des struthiolaires, des cérites turriculées." The list continues. Perhaps the
most extreme example of such "anatomizing" is to be found in the chapter
"La Mer et le vent" (sometimes omitted by editors), where Hugo studies
winds and currents on a global scale, but even without this chapter we can
find elsewhere similar examples: "Tous les rumbs sont là: le vent du Gulf-
Stream qui dégage tant de brume sur Terre-Neuve, le vent du Pérou, . . . les
tourbillons de Fer des mers de Chine, le vent de Mozambique."

Nor is the taxonomy limited to natural phenomena. Hugo lists with
painstaking care man-made objects as well. We learn the location of just
about every navigational seamark in the area, the technical name for many
parts of a steamship, and going beyond objects to language itself, Hugo tells
of the transformations that have taken place in nautical terminology over
the preceding century. As we move further toward the human, Hugo cata-
logues the superstitions that abound in the Channel Islands, lists all the jobs
that the thief Rantaine had held around the world (more, really, than needed
to explain his character), and gives details about the sociology of the Channel Islands (e.g., its system of titles, how one begins as "Vésin"—"voisin"—
and works up, if successful, through "Mess" to "Monsieur").

The fact that all this classification is present is obvious to any reader.
What is less clear is its purpose. In his "Présentation" to the fiction in the
Massin edition, Jean-Luc Mercié suggests that the listing of all these concrete details is one way in which Hugo tries to counterbalance the tendency
of the fiction to create a dreamlike, even an hallucinatory universe and
anchor that universe in solid reality. This conclusion is valid enough, but
Hugo has a larger purpose. Speaking of the oddities of marine life, he
comments on the scientific method: "Ces étranges animaux, la science . . . se
décide à les étudier; elle les dissèque, elle les classe, elle les catalogue. . . .

Cela fait, elle les laisse là. Où la science les lâche, la philosophie les reprend."
Hugo adopts this very procedure within his story. He is not content to name
objects, he also uses them as a point of departure for metaphysical specu-
lation. For instance, after having listed the mysterious phenomena visible in
the night sky, the "vastes évolutions d'astres, la famille stellaire, la famille
planétaire, le pollen zodiacal, . . . l'atome errant, le germe épars," he asks:
"Que faire de ces phénomènes?" His answer is philosophical, approaching
the concept of the Great Chain of Being that he articulated in more detail in
"Ce que dit la bouche d'ombre." By seeing all creation as expanding from
rocks and grasses to the clouds, and beyond them to the stars, Hugo is
expressing his faith that the myriad objects of nature are more than a jumble
of random matter: "Leur résultante se dégage majestueusement, Dieu." And
Hugo's God acts in human affairs. The scene in which Gilliatt, exhausted
and apparently defeated by his struggle, is forced to beg the Infinite for
mercy is brief but important. It shows that God is there watching over the
hero and that "un désarmement de l'Inconnu" is possible. This vision of
God as Lord of all creation, yet also committed to the protection of the
individual hero, is typical of the epic vision.

There is still another function to Hugo's encyclopedism. Nature is in a
state of perpetual transformation. *Les Travailleurs de la mer* opens with the
ringing assertion: "L'Atlantique ronge nos côtes." Even land itself, apparently so solid, has been in a state of constant change since the beginning of
time. Reefs are created then destroyed; even a whole island can be formed—
Jersey was once attached to France, Hugo reminds us. But all these transformations have no purpose in history. When *man* changes the land, however, a moral dimension (appropriate in a universe ruled by God) is added.
"L'Homme est un rongeur. Tout sous lui se modifie et s'altère, soit pour le
mieux, soit pour le pire." Seen in this light the enumerations of man-made
objects take on meaning within the general framework of the epic of man's
evolution toward a better world. The old sailing terms, for instance, give
way to more modern terms, which in their turn become useless as steam
replaces sail. Hugo's list of the parts of the engine are thus a declaration of
technological progress. The superstitions given in the early chapters have a
somewhat analogous function. At first Hugo seems merely to be making the
old beliefs concerning sorcerers on the Islands amusing in their absurdity:
"Un autre [sorcier] va jusqu'à avoir dans sa maison sur une planche trois
bouteilles étiquetées B. Ces faits monstrueux sont constatés." But humor
dissolves into horror with Hugo's final example. When a pregnant "witch"
had been burned alive under the reign of Mary Tudor, "elle accoucha dans
la braise du bûcher. La chronique dit: 'Son ventre éclata.' Il sortit de ce

ventre un enfant vivant: le nouveau-né roula hors de la fournaise; un nommé House le ramassa. Le bailli Hélier-Gosselin, bon catholique, fit rejeter l'enfant dans le feu." The change of tone from levity to horror has a movement toward darkness, but in history Hugo sees the possibility for a contrary movement, a progression away from the obscurantism of religious fanaticism which gives way, bit by bit, to enlightenment. As for Hugo's listing in detail all the jobs that Rantaine had held around the world and Mess Lethierry's tales (mostly fanciful) of the remarkable things he had seen on his voyages when he was younger, they serve in part the same function as Hugo's listing of winds and currents around the globe. They enlarge the scope of the action from the tiny Channel Islands and, in the spirit of the epic, provide another example of its sense of scope.

In short, when viewed thematically or in terms of content the diverse parts of *Les Travailleurs de la mer* have created a unified epic. Not that "progress" is easily achieved at every level. Men as individuals are not guaranteed success or happiness. Clubin and Rantaine are evil and fail, of course, but even Mess Lethierry and Gilliatt, true heroes, are limited. The former is powerless to save his ship and at the end loses his niece to a man he cannot admire; the latter loses the girl he loves and commits suicide. Here Hugo's "anankè suprême, le cœur humain," operates to limit personal triumph. Men acting collectively, however, can conquer the unknown (and it is this fundamental idea that explains both the plural of "Travailleurs" and the word "mer" of the title.) Thanks to their will and energy all creation, all the objects that Hugo lists, will come under man's dominion with the approval of divine Providence. The epic is complete in historical terms with just enough tragedy present—as is often the case in the best epics—to prevent the work from degenerating into propaganda.

The coherence of all these patterns is not immediately apparent to the casual reader, because from the viewpoint of linear narrative the diverse parts are isolated from each other. For example, a chapter like "La Vieille Langue de mer" is self-contained and has not a hint of a plot. The sections on flowers, grasses, reefs, and storms are tucked away, either in the prefatory "Archipel de la Manche" or in separate sections of the main fiction with the result that they seem pointless, merely exercises in pedantry. Similarly, the social epic disappears when Gilliatt goes out alone onto the reef and the psychological struggle takes over. Thus the fusion of epic parts in *Les Travailleurs de la mer* is left incomplete, and at times it is even difficult to see that one is dealing with an epic at all. Because this very process of compartmentalization works against the fundamental principle of totality and against the fusion of form and content that the epic tries to create, I have subtitled this essay "*Towards* an Epic Synthesis." Joyce and Proust and other giants of the early twentieth century were able to organize their fiction so that it created a harmonious totality both thematically and narratively. In *Les Travailleurs de la mer* Hugo did not.

SUZANNE NASH

The Allegorical Nature and Context
of Les Contemplations

The ideal of writing a long allegorical poem was in no way alien to current romantic thought. During the first half of the nineteenth century—especially before the abortive revolution of 1848—the notion of a utopian world to be realized through the inspired teaching of the poet was a popular one in France. Hugo, Lamartine, and Vigny were all dedicated to the belief in the redemptive power of language as a means of altering the course of history. Unlike traditional metaphysical poets, the younger generation of romantics believed that once man understood his place within the Divine Scheme, he would and should alter his conduct in such a way as to help realize the city of God in the here and now. For them politics was very much a part of the poet's domain. It is not surprising to see that both Lamartine and Hugo were active in French government or that they read Lamennais and de Maistre with as much care as they did Shakespeare or Schiller.

Lamartine, like Hugo, dreamed of writing "the great predestined poem of the nineteenth century which was to explain man to himself, by throwing onto the poetic screen the birth, the growth, the vicissitudes of the destinies of the human race."

> Elle [la poésie] ne sera plus épique; l'homme a trop vécu, trop réfléchi pour se laisser amuser . . . la poésie sera de la raison chantée, voilà sa destinée pour longtemps; elle sera philosophique, religieuse, politique, sociale, comme les époques que le genre humain va traverser.
>
> (*Des Destinées de la poésie, Les Méditations*)

From Les Contemplations *of Victor Hugo: An Allegory of the Creative Process.* © 1976 by Princeton University Press.

The resemblance of this passage to Hugo's preface to *Les Contemplations* is striking. The romantic exaltation of self leads to a communion with a collective, historical self. These are messianic poets dedicated to preparing the public for a utopian future.

With *Les Contemplations*, then, Hugo places himself intentionally within a didactic allegorical tradition. In his preface he informs the reader that he is telling the story of human destiny and describes the traditional allegorical theme of man's voyage from life to death and redemption. In "Autrefois" he invokes two important allegorists whom we know from his poem "Les Mages" he considered to be his literary ancestors: Milton in 1.4 and Dante in 3.1. That he sees himself as the nineteenth-century French reincarnation of Dante is evident from the key position of this poem at the beginning of "Les Luttes et les rêves," the book that describes the hell of contemporary existence. Its title, "Ecrit sur un exemplaire de la Divina Commedia," implies that the poem was dictated to Hugo by Dante's own spirit. The identification of Hugo with Dante is further strengthened by the theme of the transmigration of souls and the final triumphant line: "Maintenant, je suis homme, et je m'appelle Dante." This dependence upon another human but prophetic guide is a theme of traditional allegory and reflects the relationship Hugo has already set up between himself and the reader in the preface, where he insists that his life is really our life as well. "Prenez donc ce miroir et regardez-vous-y." The prefatory poem of *Les Contemplations* dramatically introduces the traditional daemonic or divinely inspired agent, who will be our guide, as the poet. The hero of the romantic quest is not only a man of action, but a contemplative consciousness as well. In fact, for the romantic recasting of the allegorical tale, redemption lies in the hero's image-making powers.

> Un jour je vis, debout au bord des flots mouvants,
>   Passer, gonflant ses voiles,
> Un rapide navire enveloppé de vents,
>   De vagues et d'étoiles;
>
> Et j'entendis, penché sur l'abîme des cieux,
>   Que l'autre abîme touche,
> Me parler à l'oreille une voix dont mes yeux
>   Ne voyaient pas la bouche:
>
> "Poète, tu fais bien! Poète au triste front,
>   Tu rêves près des ondes,

> Et tu tires des mers bien des choses qui sont
>   Sous les vagues profondes!
>
> La mer, c'est Seigneur, que, misère ou bonheur,
>   Tout destin montre et nomme;
> Le vent, c'est le Seigneur; l'astre, c'est le Seigneur;
>   Le navire, c'est l'homme."

The three levels of existence—individual, historical, and metaphysical—are all evoked by the age-old figure of the ship. The poet, like the sails of the ship, has been filled with the breath of Divinity. Thus the literary voyage the reader is about to undertake must be viewed as an act of faith. As Hugo later says in "La Contemplation suprême": "L'héroisme est une affirmation religieuse."

Thus if one is to take Hugo's chapter organization, preface, and poeticized dates seriously, *Les Contemplations* as a whole seems to constitute a narrative that affirms the providential nature of creation. It is a sacred book, a kind of new Scripture, in that it claims to reveal that obscure but ideal order to us. The meaning of individual poems is deciphered by the ordering consciousness of 1855. Mythic chronology emerges from under historical chronology as the poet-decipherer scratches away at the palimpsest of his own life. The poet of 1855 is able to see that order because he is "dead"— that is to say he himself has passed through all stages of human destiny and has turned back to tell the tale.

> C'est une âme qui se raconte dans ces deux volumes. *Autrefois,*
> *Aujourd'hui.* Un abîme les sépare, le tombeau.
>   (Preface to *Les Contemplations*)

If it is plausible, then, that Hugo's collection constitutes an integrated allegorical narrative rather than a loosely bound assortment of separate works, it is important to determine more precisely the nature of the quest. I have already suggested that the daemonic guide is a contemplative consciousness rather than a man of action. The title Hugo chose for his collection emphasizes at the outset the focus of the work.

The individual poems, or, by extension, the six books, are to be understood as separate contemplative experiences which together lead to the revelation of an Ideal Logos; hence the plural, Les Contemplations. The abstract notion of contemplation is thus objectified and naturalized into a series of perceivable experiences. Each book focuses on a new level of an evolving spiritual and poetic awareness: book 1—organic nature, book 2—

earthly love, book 3—society, book 4—personal suffering, book 5—prophetic duty, and book 6—supernatural reality. Thus the collection begins
and ends with the world outside the subjective consciousness
(nature–surnature), but the metaphysical significance of that world cannot
be felt until the poetic imagination has acted upon it. Hence the romantic
inwardness characteristic of Chateaubriand or Rousseau, for example, is
merely an important stage in the quest that leads beyond the alienation of
human thought. Hugo's presenting the reader with the poet as his guide
would suggest that the reader is being introduced into a structure that
reflects the image-making process itself, that is to say, into an allegory of the
poetic process. There is external evidence to support this view.

A few years after the publication of *Les Contemplations*, Hugo wrote
a series of prose works in which he discussed the steps in the creative
process. In "Philosophie. Commencement d'un livre" he divides the experience of metaphysical contemplation into three stages: "observer,"
"penser," "prier." First one can observe with the naked eye the magnificence of creation. After this period of enthusiastic observation, there follows
a terrible sense of alienation:

> Une fois l'éblouissement de cette quantité de soleils passé, le
> coeur se serre, l'esprit tressaille, une idée vertigineuse et funèbre
> lui apparaît . . . l'état normal du ciel, c'est la nuit. . . . Cet im-
> mense monde que nous voyons et dont nous sommes, serait donc
> l'enfer?

The final stage, that of prayer, is described as the rediscovery of natural
order and the communication of it to the alienated world of men. That
order is now "supernatural" and the contemplator is reborn as a kind of
cosmic self:

> Le cerveau s'écroule; ceci s'en va. Où? Dans le prodigieux
> réceptacle du moi impérissable, dans la solidarité pensante de la
> création, dans le rendezvous des consciences, distinctes, quoique
> en communion; dans le lieu d'équilibre des libertés et des
> responsabilités; dans la vaste égalité de lumière universelle où les
> âmes sont les oiseaux des astres, dans l'infini.

These three stages which result in the birth of a visionary work correspond to the "sourire," "sanglot," "bruit du clairon" evolution outlined in
the preface to *Les Contemplations*. One can find them represented in books
1–2, 3–4, and 5–6 respectively. The work Hugo put together from the
poetic fragments of his past is both a spiritual way and a poetic *grimoire*.

That *Les Contemplations* is really a religio-poetic allegory becomes clearer when one compares its formal organization to the metaphysical system as it is described in the final revelatory poem, "Ce que dit la bouche d'ombre." It is no accident that the reader is not given this key until the very end of the initiatory experience, for otherwise he would suffer no transformation. He would remain fixed in the alienated stage of "penser" in his relationship to the work. Angus Fletcher [in *Allegory*] has commented upon the cryptic nature of all allegorical literature:

> If the style was and still remains difficult, that puts it in the main tradition of prophetic literature. . . . The poet can always justify his obscurity . . . because he claims to be presenting an inspired message. This is not mere allegorical cleverness. It is the attitude of the prophet who in turn is reading the mind of some higher Being. . . . *Allegory thus would reach its highest plane in a symbolism that conveys the action of the mind* [my italics].

Very briefly, then, here is a description of the metaphysical system outlined in "Ce que dit la bouche d'ombre." At the moment of Creation, imperfection or evil is born. Otherwise Creation would be indistinguishable from God or Perfect Unity. Nevertheless, at the very beginnings of Creation, this imperfection is nearly invisible. Matter consists of diaphanous angelic forms through which Divinity shines forth. Yet it is the nature of Creation that imperfection create more imperfection, and that the increasing weight of matter pull it further and further away from original purity. Thus there is established a ladder of being: angels or spirits are at the top, and the heaviest, mute forms at the bottom. Man exists somewhere in the middle, and he is distinguished by his consciousness which is a reflection of the original, Divine Logos. Thus, within Hugo's scheme of things, the cause of the Fall—the desire to know—is the source of man's potential redemption. He is in fact free to choose between a life devoted to the material existence, which reflects his fallen condition, and a life devoted to the contemplation of that superior and immaterial reality from which he issued. His soul is the reflection of that reality. Indeed, all things in the chain of being have souls and hence must be treated lovingly, but only man is capable of bringing about his own transcendence. Contemplation of his own essence and contemplation of God are synonymous. By turning material reality into communicable thought, that is to say by poeticizing his life, man moves closer to those divine origins. Thus God can be perceived by the highly developed contemplative genius through his imperfect and imprisoned material self.

This ideated reality (the poem or work) takes its place in the objective universe and serves as a medium through which the reader can be led in his turn to a superior level of experience. Indeed, once assimilated into the reader's imagination, it will become part of some future symbolic construct. For Hugo each chapter in this continuing narration, passed on from consciousness to consciousness, adds a new step up from the depths of the original Fall symbolized by [his daughter] Léopoldine's death.

The importance Hugo places upon individual freedom within a divinely ordered universe helps to explain further his deliberate attempt to obscure the lines of the narrative and hence to render impossible any "this means that" reading. Like Dante's pilgrim, the reader "awakes to find himself in a dark wood." Book 1 ("Aurore") is by far the most confusing. Besides narrative complexities there are many other obscuring devices. . . . It is only after he completes the entire journey that the reader can see the typological significance of that first book. "Autrefois" and "Aujourd'hui" are temporal words which suggest the historical dialectic of the Old and New Testaments. But in the mid-nineteenth century Divine Order is even more mysterious and distant than it was for Dante's reader in 1300:

> The unquiet heart of the Christian pilgrim has grown quiet, and the very notion of a journey of the mind and heart to God in this life now requires such an effort of the historical imagination as would have been a veritable scandal to the medieval mind.
>
> (Charles Singleton, "The Allegorical Journey,"
> *Dante Studies 2, Journey to Beatrice*)

Society can no longer recognize the spiritual quality of its own heroes. Quasimodo, Gilliatt, Gwynplaine are monstrous to the profane eye.

Although intentional mystification is true of much allegorical fiction, in Hugo's case the shrouding of truth is directly related to his notion of freedom. The reader is expected to achieve insight into a larger, Cosmic Order through his own existential experience. Hugo's use of complex allegory assures the active intellectual and emotional participation of the reader, who is forced to make constant interpretive choices in order to find his way. Never is he offered the direct explanation provided by the abstractions of simple allegory.

Hugo as nineteenth-century allegorist obscures his meaning not just in order to prod his reader into an active interpretive role. He does so because chaos and disorder characterize the particular historical reality in which he finds himself. Thus his work assumes the *form* of history. One of his last great efforts was to bring meaning to the seemingly most monstrous year of all—*Quatrevingt-treize*. Disappearings, rifts, and darkenings proliferate throughout Hugo's work. In the last pages of *Les Misérables* we are told that the words on Jean Valjean's gravestone were eventually erased by time; in the first chapter of *Les Travailleurs de la mer,* that Gilliatt's name written in the snow by Déruchette had fallen into "une profondeur obscure." The mysterious architecture of *Notre-Dame de Paris* is built upon a word long since effaced from the wall of the cathedral. Yet none of these are final endings, but rather moments of apocalypse, promising a new, utopian world to come. Time repeatedly and persistently wipes away the original message. Every century must find a poet to reconstruct that message according to the reality within which he lives. Hugo imagined himself to be the scribe chosen for the nineteenth century. Every one of his works after 1851 is an elaborate allegorical structure within which he inscribes the providential significance of historical reality.

Chateaubriand, Hugo, and Baudelaire all used allegory with a high degree of self-consciousness. Their relationship to one another and to French romanticism generally can, perhaps, be grasped in terms of their use of this trope.

When Hugo mentions in the preface to *Les Contemplations* that his book could just as well have been called "*Les Mémoires d'une âme,* si le mot n'avait quelque prétention," he alludes to a romantic genre represented by Rousseau's *Confessions* or Chateaubriand's *Mémoires d'outre-tombe,* a genre that by its very nature stresses the importance of individual genius. Yet despite his boyhood statement, "Je veux être Chateaubriand ou rien!" it is apparent that by the 1850s Hugo considered his ideology more fully evolved than that of his early hero. A comparison of Hugo's preface with Chateaubriand's "Avant-propos" to *Les Mémoires d'outre-tombe* reveals his intention to move beyond the cult of the idiosyncratic and personal toward the realization of a mystical and universal self. Chateaubriand was loath to give himself up to history:

> La triste nécessité qui m'a toujours tenu le pied sur la gorge, m'a forcé de vendre mes Mémoires. Personne ne peut savoir ce que j'ai souffert d'avoir été obligé d'hypothéquer ma tombe. . . . Par un attachement peut-être pusillanime, je regardais mes Mémoires comme des confidents dont je ne m'aurais pas voulu séparer.

Hugo says:

> Nul de nous n'a l'honneur d'avoir une vie qui soit à lui. Ma vie

est la vôtre, votre vie est la mienne, vous vivez ce que je vis; la
destinée est une. Prenez donc ce miroir et regardez-vous-y.

That he had Chateaubriand in mind is clear when one compares the diction
of the two introductions:

Chateaubriand:

> Les rayons de mon soleil, depuis son aurore jusqu'à son couchant,
> se croisant et se confondant, ont produit une sorte d'unité
> indéfinissable; mon berceau a de ma tombe, ma tombe a de mon
> berceau.

Hugo:

> C'est l'existence humaine sortant de l'énigme du berceau et
> aboutissant à l'énigme du cerceuil; c'est un esprit qui marche de
> lueur en lueur en laissant derrière lui la jeunesse, l'amour,
> l'illusion, le combat, le désespoir, et qui s'arrête éperdu "au bord
> de l'infini." Cela *commence* par un sourire *continue* par un
> sanglot, et *finit* par un bruit du clairon de l'abîme [my italics].

The tragic circularity of the first gives way in the second to a mystical
progression toward salvation.

A study of the typological relationship of *Atala* and *René* reveals that
Chateaubriand's use of allegory reflected his growing disillusionment. *Atala*
can be read as a contemporary rewriting of *Genesis*. The book begins with
the narrator's description of what was once a "new" paradise:

> La France possédait autrefois, dans l'Amérique septentrionale,
> un vaste empire qui s'étendait depuis la Labrador jusqu'aux
> Florides, et depuis les rivages de l'Atlantique jusqu'aux lacs les
> plus reculés du haut Canada.
>
> Quatre grands fleuves, ayant leurs sources dans les mêmes
> montagnes, divisaient ces régions immenses.... Ce dernier
> fleuve, dans un cours de plus de mille lieues, arrose une délicieuse
> contrée que les habitants des Etats-Unis appellent le nouvel Eden.

The action itself is, of course, postlapsarian. The reader watches Atala fight
against the notion of sinfulness that is her maternal heritage as she and
Chactas wander through the wilderness in search of a new beginning.
Chateaubriand takes his characters further and further from that Original
Oneness, even repeating their tragedy of separation in yet more distorted
form in *René*. In the end we hear from one of the last survivors of Chactas's

tribe that René died a witness of "civilized" man's destruction of the "new Eden." René is characterized in the second novel as even more hopelessly alienated than Chactas, for he has become a prisoner of his own imagination, utterly incapable of connecting with anyone outside of himself. Chateaubriand's use of allegory, which points toward an endless spiral away from Paradise into pure subjectivity, will find a parallel in Baudelaire's work.

Hugo, on the other hand, would take language beyond the necessary stage of inwardness characterized by the genre of the memoir, or the incestuous introspection of Chateaubriand's quest, to a direct apprehension of Divinity. This ultimate stage of enlightenment that he later calls "la contemplation suprême" reunites the alienated human soul with a heightened or supernatural world beyond the restrictions of time and space.

It is the second-generation romantic poets' belief in the redemptive potentiality of human consciousness that separates them dramatically from Baudelaire and that inspires Hugo's letter written after Baudelaire's publication of his essay on Gautier:

> Vous ne vous trompez pas en prévoyant quelque dissidence entre vous et moi. Je comprends toute votre philosophie . . . je fais plus que la comprendre, je l'admets; mais je garde la mienne. Je n'ai jamais dit: l'art pour l'art; j'ai toujours dit: l'art pour de progrès. Au fond, c'est la même chose, et votre esprit est trop pénétrant pour ne pas le sentir. En avant! C'est le mot du progrès; c'est aussi le cri de l'art. Tout le verbe de la poésie est là. *Ite.* . . . L'art n'est pas perfectible, je l'ai dit, je crois, un des premiers; donc je le sais; personne ne dépassera Eschyle; personne ne dépassera Phidias; mais on peut les égaler; et, pour les égaler, il faut déplacer les horizons de l'art, monter plus haut, aller plus loin, marcher. Le poëte ne peut aller seul, il faut que l'homme aussi se déplace. Les pas de l'humanité sont donc les pas mêmes de l'art.—Donc, gloire au Progrès. C'est pour le progrès que je souffre en ce moment.

Baudelaire utterly rejects this utopian optimism, later to be so vigorously expressed in *Les Misérables.* For him man is tainted once and for all with the sin of existence.

> Hélas! du Péché Originel, même après tant de progrès depuis si longtemps promis, il restera toujours bien assez de traces pour en constater l'immémoriale réalité.
>
> ("*Les Misérables* par Victor Hugo")

The younger and more disillusioned poet sees man frozen within his own alienated imagination, forever dreaming about an unattainable ideal. Like the swan's or Andromaque's nostalgic dreaming in "Le Cygne," allegory no longer expresses the power of human consciousness to communicate redemptively and to alter the course of human events, but rather enunciates the poet's resignation before the ultimate failure of language to carry us beyond its own self-referential constructs. Poetic language with its dizzying, infinitely allusive character signifies for Baudelaire man's state of permanent exile within the pure temporality of impermanence.

> Paris change! mais rien dans ma mélancolie
> N'a bougé! palais neufs, échafaudages, blocs,
> Vieux faubourgs, tout pour moi devient allégorie,
> Et mes chers souvenirs sont plus lourds que des rocs.
>
> Aussi devant ce Louvre une image m'opprime:
> Je pense à mon grand cygne, avec ses gestes fous,
> Comme les exilés, ridicule et sublime,
> Et rongé d'un désir sans trêve! et puis à vous,
>
> Andromaque, des bras d'un grand époux tombée,
> Vil bétail, sous la main du superbe Pyrrhus,
> Auprès d'un tombeau vide en extase courbée;
> Veuve d'Hector, hélas! et femme d'Hélénus!

Hugo, the exiled poet to whom Baudelaire dedicates his poem, is for him one of those sublime but ridiculous fools who continue to believe in an absent Presence.

Baudelaire's nostalgic despair recalls that of Chateaubriand, the very poet beyond whom Hugo tried to move. Baudelaire's admiration for that other great dandy seems to be unrestricted. "Chateaubriand a chanté la gloire douloureuse de la mélancolie et de l'ennui," he says in *Théophile Gautier*. The ennui that pervades *Les Fleurs du mal* is curiously akin to the paralyzed brooding upon the past of "le grand René." Both poets are like the swan, their necks twisted backward toward an idealized past.

Whereas Hugo would have the bouquet of verses he sends to Villequier from his island of exile carry with them the mediating power of prayer, Baudelaire's verses remain flowers born out of the imperfection of existence ("les fleurs maladives") symbols of the tomb of language itself. To contemplate them is to contemplate one's own mortality: "Auprès d'un tombeau *vide* en extase courbée." The movement away from temporal existence— *anywhere out of this world*—toward a moment of ideal harmony, a kind of musical-pictorial stasis, and the fall back to an ironic awareness of the solipsistic nature of his quest constitute the structure of a significant number of Baudelaire's poems and of the first part of *Les Fleurs du mal* ("Spleen et Idéal"). The mane of hair, the cadaver, the swan, are all symbols that postulate an order greater than themselves and begin the voyage by which the poet hopes to attain to that Ideal Order. But the symbol, despite its power to point toward an Ideal Unity, reveals itself in a seductive sensual form ("comme une femme lubrique"), and thus inevitably draws the poet back to the evanescent world of his own fallen condition from which he hoped to escape. Like the dog in "Une Charogne" he returns to sniff the intoxicating odor of mortality. The last stanza of that poem is spoken in the mode of the sixteenth-century carpe diem love poem, but with the irony of the disillusioned postromantic poet:

> Alors, ô ma beauté! dites à la vermine
>   Qui vous mangera de baisers,
> Que j'ai gardé la forme et l'essence divine
>   De mes amours décomposés!

Thus form (composition) in Baudelaire's work contains within it, as its subject, the worm of time, the destruction ("décomposition") of idyllic duration.

It is paradoxical that allegory is the mode that translates both Hugo's messianic poetics and Baudelaire's disillusioned idealism. Unlike symbol, allegory does not attempt to render divinity incarnate. Its apprehension involves the reader in an experience of temporality fundamentally different from that which attends his enjoyment of symbolic expression. Allegory requires a sequential reading of the text and hence the reader's historic consciousness—his ability to recognize the allusive and conventionalized nature of art. The use of allegory, then, reflects for both writers preoccupation with the inescapability of the temporal dimension. Hugo sees the present within a meaningful continuum emerging from the past and moving toward the future; Baudelaire sees duration as an ideal state, with death and disillusionment as an inescapable conclusion to that ideal. Whereas Baudelaire uses allegorical diction to state poetically the failure to achieve transcendence through symbolic language, Hugo's allegorical narrative encloses within it the assertion of Unity, of Divine Duration. The difference between the two poets, then, is that for Baudelaire the recognition of man's temporal nature constitutes a fall from the ideal promised by the symbol, and for Hugo it begins man's struggle toward spirituality within the framework of a poeticized history, a struggle that can be communicated allegorically—from consciousness to consciousness.

JEFFREY MEHLMAN

Revolution and Repetition
in Notre-Dame de Paris

Our *tocsin* is as well a heliotrope, a movement toward the sun (Phoebus) that fails to attain it, a flawed turning toward the source: a blot against the sun. But that was precisely the situation of the *tocsin* in "Aures habet, et non audiet." It figured there as an intermittent blackness silently blocking out the sun. Pierre Gringoire as clown: "Que voulez-vous? c'est une éclipse." Heliotrope/tocsin; flower/bell: we encounter here a movement of reversal of shape which is that of the oscillating bell itself. A second meaning of heliotrope is bloodstone. The *Oxford English Dictionary* quotes Philemon Holland: "The pretious stone Heliotropium is a deepe greene in manner of a leeke garnished with veins of bloud." La Esmeralda is, then, a heliotrope swollen animate. Having progressed from La Esmeralda to *tocsin* to heliotrope, we find we have come full circle with the return of a "deepe greene" stone. Our writing machine is then the pure and unending movement of metaphoricity from term to term in our circular chain. But these results converge with those of Derrida's remarkable inquiry into the status of metaphor in the history of philosophy. From Aristotle to Nietzsche, he demonstrates that the metaphor of the heliotrope, a failed movement toward an elusive source, is the metaphor of metaphoricity itself: "Métaphore veut donc dire héliotrope, à la fois mouvement tourné vers le soleil et mouvement tournant du soleil" ("La Mythologie blanche," in *Marges*). Heliotropism is for Derrida the infinitely cascading medium of metaphoricity within which a certain non-teleological death of philosophy may be effected. For us it

From *Revolution and Repetition: Marx, Hugo, Balzac.* © 1977 by the Regents of the University of California. University of California Press, 1977.

takes its place through La Esmeralda in a complex writing machine. But to invoke such a machine in the context of *Notre-Dame de Paris* is inevitably to conjure up the printing presses of "Ceci tuera cela," that is, to work toward the undermining of that other onto-theological monument, the cathedral itself.

La Esmeralda as character leads both Claude Frollo and Quasimodo to their doom. But as writing machine she visits a more threatening death on these characters. For brought to a certain pitch the primordial metaphoricity we have invoked is corrosive of that minimum of homogeneity without which the very notion of "character" loses its consistency. The case of the archdeacon is particularly instructive. At an important juncture in the novel, Claude, brooding with a colleague in alchemy in his study within the cathedral, observes a fly foiled in an attempted flight out of the edifice toward the sun. It is caught in a spider's web and quickly devoured. Claude's impassioned commentary:

> Voilà un symbole de tout. Elle [la mouche] vole, elle est joyeuse, elle vient de naître; oh! oui, mais qu'elle se heurte à la rosace fatale, l'araignée en sort, l'araignée hideuse! Pauvre danseuse! pauvre mouche prédestinée! Maître Jacques, laissez faire! c'est la fatalité! Hélàs! Claude, tu es l'araignée. Claude, tu es la mouche aussi! Tu volais à la science, à la lumière, au soleil, tu n'avais souci que d'arriver au grand air, au grand jour de la vérité éternelle; mais, en te précipitant vers la lucarne éblouissante qui donne sur l'autre monde, sur le monde de la clarté, de l'intelligence et de la science, mouche aveugle, docteur insensé, tu n'as pas vu cette subtile toile d'araignée tendue par le destin entre la lumière et toi, tu t'y es jeté à corps perdu, misérable fou, et maintenant tu te débats, la tête brisée et les ailes arrachées, entre les antennes de fer de la fatalité!—Maître Jacques! maître Jacques! laissez faire l'araignée.

Claude Frollo is, then, caught up in the heliotropic metaphor. And the failure inscribed in that movement is here attributed to the web—or text—of fate. But *fate* itself, in its written form, is, of course, a highly charged word in the novel. The preface evokes the disappearance of the word ANANKE etched into the wall of the cathedral, and concludes: "C'est sur ce mot qu'on a fait ce livre." Writing the novel is thus tantamount to restoring that word or text (the web of *fate*), the medium through which the heliotrope consummates its failure.

We should note here how closely Frollo's heliotropic scenario prefigures a crucial subsequent episode in the novel: La Esmeralda's seduction by Phoebus and victimization by Claude. And yet the point to be made in the case cited is that Claude is *both* fly and spider. At this point in the novel he is less a figure in an allegorical drama than the sheer capacity for displacement in a fantasmatic scenario. And it is that radical metaphoricity which is a measure of the havoc wreaked by the heliotrope on what one no longer feels quite justified in calling the "character" of Claude Frollo.

And what of Quasimodo? The reader's experience of the novel is marked by a growing realization of a certain subsitutability of the hunchback for La Esmeralda. For Quasimodo was the child abandoned by the gypsies in place of the abducted La Esmeralda. Even at the level of their names one begins to see a certain contamination of the sublime by the grotesque, a surprising equivalence between the two. For Quasimodo, we are reminded, means "à peu près." La Esmeralda is addressed by her beloved, who can never quite recall her name, as Similar. Similar, Quasimodo: close, but not quite. The novel thus elaborates a surprising interchangeability between the epitomes of the sublime and the grotesque. This is underscored in the chapter entitled "Une Larme pour une goutte d'eau." When La Esmeralda brings water to the pilloried Quasimodo, he emits a telling tear: "Alors, dans cet oeil jusque-là si sec et si brûle, on vit rouler une grosse larme qui tomba lentement le long de ce visage difforme et longtemps contracté par le désespoir." The episode is a sentimental illustration of the process Freud termed "anaclisis [*Anlehnung*]": the movement whereby a fantasmatic and "partial" object is generated "marginally" in excess of the satisfaction of an instinct. The very subjectivity of Quasimodo is metonymically focused on that drop and its substitutions. For when *his* turn comes to reciprocate the gypsy's kindness, Hugo evokes his exploit as follows:

> Il enjamba la balustrade de la galerie, saisit la corde des pieds, des genoux et des mains, puis on le vit couler sur la façade, comme une goutte de pluie qui glisse le long d'une vitre, courir vers les deux bourreaux avec la vitesse d'un chat tombé d'un toit, les terrasser sous deux poings énormes, enlever l'égyptienne d'une main, comme un enfant sa poupée, et d'un seul élan rebondir jusque dans l'église, en élevant la jeune fille au-dessus de sa tête, et en criant d'une voix formidable: Asile!

At his most intense, Quasimodo is nothing but the sheer mobility of that "partial object" in its circuit of exchange: raindrop for tear (for a drop of water). Thus it is that La Esmeralda-Similar, our "writing machine," continues to tear apart the characters of the novel. We have already seen Claude

Frollo inscribed as heliotrope. It remains for us to see Quasimodo transformed into a silent *tocsin*.

That operation occurs in one of the most memorable chapters of the
book, one in which Hugo presents what I should be inclined to call an
exemplary *theory* of textuality. "*Théorie*: (repris au xviiie siècle au grec
theoria, 'procession'). *Antiq*. Députation envoyée par une ville à une fête
solenelle.—*Par ext*. Groupe de personnes qui s'avancent les unes derrière les
autres." We shall do well to adopt this entirely secondary meaning of theory
for it admirably captures the silent procession of *truands,* the delegates of
the city of thieves, as they cross the bridges of the Seine to converge upon the
cathedral: "L'immense multitude parut se former en colonne. . . . Dix min-
utes après, les cavaliers du guet s'enfuyaient épouvantés devant une longue
procession d'hommes noirs et silencieux qui descendait vers le Pont-au-
Change." Such is this army of the night, "cohue de morts, muette, impalpable . . . effrayant troupeau d'hommes et de femmes en haillons, armés de
faulx, de piques, de serpes." Its members have come to besiege the masterpiece, cathect the cathedral: to liberate La Esmeralda, a certain movement
of metaphoricity imprisoned within the monument. Now what is remarkable is the form that the onslaught eventually takes. The *truands* scale the
walls of the cathedral: "Aucun moyen de résister à cette marée ascendante
de faces épouvantables. La fureur faisait rutiler ces figures farouches. . . .
On eut dit que quelque autre église avait envoyé à l'assaut de Notre-Dame
ses gorgones, ses dogues, ses drées, ses démons, ses sculptures les plus
fantastiques. C'était comme une couche de monstres vivants sur les monstres
de pierre de la façade." What we are invited to witness is not a penetration
to the heart of the masterpiece but a bizarre simulation of its surface. But
what is our *tocsin* if not a certain silent vibration cut off from its *end* as
sound? And what our heliotrope if not a wavering that fails to attain its
source? Indeed the "practice" which is indistinguishable from our own
textual "theory" has consisted in playing off surface (of *Quatrevingt-treize*)
against surface (of *Notre-Dame de Paris*), of replicating the *tocsin* of the
later novel, through the most rigorously superficial of resemblances, into a
perfectly monstrous *toque-sein*. It is in that context that we are inclined to
consider the *crowning* image of the entire sequence. Quasimodo, in the
delusion that he is protecting La Esmeralda from her would-be ravishers,
prepares a fire atop the cathedral to melt the lead he eventually pours on the
besiegers of the cathedral. "Et parmi ces monstres ainsi réveillés de leur
sommeil de pierre par cette flamme, par ce bruit, il y en avait un qui marchait
et qu'on voyait de temps en temps passer sur le front ardent du bûcher
comme une chauve-souris devant une chandelle." The odd alternation of

light and eclipse is metaphorized as a "phare étrange" and greeted by the assembled outlaws with a "crainte religieuse." But the object of this terror reproduces quite precisely the configuration of the silent *tocsin* of *Quatrevingt-treize*. The image in the earlier novel comes as the culmination of a series of protective strikes by Quasimodo from above: "la grêle de moellons commença à tomber, et il leur sembla [aux truands] que l'église se démolissait d'elle-même sur leur tête." Quasimodo become *tocsin* is thus the goal of a silent procession, of a "theory" of textuality. Become "writing machine," he presides blindly, above all deafly, over the very process whereby the cathedral seems to dismantle itself.

Such as well is the goal of our own textual theory: a perverse replication or repetition-in-difference of the surface, making the limits of the masterpiece tremble in a movement of silent alternation. It is an effort to coincide with that infinitely superficial stratum of the text whereby it begins undoing or dismantling itself. It calculates its effects solely in exhilaration, in the energy released by the transformations achieved. But this theory is a practice as well, or rather, it is insufficiently stable to be able to sustain that metalinguistic distance without which the distinction theory/practice is unthinkable. As Hugo has it in *Notre-Dame de Paris*, the outlaws, in their very effort to liberate that dimension of radical metaphoricity (La Esmeralda) from the masterpiece, simultaneously fail to attain their object and find *themselves* appearing as grotesque duplications (or metaphors) of the surface of the cathedral (as masterpiece). Our (Hugo's?) "theory," then, is a practice that may be defined through the perverse rigor with which it *misses* its object. To borrow a pun from *Les Misérables*, it is less a philosophy of literature than a *filousophie* of textuality.

Now oddly enough the entire sequence initiated by the "theory" of outlaws is described by Hugo as premonitory of 1789. For the storming of the cathedral is observed with remarkable calm by Louis XI from his apartment in the Bastille. His composure is the result of a misinterpretation. He believes that the populace is attacking not the royal cathedral but a feudal bailiwick: "Ah! mon peuple! voilà donc que tu m'aides enfin à l'écroulement des seigneuries!" While still under this misconception, the king has the following exchange with a Flemish visitor attuned to the mood of the people:

> Je dis, sire, que vous avez peut-être raison, que l'heure du peuple n'est pas venue chez vous.
>   Louis XI le regarda avec son oeil pénétrant.
>   —Et quand viendra cette heure, maître?

—Vous l'entendrez sonner.

—A quelle horloge, s'il vous plaît?

Coppenole avec sa contenance tranquille et rustique fit approcher le roi de la fenêtre.—Ecoutez, sire! Il y a ici un donjon, un beffroi, des canons, des bourgeois, des soldats. Quand le beffroi bourdonnera, quand les canons gronderont, quand le donjon croulera à grand bruit, quand bourgeois et soldats hurleront et s'entretueront, c'est l'heure qui sonnera.

Shorly thereafter Louis is shocked to discover that the object of the attack is his cathedral and moves to crush the revolt pitilessly.

The besieging of the masterpiece by the most heterogeneous elements in society is thus plainly, for Hugo, a premonition of the Revolution. One senses in this somewhat improbable parallel between the events of 1482 and 1789 that liberal teleology of history which would see in the year of the bourgeois revolution a culmination of all that preceded it. But such a juxtaposition of the two years has a precise basis in the textual activity of our author. For shortly after the completion of *Notre-Dame de Paris,* he was, in *Littérature et philosophie mêlées* (1834), to reproduce the constellation of traits that had crystallized as Quasimodo in the figure of the great orator of the revolution, Mirabeau: "homme avorté," "créature disloquée," "mâle monstrueux." Like Quasimodo, Mirabeau is associated with the spirit of the People. The lawyer of Aix was, in fact, for Hugo "the most complete symbol" of the People in 1789. The difference, of course, is in the degree of articulateness of the two. The mythographers of Hugo's *oeuvre* join the poet here in his teleology of 1789. Thus P. Albouy: "Au xve siécle, le peuple, difforme encore et proche de la brute, ne sait pas parler. Mais son jour viendra, prédit par le chaussetier gantois, Jacques Coppenole, qui prophétise, devant Louis XI, la chute de la Bastille." The *end* of history is incarnate in the *logos,* the "Verbe" emergent at last from the deformed mouth of Mirabeau. The virtual muteness of Quasimodo is a falling short of that phonic plenitude.

But what of 1793? Our reading of *Quatrevingt-treize* mediated nothing so much as a deconstruction of the logocentric scheme which Albouy has (justifiably) extracted from his juxtaposition of Quasimodo and Mirabeau. The later novel would afford us the means to reinscribe the relation between the silence of the bell-ringer and the eloquence of the orator. The cult of 1789 in Hugo would serve to repress the textuality of 1793. We have seen Quasimodo become silent *tocsin* atop Notre-Dame. Hugo interprets that warning signal affirmatively as an anticipation of the storming of the

Bastille: only then will the hour of the people have *sounded*. But in our retrospective reading the *tocsin* of the earlier novel is clearly a component in the "writing machine" of 1793. Indeed, in an important way, the "warning bell" of 1482 *repeats* that of the later novel. In a certain undecidability between the mute bell of 1482 (anticipating 1789) and that of 1793 (the death knell of the liberal revolution), the ideals of 1789, logocentric and *bourgeois* through and through, are disoriented, made to suffer a devastating disarticulation. An entire teleology of history is disrupted. Such is the unintended force of Hugo's textuality. It is to a final effort to domesticate that energy within *Notre-Dame de Paris* that we now shall turn.

In the benighted battle between Quasimodo and the *truands,* the struggle for possession of La Esmeralda, . . . she escapes. Or rather, she is abducted by a desperate Claude Frollo in disguise. As the novel draws to a close, the *end* of her evasion becomes clear: she is moving toward a discovery of her own identity. The cascading movement of metaphoricity itself (*tocsin* and heliotrope), crystallized in the imaginary unity of a character, would here be reduced, come to rest in a revelation of selfhood. A discussion of the circumstances of that discovery requires reference to a character we have not yet mentioned. For after Claude Frollo despairs of ever winning the affection of La Esmeralda, he delivers her into the punitive custody of Gudule, while he makes off to fetch the royal authorities. Gudule is a wretched penitent who has retreated in misery from the world after her one joy in life, an infant daughter, was kidnapped by a band of gypsies. Her one vestige of the child is a single slipper which she now cherishes in the penitent's cave she occupies in Paris. Above that retreat are inscribed the edifying words: TU, ORA. But in view of the sinister character of the cave, the public has transformed those words into a demeaning name for the retreat: "Trou aux rats." The one emotion Gudule still seems capable of is rage at the most visible gypsy in the book, La Esmeralda, whom she frequently sees dancing in the square adjacent to her cell. Whence Claude's confidence in delivering La Esmeralda into Gudule's custody. Events move rapidly toward the melodramatic moment of recognition. Gudule shrieks her rage, then her desperate love for her child, and finally manifests the slipper. Whereupon:

> —Montrez-moi ce soulier, dit l'égyptienne en tressaillant. Dieu! Dieu! Et en même temps, de la main qu'elle avait libre, elle ouvrait vivement le petit sachet orné de verroterie verte qu'elle portait au cou.
>
> —Va! va! grommelait Gudule, fouille ton amulette du démon!
> Tout à coup elle s'interrompit, trembla de tout son corps et cria

avec une voix qui venait du plus profond des entrailles:—Ma
fille!
    L'égyptienne venait de tirer du sachet un petit soulier absolu-
ment pareil à l'autre.

Victor Hugo hélàs . . . Before pursuing the analysis it is worthwhile pausing
to savor the intolerable sentimentality of the scene. Shortly thereafter, the
royal guard arrives led by none other than Phoebus. La Esmeralda, secreted
in the recesses of Gudule's cave, cannot resist a last heliotropic move. In a
passage already quoted, she betrays herself by turning toward Phoebus and
shouting his name—just as he disappears from view. In this final heliotropism, what is lost is both object (Phoebus) and subject: as a result of her act,
she is captured and soon put to death.
    How are we to read this final sequence? We may begin by noting how
closely the pair of slippers corresponds to that dimension which Lévi-Strauss,
then Lacan have isolated as the *symbolique*. E. Ortigues's evocation of the
tessera of antiquity is a convenient guide here: "Le symbole est un gage de
reconnaissance, un objet coupé en deux et distribué entre deux partenaires
alliés qui devaient conserver chacun leur part et la transmettre à leurs descendants, de telle sorte que ces éléments complémentaires à nouveau
rapprochés, permettaient par leur ajustement réciproque de faire reconnaître
les porteurs et d'attester les liens d'alliance contractés antérieurement. Le
sum-bolon consiste dans la corrélation entre des éléments sans valeur isolée,
mais dont la réunion (*sum-ballô*) ou l'ajustement réciproque permet à deux
alliés de se faire reconnaître comme tels" (*Le Discours et le symbole*). A first
reading of the novel's conclusion, then: to be confronted with the contents
of the *toque-sein,* to discover the *identity* of a character who has gone by the
palpably false name—*toc-seing*—of La Esmeralda is to encounter a certain
ludicrousness of the scenario informing the very notion of the *symbolique*.
It is perhaps as well to prefer the receptacle, the residue: to affirm the *tocsin*
or writing machine as containing or exceeding the *symbolique*. It is perhaps
even to suspect that Hugo invites as much in his plotting of La Esmeralda's
last "heliotropism," a thoroughly metaphorical movement fundamentally
destructive of her newly acquired identity.
    The *symbolique* of the structuralists is that dimension of unconscious
structure through which the values and desires of a society are transmitted.
As such, it occupies within the thought of our contemporaries a role not
unlike that other structure bearing and preserving the traditions of a culture: the cathedral of Notre-Dame in Hugo's novel. In positing the
symbolique as contained by the writing machine, may we not then be deal-

ing with a phenomenon analogous to that odd replication of the surface of the cathedral through which that monument was besieged? Such is the hypothesis I shall attempt to sustain in the ensuing analysis. In fact, I shall be discussing the "besieging" of a specific component of the *symbolique*, the concept of "castration." For that category, originally the theme of an "infantile sexual theory," is the cornerstone of the *symbolique*. The castration complex, coming at the culmination of the Oedipal crisis, marks the child's entry into the intersubjective structure of exchange known as the *symbolique*. To exceed and dislocate the notion of castration, to work one's way out of the order it *structures*, is thus perhaps to move in an analytic medium that can no longer be called "structuralist."

As our analysis of the textual "theory" of *Notre-Dame de Paris* converges with the issues of a crucially contemporary debate, we should do well to situate briefly the terms of that crux. In the interpretation of Freud that has loomed so large in the intellectual life of France in the last ten years, the notion of "castration" has enjoyed special privilege. The specific reasons for its attractiveness are clear. It is a theory of (sexual) difference, catastrophic to every image of (ego's) integrity, a cornerstone of the structural unconscious. There were few categories in the history of Western thought better suited to the structuralist project than Freud's "castration." Indeed, when asked informally by bewildered Americans what French structuralism was, after all, all about, one was hard put to find a more usefully concise response than the flippant observation that there were two kinds of people in the world: those who when they read Freud find the most potentially liberating or exhilarating category to be bisexuality and those for whom it was castration. The Americans were among the former; the French (structuralists) among the latter. Lacan and those around him were distinguished by their willingness to take seriously Freud's remark that the castration complex was the "bedrock" beyond which one could not go.

Yet whatever the analytic yields accruing to the French from their privileging of "castration," the affirmation of that category entails a major drawback for any intellectual enterprise aspiring to a stance that might be called radical. For to the extent that the castration complex marks the (logical) moment of the subject's insertion into structure, any affirmation of castration runs the severe risk of sounding flatly adaptative. (Indeed, the heavily normative aspects of Freud's theory of sexuality are intimately bound up with the castration complex.) Much of the aftermath of structuralism may be read in terms of degrees of ambivalence toward the duplicity of castration: at once radical theory of *difference* and medium through which subject is made to adapt to structure. Thus Deleuze and Guattari, for example, in a celebrated volume [*L'Anti-Oedipe*], have attempted to laugh away castration—and, ultimately, Freud with it—as the "ideology of lack." The risk run in such a move is that in writing off Freud, one may quite simply have eliminated the interpretative medium in which the question of sexuality may be *thought* with maximal intensity. One suspects that if "castration," with all the traps that it poses, is to be "overcome," it will be by engaging the intricacies of Freud's texts and not by laughing them away. For that reason, our own approach to the fundamentally open question of castration shall be through a consideration of the key discoveries of an inquiry far less publicized than that of Deleuze and Guattari, the lectures of castration delivered by Jean Laplanche. For Laplanche, I believe, by dealing with the letter of Freud's text, has waged the most convincing combat against the interpretative tendency that would see in "castration" the repressed *par excellence*. Whereas the authors of the *Anti-Oedipe* would laugh castration away, Laplanche manages to retain it . . . in the very element of its ludicrousness.

It will perhaps be objected that we are moving all too rapidly away from our reading of Hugo. But, in fact, our reason for invoking the most striking results of Laplanche's analyses is that they provide a remarkably efficient summary of our own conclusions regarding Hugo. We approach here a certain withering of the all too academic question of the relation between Psychoanalysis and Literature. For our answer to that question of theory will be a demonstration of the way in which a transformation of psychoanalysis may be made to help effect a certain displacement of literature as well. The abstract problem of theory gives way to a concrete textual analysis that is undecidably psychoanalytic or literary. "Psychoanalysis" and "Literature": terms to be inscribed on the "opposite" sides of a Möbius strip.

What follows, then, are three important developments from Laplanche's ongoing inquiry into the perverse rigor with which Freud's most virulent discoveries are perpetually escaping him, undergoing repression. They turn on the question of castration and may be seen to be literally inscribed in Hugo's text.

I

A prerequisite for an understanding of castration is an examination of the crucial shift in Freud's theory of anxiety. The initial "naive" theory, elaborated at the beginning of the century in the context of a discussion of "actual neuroses," posits anxiety as a deviant form of discharge of dammed up libido. The theory is economic and comes close to being purely physiological in orientation. In the absence of libidinal discharge, the ego is threatened with submergence by a free-floating form of affect, a tension virtually without quality: anxiety. It is what Freud calls a poison, a toxin.

For that reason, it should be noted, "actual neuroses" were not deemed particularly amenable to psychoanalytic treatment. Unlike the "psychoneuroses," to which they were opposed, they could not be traced etiologically to some motivating occurrence in the patient's past. Oddly enough, the theory of anxiety does not become fully "psychoanalytic" until the emergence of the second, more "sophisticated" theory in 1924. Anxiety was then integrated into a theory of defense, more historical than economic in character. It existed above all as "signal-anxiety," a distressing warning of some objective danger which, like a vaccination, would mobilize the defenses of the "psychical organism." Anxiety was no longer the result of repression but the motivating force behind it. To the extent that the prototype of such a danger might be the submergence of the infant at birth through a rush of energy, a virtual self-intoxication, the first theory might still function significantly within, or behind, the second. But gradually the peril *par excellence* was posited by Freud to be castration: "a true external danger." The first theory was deemed "superficial," and partially abandoned. Anxiety was not essentially a poison, a toxin; it was a warning-signal, a tocsin.

We return now to the early theory, specifically to its structure: the liberation of a form of free-floating affect through deviation from a process of instinctual gratification. For in its structure, the "naive" theory reproduces that of one of the most potent and little noticed conceptual configurations in Freud's theory of sexuality: that of *Anlehnung* (anaclisis), the movement, in the *Three Essays,* whereby unconscious sexuality itself (as *Trieb* or drive) is generated as a free-floating form of affect through deviation from a process of instinctual gratification. At the level of structure, then, the first theory begins to appear far less naive.

A second remark on the early theory: within the context of the "toxic" interpretation of anxiety, Freud posited a specific mechanism of defense, phobia. It consists in the focusing of anxiety on some purely arbitrary, external reality perceived as a danger. The prototype would be Little Hans's fear of being bitten by horses. A phobia, in fact, is capable of structuring the entirety of the subject's perception of time and space around the elected object.

It is at this point that the most surprising reversal may be operated. For consider: (1) the latent "sophistication" of the "naive" theory as a structural repetition of *Anlehnung*; (2) the perfectly futile, unreal, and increasingly rare nature of the castratory scenario that Freud posits as the grounding reality for his later theory of anxiety; (3) the dimension of phobia within the earlier formulation as a theory of imaginary dangers forged in order to focus, bind, and externalize the free-floating affect of anxiety. Taken together these three elements lead us to the speculative conclusion that the entire second theory, centered as it is on the "true external danger" of castration, is interpretable as a phobic formation within Freud's own discourse. The rational fear of father's knife, posited by Freud, is every bit as ludicrous as Hans's fear of horses. Whereupon we would suggest that the second theory of anxiety functions as a restricted economy within the general economy of the first, that the first, once interpreted, mediates nothing so much as a theory of the inevitability of the error entailed by the second. The second theory, in brief, is the form taken by the repression of the first, a repression which the historians of psychoanalysis have helped only to consolidate.

But what is Victor Hugo's relation to all this? Our point of departure was the joining of La Esmeralda's slippers, the scenario informing the *symbolique*. Castration, we have said, is the cornerstone of the structural unconscious. Our reaction to the episode in Hugo was embarrassment. The result of the analysis of Freud just undertaken was the affirmation of a certain (phobic) ludicrousness of the castratory scenario as the second theory of anxiety came to be centered on it. La Esmeralda drew her slipper out of what a certain silent contamination allowed us to call *tocsin, toque-sein, toc-seing:* a writing machine. It was that metaphorical duplicity of the container that led us to posit the writing machine as *exceeding* the dimension of the *symbolique*. In our reading of Freud, what allowed us to dismantle castration, to intuit a certain ridiculousness in the way it functions, was the odd shift in Freud's theory of anxiety, the bizarre interplay between anxiety as toxin and anxiety as tocsin. But what is the toxic element in Freud which we came to affirm as constitutive of a general economy if not the free-floating play of unbound affect as it shifts from representation to representation? To say as much, to invoke a silent gliding of terms in relation to their (affective) meanings—say, tocsin replacing toxin as the "meaning" of anxiety—is to sense the extent to which Freud's own text at its most intense functions as a (theory of a) marvelously duplicitous writing machine. We have besieged "castration" much as Hugo's *truands* besieged the cathedral or as the *tocsin* contained the *symbolique:* by giving full play to a certain shiftiness in the apparently secondary element of castration *anxiety,* by doubling the surface. If castration, nevertheless, emerges from this analysis as a necessary construct (or phobia), it will be in the restricted sense in which *Notre-Dame de Paris*, a printed text, may be regarded, despite "Ceci tuera cela," as intended to glorify another construct: Notre-Dame de Paris.

II

With the passing of the castration complex, in Freud's scheme, the "superego" comes into existence. Now, along with that interpretative tendency in psychoanalysis that would delibidinize anxiety, turn it into a displaced fear, there is a pressure to see in the superego an almost abstract system of logical and ethical imperatives. For if anxiety can be reduced to a fear of punishment by castration, what would be internalized as superego would be a law—or laws—sustained by that fear. It is in this context that we would consider briefly Laplanche's discussion of the Rat-Man. For the Rat-Man's obsessional neurosis, riddled with questions of guilt, remorse, and indebtedness, is a kind of matrix in which the problematic of the superego is treated before the term itself surfaces in Freud's writing. Now the key point is that the concrete form in which the superego *enters* Freud's thought is as the obscene rats which would *penetrate* the anuses of those beloved by the Rat-Man were he not to acquit himself of a thoroughly imaginary debt. As the Rat-Man discloses his "great obsessive fear," Freud notes, his expression reveals what can only be interpreted as "horror at pleasure of his own of which he himself was unaware." The upshot of Laplanche's analysis is to relibidinize the concept of the superego: "Le surmoi apparaît parfois comme un rat, jouisseur, cruel, image même de la pulsion. De sorte que le conflit moral, torturant, implacable, apparemment assimilable à un conflit qui serait élevé, ne fait que recouvrir une lutte 'cruelle et lubrique' où le châtiment suprême est aggloméré toujours avec la jouissance suprême." The rats would function as phobic objects no longer available to any disguise of their horrendously libidinal nature.

Victor Hugo? Let us recall the *scene* in which the *sum-bolon* is revealed in *Notre-Dame de Paris*. La Esmeralda draws her slipper from the *toque-sein* at the entry of the penitent's cave, "cavité noire, sombre et humide." Inscribed above is an edifying call to prayer and remorse: TU, ORA; whence the popular name for Gudule's retreat: "Trou aux rats." The introduction of the *symbolique* thus takes place within a duplicitous field of script, oscillating, beyond any possibility of synthesis, between the appeal to conscience of TU, ORA and its obscenely anal reinscription as "Trou aux rats." The *symbolique* enters Hugo's novel in exactly the same manner, through the very same orifice, as the superego penetrates into Freud's thought: midst excrement and puns. Puns, we recall: "la fiente de l'esprit qui vole." Consider the moves of our *tocsin*, the allegedly humble bearer of the Law. In *Quatrevingt-treize*, we found it ripping apart the acoustic circuit of mouth and ear. For La Esmeralda it became *toque-sein*. Now, with Gudule, it is anal. The circuit of the Law ("castration," the "symbolique") would seem to be indistinguishable from the possibilities of perversion itself.

III

Laplanche's third incursion against the restrictive normativity of Oedipus and castration concerns the formation of the superego through parental identification. In the normal Oedipal situation, the boy, failing to attain his desired (maternal) object, renounces his desire and identifies with his father. Now ultimately, the only theory of identification concretely sustained by psychoanalytic practice concerns identification with the lost love object. But precisely to that extent Freud, in the third chapter of *The Ego and the Id,* is forced into the paradoxical affirmation that the "normal" identification runs contrary to "our expectation." For according to the theory, the boy should end up identifying with his mother. Because of this dilemma, Freud seems almost relieved to encounter the negative or homosexual Oedipal position, for it would allow the boy to emerge from the Oedipal crisis with a "normal" paternal identification.

Laplanche's solution to the problem suggests that every Oedipus complex is both positive and negative, and that, paradoxically, it is the positive Oedipal position which results in a homosexual identification and the negative one which issues in a normal or heterosexual one. What such a chiasmatization of the Oedipus complex eliminates is any possibility of interpretation in terms of an apprenticeship in love. For the heavily normative trend in Freudian sexual theory is rooted in the ultimately behaviorist notion that one *learns* one's sexuality, for better or for worse, in the Oedipal moment, that one will love in perpetuity more or less as one has loved Oedipally. And with the idea of a sexuality that is learned comes the possibility of a failure to learn the lesson, of a botched apprenticeship. But in the model presented, one by no means learns one's sexuality; rather, one identifies—chiasmatically—into it. One will end up loving precisely as one *did not love* (predominantly) during the Oedipal moment. The question of Oedipal identification is opened to the freedom and rhetorical complexity of dream-work. As the behaviorist interpretation is dissolved, the entire problem of the resolution of the Oedipus complex invites reconceptualization in far less moralistic terms.

Consider now the conclusion of *Notre-Dame de Paris.* Claude Frollo, in his move to punish La Esmeralda, absents himself just long enough for the melodramatic reunion with Gudule to take place. That situation alone would confirm our interpretation of Cimourdain as mother at the end of

Quatrevingt-treize, for it is as though the vindictive pair in the earlier novel were conflated in the later one: Cimourdain is a condensation of Claude Frollo and Gudule. Plainly, Hugo is drawing on identical imaginative resources in the conclusion of each novel. And to that extent, we may imagine a superimposition of the two as an intertextual entity possessing a certain autonomy and in itself worthy of consideration. But in that case, at the moment of the introduction of the *symbolique* (in *Notre-Dame de Paris*), we find the composite character La Esmeralda-Gauvain confronting the maternal-paternal-amorous-punitive instance of Gudule-Frollo-Cimourdain. That is, our intertext would seem to offer every possibility of sexual identification, a matrix sufficiently complex to be open to just those chiasmatic effects posited by Laplanche in the case of Freud. Surely, with the infinitely perverse La Esmeralda at the heart of the action, one is not running too risky a wager in positing at least the virtuality of their occurrence. The elaboration of our *tocsin,* we have suggested, has been implicitly a reading of one of the most remarkable and demanding texts to have emerged from France in recent years, Jacques Derrida's *Glas.* That implicitness is perhaps worth respecting, since one is hard put to imagine a metalanguage at present capable of explicitly *comprehending* that text. Still, a series of necessarily schematic remarks on *Glas* may help to clarify its relation to our own undertaking, and indeed bring into better relief the analyses pursued above.

1. *Glas* is first of all an effort at a materialist dismantling of the concept of sociality in Hegel. To that extent, it may be Derrida's *Marx,* a thinker whose texts have never been engaged explicitly by Derrida, but who haunts, at times more than allusively, many a page of the Frenchman's text. Our own reading of Marx, for instance, whose point of departure was what Marx called an "uncanny anonymity," might well be regarded as a commentary on the following passage: "on ne touche pas au glas, donc, sans toucher à la classe. Mais le discours codé, policé sur la lutte des classes, s'il forclôt la question du glas (tout ce qui s'y forge, tout ce sur quoi elle retentit, en particulier l'expropriation du nom partout où elle porte) manque au moins une révolution. Et qu'est-ce qu'une révolution qui ne s'attaque pas au nom propre."

2. Now the concept of sociality deconstructed by Derrida is above all that of the family. For his analysis is directed at both the concept of the family and a certain familialism of the concept, at that level of Hegel's discourse at which "l'ontologie ne se laisse plus décoller du familial." Indeed, the Marxian title that recurs most often in *Glas* is *The Holy Family.* But the attack on Hegel's "family" soon takes the form of a dismantling of

the Freudian concept of castration: "Je l'ai toujours dit, répondrait Hegel aux docteurs de la castration." It is worth noting that what we have called Derrida's *Marx* should take the odd form of a reading of Freud. For one suspects that at this juncture in the history of reading, the interpretative medium within and against which the most radical moves may be effected is the works of Freud. (It was for that reason that our own reading of Marx turned on the death drive; our reading of Hugo on a dismantling of castration.) In Derrida's case, the unhinging of "castration" works against that erotico-philosophical matrix in which, "l'*Aufhebung,* concept central de la relation sexuelle, articule le phallocentrisme le plus traditionnel sur l'onto-théo-téléologic hegelienne." The erotics eventually *affirmed* in the text posit a plurality of sexual differences in opposition to *the* difference between the sexes. What is effected is a reinscription of Oedipus in which it would be possible to occupy all positions simultaneously.

3. The structure of Derrida's dismantling consists in actively *losing* Hegel's text in that of Jean Genet, most particularly in *Notre-Dame des fleurs*. Whence the typographical oddity of the book: a column on Hegel set against a column on Genet. *Glas,* then, would disperse the construct of metaphysics in a poetico-erotic thieves' carnival of perversity, a world of *argot.* We need only allude here to the philosopher Gringoire lost in the Cour des Miracles: "Me voilà donc en habit d'histrion, comme saint Genest. Que voulez-vous? c'est une éclipse."

4. The movements by which the dialectics of Hegel are lost in the "galactics" of Genet is assimilated by Derrida to that of a silent bell, a written text: "entre les deux, le battant d'un autre texte, on dirait d'une autre logique!" (Recall the entry of Gringoire into the Cour des Miracles, of Lantenac into the Vendée.) The movement of *Glas* is that of writing as *tocsin/toc-seing:* "Il rejoue la mimesis et l'arbitraire de la signature dans un accouplement déchaîné (toc/seing/lait), ivre comme un sonneur à sa corde pendue." We are approaching La Esmeralda, our *toque-sein,* here: "Le glas tinte à proximité de la tétine"; "quelle forme lactifère reconnaître au tocsin?"

5. The two other principal media through which Derrida's disarticulation of castration is pursued are plants (*Notre-Dame de fleurs*) and minerals. "Ce discours sur la différence sexuelle . . . exclut les plantes." "Au programme depuis toujours . . . , l'anthoedipe arrive à chaque saison comme une fleur." La Esmeralda, a writing machine containing a *symbolique* which it exceeds: a heliotrope. As for minerals, as matter itself, they constitute the resistance of materialism, above all, perhaps, to the ideality of a certain interiority of sound: "Le son qu'il [le minéral] émet lorsqu'il est frappé, il ne l'émet pas de lui-même, comme une voix, mais il le reçoit comme d'une source étrangère." La Esmeralda, the false name, the green stone: heliotrope.

6. *Glas* is studded with neologisms. Derrida: "J'argotise, je jargonne, j'ai l'air de produire des mots nouveaux, un nouveau lexique. Un argot seulement, un jargon." The reader may be reminded here of our reinscriptions of *tocsin* (*toque-sein, toc-seing*, etc.) A word of amplification may be of help at this juncture. What is offensive about such a procedure, I suspect, is the clarity with which it betrays the violence of interpretative activity. For we persist in regarding texts as monuments which must not be defaced. And yet the model of reading that has oriented the analyses above, and that has guided Derrida's efforts in *Glas* as well, I believe, would see in a text the point of intersection of a number of interpretative forces. A text is less a monument than a battlefield. The interpreter's task, then, is to situate his own efforts strategically at the crux of that struggle and to ally himself with that stratum of the text generative of the greatest intensity. But to the extent that one has been able to work within the node or matrix of the various forces, the pursuit of the "battle" will take the form of a rigorous positing of the lines along which and the conditions under which the work may be *rewritten*. It is that process of rewriting the language—of the text—that is referred to in Derrida's affirmation: "j'argotise."

SEI EIN KLINGENDES GLAS,
DAS SICH IM KLANG SCHON ZERSCHLUG.
—RILKE

Victor Hugo's *Glas*? The element within which to think through our own modernity? The suggestion seems ludicrous. Yet however outrageous, it is hardly original; it is indeed the organizing subtext of Mallarmé's important essay, *Crise de vers*. That text deals with the fallout of a specific event, the death of Victor Hugo. "Un lecteur français, ses habitudes interrompues à la mort de Victor Hugo, ne peut que se déconcerter." Hugo's accomplishment had been in reducing all discursive forms to the line of verse: "Hugo, dans sa tâche mystérieuse, rabattit toute la prose, philosophie, éloquence, histoire au vers, et comme il était le vers personnellement, il confisque chez qui pense, discourt ou narre, presque le droit à s'énoncer." Meanwhile, as though unconsciously, within the language, a shattering of Hugo's hegemony was silently in preparation: "Le vers, je crois, avec respect attendit que le géant qui l'identifiait à sa main tenace et plus ferme toujours de forgeron, vînt à manquer; pour, lui, se rompre." The breakup of the classical line of verse, a new poetic mobility, was concomitant with Hugo's death, and our modernity—"Jugez le goût très moderne"—is nothing but that dispersion.

ALEXANDER WELSH

Opening and Closing Les Misérables

Is it really the case, as the foregoing argument of J. Hillis Miller suggests, that the question of whether a narrative closes is inherently undecidable? The arbitrariness and contradictions of novelistic endings have often been remarked—still, are the occasional embarrassment of readers and the jokes of some novelists about endings evidence of an insolvable conundrum? Above all, if one concedes that illogic plays a part in the difficulties experienced in ending novels, does this mean that we should forgo attempts to generalize about a given period in terms of its fictions? These are questions well worth posing, and perhaps the best way of responding to them in a short space is to point them toward a great novel like *Les Misérables*. In truth there is no other novel quite like *Les Misérables,* yet it is also prototypical of an age. Without some such concrete instance it is hard to understand what is different about the endings of such works as *Tristram Shandy* or *Ulysses*—or of that nineteenth-century exception to rules, *Dead Souls*.

Miller's position is not as drastic as it is witty, and at least three of the arguments he brings to bear on the problem invite qualification. The beginning, middle, and end of a continuous stretch of narrative may require—and usually receive—stipulative definition, as in the division of a play into acts. To argue that the merging of the action in all three parts, or the merging of the whole with events that precede or follow, makes beginning and ending indeterminate is like saying that the terms East, Midwest, and West have no clear denotation because the regions they represent merge imperceptibly on

From *Nineteenth-Century Fiction* 33, no. 1 (June 1978). © 1978 by the Regents of the University of California.

the map, or that the tides that lap the shores of the continent obscure the distinction between dry land and wet. Similarly, the argument that analysis, "if carried far enough," leads to an impasse must at some point yield to convenience, as is recognized in all sciences. The appropriate level of analysis depends on the uses of literary investigations. And thirdly, though metaphors for narrative derived from spinning and weaving seriously call for the investigation that Miller is undertaking, they do not render narrative closure meaningless. It would be good to know in what craft the word "unravel" became equivalent to "ravel," but surely the significance of these two terms—as a structuralist perspective would confirm—is their opposition. In separate contexts the terms may be interchangeable, but used in the same sentence, as in "one should ravel up the plot before unraveling it," they distinguish sequentially two conditions of yarn. With such practical qualifications, Miller's perceptions of the paradoxes of beginnings and endings are consistent, it seems to me, with anything I might say about *Les Misérables*—except that one cannot safely speak of the *aporias* of closure in the case of Victor Hugo, a writer who is never at a loss for words even in the depths of self-contradiction.

The main difference between my point of view and Miller's is that I see the "impossibility" of Hugo's ending, and that of the endings of most nineteenth-century novels, as resulting not from violations of logic but from contradictions of desire. When Miller refers in an aside to Trollope as "a novelist of closure if there ever was one," I believe he acknowledges the same general phenomenon that I wish to describe: an intensification of the sense of an ending in order to account for the disruption of the narrative and to satisfy contradictory desires. The narratives we are concerned with are in the first place constructions of desire, the making of things come true. A little paradigm from *The Mikado* contrasts such fictions with hypothetical fact:

> See how the Fates their gifts allot,
> For A is happy—B is not.
> Yet B is worthy, I dare say,
> Of more prosperity than A!

This stanza postulates an inequality of proportions such as might be perceived or invented by any novelist—a true or imagined story of injustice. The story represented thus far is transformed by desire in the second stanza of the song, and to accomplish this transformation the narrator speeds up the action and blatantly usurps the role of Fortune, or of what we might call History:

If I were Fortune—which I'm not—
B should enjoy A's happy lot,
And A should die in miserie—
That is, assuming I am B.

It will be noticed that this "pure fiction" (by which we mean the impure fiction of desire) introduces in the death of A a much more definite ending than the hypothetical situation posits or implies. W. S. Gilbert's model fiction specifies also the conduit of desire, which is the identification of the author (and readers) with one of his characters, the hero B. The ending is thus openly problematic: the theme of the first stanza is injustice, and that of the second ostensibly justice, but justice for B is almost certainly injustice to A. No sooner has B prospered from the insidious operation of wish-fulfillment than A seizes our attention again. That A should die in misery and B live happily ever after is the story of *Les Misérables* in a nutshell.

Beginnings and endings of narrative have much in common since both are arbitrary disjunctions in a sequence of events that is presumed continuous, extending before and after the events that are narrated. We also have to imagine a surrounding space for each narrative, so that one narrative is arbitrarily separated from another, these beginnings and endings from those. Stories do not end in medias res in quite the same way they begin in medias res, however, because of the direction of time. Thus Aristotle writes matter-of-factly of the complication in a play extending before the action proper but not of the dénouement extending after, even though many of the stories enacted on the Greek stage had known sequels. The beginning disjunction weighs heavily in the impact of an action upon the audience, but the ending is felt to be decisive because every event precludes every other event in time. Things happen this way and not that, but only when the happening is over do we know this. The events contributing to an action spread themselves comfortably in past and present time. "See how the fates their gifts allot": the inventor of a fiction and his audience can see as much or as little of this complication as they choose. Choices from the known "facts," events that are over and done with, result in beginnings; but endings, with respect to beginnings, always come later and are choices of something unknown. Hence the diffidence and conditional mood of Gilbert's second stanza, which hedges the decisive wish, "A should die." It makes no difference whether the action is raveling or unraveling its way from past to future: the ending with respect to the beginning is always an image of the future. The reason that endings are often boldly assertive, therefore, is that they are merely assertive—for we are never privileged to experience what will happen next until it happens. Every narrative ending stated as decisive is actually prophetic.

A far more attenuated and sophisticated model for a fiction than Gilbert's is Diderot's *Jacques le fataliste et son maître,* in which "Jacques" and "Le Maître" serve as independent variables A and B. Diderot's model begins, in fact, simply with pronouns framed into questions: "How had they met? By chance, like everyone. What were their names? What does it matter to you?" The answers to the next two questions in sequence show the difference between beginnings and endings: "Where were they coming from? From the nearest place at hand. Where were they going? Does one know where one is going?" In short, there are readily available answers to the question of where to begin: in theory at least the narrator can trace steps backward as far as it suits him, and if the exposition presents practical difficulties, he can refer to the previous instant when the characters were nearly in the same position that they occupy now. But the future is in question. Throughout his model fiction Diderot teases the reader by resisting the sense of ending, the hold of which on the reader's imagination is always prophetic. The running argument between Jacques, who believes every event is fated, and his master, who whimsically trusts to free will, provides a philosophical ground for this demonstration, but the true argument is between the narrator who refuses to give any hint of an outcome to the action and the reader who expects him to write a conventional story. Any reader who feels frustrated by *Jacques le fataliste* (as readers must) experiences a desire that is, minimally, the desire to make a future present. Consider then the usefulness of novels in foreclosing the future in the nineteenth century, a period in which the future was popularly advertised as far more important to mankind and to individuals than was the present. A few dates and reflection on the concurrent development of the faith in history will place these matters in perspective.

Jacques le fataliste, which so frankly challenges narrative conventions that it may be thought of as an anti-novel, was completed sometime in the 1770s and not published until 1796. As early as 1784 Kant published his essay on the idea of universal history in harmony with *"the purpose of nature itself,"* in which he compared his new emphasis on the ends of history to the way in which novels ordinarily proceed toward rational ends:

> It is admittedly a strange and at first sight absurd proposition to write a *history* according to an idea of how world events must develop if they are to conform to certain rational ends; it would seem that only a *novel* could result from such premises. Yet if it

may be assumed that nature does not work without a plan and purposeful end, even amidst the arbitrary play of human freedom, this idea might nevertheless prove useful. And although we are too shortsighted to perceive the hidden mechanism of nature's scheme, this idea may yet serve as a guide to us in representing an otherwise planless *aggregate* of human actions as conforming, at least when considered as a whole, to a *system.* ("Idea for a Universal History with a Cosmopolitan Purpose")

This turn toward the future anticipates the great system-building theorists of the nineteenth century, including Hegel, Saint-Simon, Comte, Marx, and Spencer. Moreover, Kant repeatedly stresses that the construction of a universal history must rely on discovering the purpose of nature, since human history is, frankly, chaotic. In advance of key discoveries of geology and evolutionary science, this commitment is also founded on desire, as is evident from the first proposition in Kant's essay:

> *All the natural capacities of a creature are destined sooner or later to be developed completely and in conformity with their end.* This can be verified in all animals by external or anatomical examination. An organ which is not meant for use or an arrangement which does not fulfil its purpose is a contradiction in the teleological theory of nature. For if we abandon this basic principle, we are faced not with a law-governed nature, but with an aimless, random process, and the dismal reign of chance replaces the guiding principle of reason.

In the century that followed, the discoveries of science, or natural history, seemed to confirm the arguments from desire.

Hugo's immense novel was begun as "Les Misères" in 1840 and published in Brussels and Paris in 1862. It thus could profit from the novelistic enterprises of Scott and Balzac as well as the developmental thesis that culminated in Darwin's *Origin of Species* in 1859. *Les Misérables* is in truth a vast compendium of nineteenth-century beliefs, especially of the faith in history. It is the epitome of what Donald Fanger would call romantic realism and what I would prefer to call in the present context historical realism. But think of it first simply in terms of our model beginnings and endings. The first paragraph of the novel states, "In 1815 M. Charles François Bienvenu Myriel was Bishop of Digne. This was a man of about seventy-five years; he took up the see of Digne in 1806." The second paragraph begins, "Although these details in no way essentially concern that which we have to tell . . ." and only fourteen chapters later, at the beginning of a second book, do we read, "In the early days of the month of October, 1815, about an hour before sunset, a man who was traveling on foot entered the little town of Digne." (Subsequent references to the novel are by part, book, and chapter number in parentheses; translations are my own.) The unnamed person is Jean Valjean—though the story of Jean Valjean might be said to have begun nineteen years earlier when he stole a loaf of bread, or perhaps when he was born, or when his parents conceived him, or when they were born, or their parents. Hugo experiences no logical difficulty in beginning where he pleases, and his deliberate specification of dates and time of day is a means of taking advantage of the axiom that everything that has happened up to now, up to the last possible moment before, can in theory be known to us. Relative to this beginning every subsequent event in *Les Misérables* is both future and unknown; hence the novelist's mastery of those events is prophetic and their enaction a fulfillment, up until the last event to be narrated or prophetically realized, the death of Jean Valjean. The last event is the most problematic of all, suffused with contradictory wishes and mysterious hints; but it is presented with little of the amplitude of confessedly irrelevant detail with which the novel begins. It is presented, in short, as decisive, for the same reasons of desire that Kant gives for endorsing "a teleological theory of nature," lest we have to confront "an aimless, random process, and the dismal reign of chance."

The last words of the novel are in fact four lines of verse, which an unknown hand wrote in pencil "years ago" on Jean Valjean's tombstone—a stone otherwise unmarked and expressly without a name:

> He sleeps. Although his lot was a strange one,
> he lived. He died when he no longer had his angel;
> the thing came of itself, simply,
> as the night forms while the day fades away.

The hint that the hero's death occurred as naturally as the passing of day into night raises a possibility the reverse of a pathetic fallacy. The idea is that human affairs shall order themselves as nature is ordered. Yet this analogy (frequently invoked in other contexts in the novel) also suggests that Jean Valjean might die over and over again each evening. That proposition, though it suits nicely the commonplace deception, "He sleeps," is hardly consistent with the statement that he died from the loss of his angel. The clause about the angel is troublesome because it very nearly says that the hero's death was unnatural. It alludes to the loss of Valjean's adopted child Cosette through her marriage, a consummation parallel to the loss of

Déruchette through marriage in *Les Travailleurs de la mer* or the loss of Esmeralda from love and death in *Notre-Dame de Paris*. Since those parallel events in Hugo's other novels precipitate in each case the hero's suicide, perhaps Jean Valjean cannot be said to die a natural death at all. In truth, to comprehend the concluding verses fully one would have to pursue a long course not only in Hugo's writings but in nineteenth-century cultural history.

Fortunately, *Les Misérables* virtually offers such a course of study in itself. Because Hugo tirelessly elaborates the action in speech and description, we have far more information (prophecy) to interpret than the plot of Gilbert's verses or the stringency of Diderot's questions allows for. Again and again the novelist preaches of the future. All of the violence, commotion, frustration, political mishap, escapes and near escapes of the action, which spans the first part of the century, will be made good in some indefinite future time. The narrator frequently promises as much in his own voice, but perhaps the most unrestrained faith in history is put in the mouth of Enjolras, a revolutionary who is about to die on the barricades in 1832. In a stirring address far too long for quotation in its entirety, this doomed young man demands, "Citoyens, où allons-nous?" He does not pose this question in order to counter, like Diderot, that we can never know. On the contrary, he supplies an answer:

> Citizens, where are we going? To science become government, to the force in things become the sole public force, to natural law having its sanction and its penalty in itself and promulgating itself through evidence, to a dawn of truth corresponding to the dawn of day. . . . Citizens, the nineteenth century is great, but the twentieth century will be happy. Then there shall be nothing like ancient history; there shall be no more fear, as today, of a conquest, an invasion, a usurpation, an armed rivalry of nations, an interruption of civilization because of the marriage of kings, a birth of hereditary tyrannies, a division of peoples by congress, a dismemberment by the collapse of dynasty, a combat of two religions butting each other like two goats of darkness on the bridge of infinity; there shall be no more fear of hunger, exploitation, prostitution through adversity, misery from unemployment, and the scaffold, and the sword, and battles, and all the brigandage of chance in the forest of events. We can almost say, there will be no more events. We shall be happy. The human race will achieve its law as the terrestrial globe achieves law . . . the

human race will be delivered, relieved, and consoled! We affirm
it on this barricade.

(5.1.5)

Since history up to now has been all confusion and disruption and injustice,
desire argues that a decisive change must be imminent. Like Kant, Enjolras
seems especially uncomfortable with the role of chance in human events and
readily prophesies that the brigands will be driven from the forest.

These revolutionary arguments depend on what M. H. Abrams calls
"Apocalypse by Cognition" rather than a knock-down struggle at the barricades. Knowledge will drive away chance; in the larger view every event
falls into its appropriate place, and this is what makes Enjolras's personal
sacrifice worthwhile. The faith represented here is similar to Herbert Spencer's in his *Social Statics:* "always toward perfection is the mighty movement—toward a complete development and a more unmixed good,
subordinating in its universality all petty irregularities and fallings back, as
the curvature of the earth subordinates mountains and valleys"; or to Henry
Thomas Buckle's in the closing words of *History of Civilization in England:*
"it shall be clearly seen, that, from the beginning there has been no discrepancy, no incongruity, no disorder, no interruption, no interference; but that
all the events which surround us, even to the furthest limits of material
creation, are but different parts of a single scheme, which is permeated by
one glorious principle of universal and undeviating regularity." Such resounding optimism apes the Christian view of history as proceeding in a
straight line from the creation to the last day, though Buckle's "one glorious
principle of universal and undeviating regularity" is somewhat repellent as
compared with God the Father.

Though consistency and even uniformity are principal demands of such
theories, it may be seen that they are not truly consistent with themselves.
Events move of their own accord, assimilating both successful and unsuccessful human efforts to control them; but they do not move forever, apparently, since they move toward an obtainable goal. Carried away by his
thought, Enjolras is tempted to predict that there shall be no more events
("On pourrait presque dire: il n'y aura plus d'événements"). He qualifies
this prophecy even as he utters it because he is half aware that he is calling
on history to destroy itself. Mircea Eliade has shown [in *The Myth of
Eternal Return*] how precarious this secularization of messianic beliefs becomes. Within a Christian framework of history, "the irreversibility of historical events and of time is compensated by the limitation of history to
time"; but no such belief in the end of time can rescue a purely secular

theory from contradiction, and Eliade is at pains to show that "at the end of the Marxist philosophy of history, lies the age of gold of the archaic eschatologies." In general, any philosophy that construes human events in endless sequence increases psychologically the need to envision an ending, more so than a philosophy that views events as cyclical, repeating themselves in distinct phases. Neither attitude toward history completely rules out the other, however, as can be seen from the appeal to diurnal cycles in Enjolras's speech ("a dawn of truth corresponding to the dawn of day") or in the verses at the end of *Les Misérables* ("as the night forms while the day fades away"). But linear shapes of history dominated nineteenth-century thought and were immeasurably strengthened by the linkage between human and natural history.

Les Misérables itself narrates a sizable number of nineteenth-century events, real and imagined. Hugo fills its pages with sermons, long and short, on progress—the main idea being that unhappy episodes like the affair on the barricades are merely temporary impediments to history. One such sermon he polishes off by calling attention to the progress of events in his novel, as if *Les Misérables* confirmed universal history and history, *Les Misérables*.

> The book which the reader has before him at this moment is, from one end to the other, in its entirety and details, whatever its intermittences, exceptions, or failings, a progress from evil to good, from injustice to justice, from falsehood to truth, from night to day, from appetite to conscience, from corruption [pourriture] to life; from bestiality to duty, from hell to heaven, from nothingness to God. The starting point: matter, destination: the soul. The hydra at the beginning, the angel at the end.
>
> (5.1.20)

Here the language of progress borrows heavily from the Christian moralization of history, and the angel presumably refers to a moral state of mankind rather than to Cosette. From hydra to angel represents the course of evolution, though a hydra does not appear in the novel unless it is Jean Valjean himself, in his own eyes a sort of moral monster for having unrepentantly stolen a loaf of bread. In a new age crime will be as obsolete as every other form of violence—or perhaps there will be no more events whatsoever.

In *The Sense of an Ending* Frank Kermode displays some of the contradictory wishes present in all contemplations of beginnings and endings. The pronounced endings of nineteenth-century novels conceal a deepening contradiction between the belief that history is endless and a desire to make an end: that is, the endings are emphatic because they are proclaimed against the narrative's own assumption of continuing development and change, during "the quite sudden and enormous lengthening of the scale of history in this period." The best example in English literature is *The Mill on the Floss,* in which George Eliot assumes a developmental perspective in order to explore family, social, and economic history, together with her heroine's growth in consciousness—with many analogies to natural and sexual selection thrown in—only to overturn her entire complex history by means of the prophesied flood at the end.

The simplest and most general form that this contradiction takes, however, is the setting of novels in past time. This frequently remarked tendency of realistic fiction of the period—and not the historical novel narrowly defined—is the true legacy of Scott to the nineteenth-century novel. By setting actions in past time novelists assured that actions could be experienced as complete. Historical realism could demonstrate the forces of history at work yet implicitly promise an untrammeled future simply by bringing the novel to a close: this future became the readers' present time. Every establishment depends upon history, but, conversely, history always threatens the establishment anew: hence the desire expressed in every ending to still the action or even to deny that more action is possible. The characters must either die or live happily ever after. Jean-Paul Sartre makes the same point in writing of the novels of the Third Republic: "the plot does not belong to that history without conclusion which is in the making but to history already made." The same might be said of the literature of the century as a whole: the plot of a typical novel "is a local change in a system at rest."

> In a stable society which is not yet conscious of the dangers which threaten it, which has a morality at its disposal, a scale of values, and a system of explanations to integrate its local changes, which is convinced that it is beyond historicity and that nothing important will ever happen any more, in a bourgeois France tilled to the last acre, laid out like a checkerboard by its secular walls, congealed in its industrial methods, and resting on the glory of its Revolution, no other fictional technique could be possible.
>
> (*What Is Literature?*)

The impression of a local change in a system at rest results from the system's having the last word. Again Kant's determination of the need for subordinating events to a system seems vindicated by novels. The frenetic discourse of Victor Hugo, like that of Spencer or Buckle, is accounted for by the need to suppress all "intermittences, exceptions, or failings."

Sartre's polemic is addressed to the need of a new sort of novel in his own time. His description of nineteenth-century novels is confirmed by another Marxist critic who approves of their conclusiveness and who contemns modern novels in part because they fail to work round to satisfactory endings. According to Georg Lukács, modern novels fail to render human potentiality concrete. In order to do so they would need to employ a more careful selection of detail, and selection must be guided by some goal:

> In all this, *perspective* plays a decisive role. . . . Objectively, perspective points to the main movements in a given historical process. Subjectively—and not only in the field of artistic activity— it represents the capacity to grasp the existence and mode of action of these movements. If literature is to render an image of life that is adequate, formally convincing and consistent, the sequence must be reversed. Whereas in life "wither?" is a consequence of "whence?," in literature "wither?" determines the content, selection and proportion of the various elements. The finished work may resemble life in observing a causal sequence; but it would be no more than an arbitrary chronicle if there were not this reversal of direction. It is the perspective, the *terminus ad quem,* that determines the significance of each element in a work of art.
>
> (*The Meaning of Contemporary Realism*)

Thus Lukács stands firmly on the side of Kant and nineteenth-century philosophy of history. One might easily conclude from his argument that no problem of where we are going arises except in literature, which is essentially propaganda. *Les Misérables* fits comfortably such views, though Lukács elsewhere fights shy of Hugo's "bombastic monumentalism."

Novelists and critics committed to purposeful history approve dramatic endings, in which the conflict arises from the potency of events and the desire to be done with them. The readiest way to express this conflict was actually to provide two endings, and here again the example of the Waverley novels proved useful. What used to be called Scott's dualism is most importantly reflected in the double fable of most of his novels, wherein the correct hero refrains from acting and survives history but certain active heroes who endorse violence or have the bad luck to stand in the way of the "whither?" of the action pointedly end their lives with the end of the novel.

Les Misérables boasts two such contrasting heroes in Marius Pontmercy and Jean Valjean. The first is a younger man who witnesses much of the action but is essentially innocent of any involvement in history and thereby prepares himself to live happily in the stillness of future time. It is he who marries Cosette. The second, equally innocent of intent to harm, is nonetheless a trespasser upon the law and—perhaps even more damning—during one part of his life an active producer of goods. It is he who rescues Cosette from treachery and servitude but loses her, naturally enough, to Marius. "If it was not for death and marriage," E. M. Forster declared, "I do not know how the average novelist would conclude. Death and marriage are almost the only connection between his characters and his plot." There are ample precedents in literature for concluding with both, and the survival of Waverley and death of Fergus Mac-Ivor in Scott's first novel created a precedent for reading the double fable as universal history. Since the vast popularity of this fable depended on representing history as completed action, the death of the maker of history was appropriate and even reassuring; and lest the achievement of history, the *terminus ad quem*, be threatened in any way, the inactive hero, the deserving, meritorious B, usually enjoys an eventless marriage.

As the nineteenth century progressed, writers began to interpret this fable as marking a division between claims of the species and claims of the individual—"So careful of the type," in Tennyson's description of nature, "So careless of the single life." *Les Misérables* and *Les Travailleurs de la mer* speak with a rhetoric of swashbuckling natural history, yet the curious outcome of Hugo's boundless optimism is that the principal combatants in his novels all bow before history as individuals. The tremendous energies of Jean Valjean and Gilliat—descendants of the monstrous Quasimodo in *Notre-Dame de Paris*—successfully conquer all physical odds but succumb helplessly in affairs of the heart. More than that, they are absolute virgins where women are concerned, though their activity is chiefly inspired by sexual longings. Rather than natural or sexual selection, a tremendous force of sublimation seems at work in these novels. The strongest persons do not survive but voluntarily step aside after saving the lives of precisely those pale heroes who breed with the women in question and continue the race. There are two possible ways of regarding such actions, which have vast sentimental value: either they represent the heroism of placing the species before oneself, or a secret longing to die childless and thereby have nothing to do with the species. On the one hand there is the dedication to natural history, so to speak, and on the other a desire to stop the world and get off.

The contradiction of desire in nineteenth-century endings may be frankly presented as marriage for one hero and death for another, or it may be veiled in allegory. Like so many nineteenth-century heroines, Cosette herself is an ambiguous virginal figure who promises both death and continuance. In *Les Misérables* her relation to both heroes brings out her two roles, which correspond to our mixed feelings about the end of individuals on earth. But in novels of a single hero the ambiguous role of the heroine, encompassing both traditional novelistic endings remarked by Forster, may often be detected in the language employed to bring the action to a close. The locus classicus of such ambiguity is (or should be) the words Dickens uses in *Little Dorrit* to describe Arthur Clennam's realization of his love and his inward accession to marriage:

> Looking back upon his own poor story, she [the heroine] was its vanishing-point. Every thing in its perspective led to her innocent figure. He had travelled thousands of miles towards it; previous unquiet hopes and doubts had worked themselves out before it; it was the centre of the interest of his life; it was the termination of everything that was good and pleasant in it; beyond there was nothing but mere waste and darkened sky.

When Dickens uses the language of "vanishing point" and "termination" for marriage, when he immediately invokes the "mere waste and darkened sky" that lie beyond, he builds into the narrative the two endings paraded before the reader in *Les Misérables* and many other novels. These are not merely difficulties with words: marriage provides a dramatic ending to a novel precisely because of the contradictions of desire that it proclaims. If we think of famous novels that do not have dramatic endings, they are often works like *Tristram Shandy*, or *Ulysses*, or *Dead Souls*—or the most endless of all, the *Tiers Livre* of Rabelais—which evade marriage as an end. At the opening of *Jacques le fataliste* Diderot also teases the reader with the question, "What would prevent my having the master married and making him a cuckold?" Though this is but one of many such questions, it happens to prefigure the miserable fragment of plot that the narrator finally doles out to us. There is nothing like unmarriage, an idea that realists have always toyed with, to express open-endedness. The question that deserves much more research is the relation of endedness to nineteenth-century convictions about human and natural history.

"Which came first, the chicken or the egg?" If this old question from natural and folk history of beginnings and endings were inherently undecidable, I suggest, it would not be a popular riddle. In truth the riddle poses some tough questions of biological evolution, but everyone understands that the answer depends on taking a certain perspective. Chickens lay eggs that grow into chickens that lay more eggs and so on—a sequence that can be imaginatively sustained backwards and forwards in time; but as far as the individual bird is concerned, it is perfectly clear that the egg precedes the chicken. Since the embryo bears traces of chickens who were not chickens as we know them today, even as a series the chicken-egg has an irreversible direction. The interest in the riddle and its implied narrative lies not in the difference in experience between chicken and egg, but in the difference between the life of the species and the life of the individual. Obviously we cannot speak for *Gallus gallus*, the domestic fowl, but only for *Homo sapiens*, the domestic person, in stating that the chief difference is that of consciousness. Individuals who are conscious of desires and of death are capable of comparing their brief lives with the continuity of the species. Individuals are also capable of wishes, and some are capable of writing novels. The species does not possess a rival form of consciousness—and that from the point of view of the individual is one of the blessed and terrifying things about the species. One of the favorite pastimes of the nineteenth-century individuals was to imagine, as Kant imagined, that the species had a purpose, as though it were a larger sort of individual to which one could turn for direction and inspiration. The novelistic result was a celebration of history but also of inaction and of an end to time.

HENRI PEYRE

After 1852: God

There was one point on which Hugo never wavered: the fact that God existed. He declared to several of his visitors and correspondents and to George Sand in particular on May 8, 1862: "I believe . . . in God far more than in myself. . . . I am more certain about the existence of God than I am about my own." But it is not clear what conception Hugo had of God, whether his God was that of the Christians or that of the Old Testament, or even the impersonal god of the Deists, that supreme watchmaker who set up the great mechanism of the universe, set it going with a flick of his hand—which Pascal derided in Descartes's work—and has rarely bothered about it since. Hugo did not express himself clearly on this point. He preferred to feel intensely and communicate the mystery of the divine impressionistically. Too much precision would be limiting and, furthermore, diminishing. Hugo could well have uttered Denis Diderot's admirable words: "Enlarge God!" In *Religions et religion*, Hugo farcically attacked the pettiness of organized religions, which are often more inspired by primitive superstitions than by a purified faith and "which often belittle what God made great."

Hugo's god is certainly not the impersonal creator envisaged by the Deists, a god who, very prudently, stays aloof from the world, refuses to listen to prayers, and does not bother about guaranteeing us any form of immortality, or even of survival, after death. Nor is Hugo's god the one naively portrayed to children, and sometimes even to adults, by a crude anthropomorphism, that god whom Xenophanes and, much later, Voltaire

---

From *Victor Hugo*. © 1980 by Henri Peyre. University of Alabama Press, 1980.

poked fun at by suggesting that if horses conceived of a god, this god must look like a horse.

Hugo declares that he does not believe in that "good old-fashioned god," in a forceful poem of *L'Année terrible,* in which he flares up at "the bishop who called me an atheist." In this polemical epistle, whose forcefulness Charles Renouvier was one of the first to point out, Hugo characterizes his religious experience. It is not that of a mystic, or even that of a Pascal, and Jesus Christ is not the intermediary between Hugo and his god. In fact, his religious experience remains abstract. But it anticipates Claudel's famous line on "someone who is within me and is more myself than I am." Hugo declares that if God is

> The being whose soul lies deep within my soul,
> The being who speaks softly to me and constantly intercedes
> In favour of the true against the untrue,

then he is a believer. When all is said and done, Hugo's god is rather similar to the voice of conscience heard by Rousseau and Kant, an intimate and living form of moral law.

On the other hand, Hugo's god is not exactly (or, at least, not invariably) the god of the pantheists, infused and diffused in nature, controlling it and becoming one with it. Formerly, the stoics, and Cleanthes in particular, and, later, poets such as Goethe and Shelley found great poetic resources in this conception of the divine. There are pantheistic elements or expressions in the works of many believers, who, however, disclaim this—in the works of Claudel, for example, and in those of Teilhard de Chardin, who liked to quote the famous words of the apostle Paul (1 Cor. 6:28) announcing that once Christ's work is completed, "God will be all things to all men." Both protested against asceticism, Christian as well as Buddhist, which had totally condemned material things. Hugo too often exalted nature as being quasi-divine and inspired by a superior presence and, at times, by an erotic quality. "God wants us to have been in love. Live and be envied," he cries to lovers in "Crépuscule" (*Les Contemplations,* 2.26). But, contrary to all logic, pantheism and faith in a personal god coexist in many people. "We are born of you," says Cleanthes to Zeus in his hymn, and St. Paul quotes this in his sermon on the Areopagus, presented in the Acts of the Apostles. Indeed, the naturalistic pantheism of the best poet among the ancient stoics had something in common with a Christian prayer.

Hugo's work provides no answers to the various questions posed by his very emotional and colorful philosophy. Indeed, there was no reason for him to write a catechism or a philosophy textbook. Did God create the

world once and for all, assigning a fixed role to each entity within it and
confining it forever within its laws? Did he provide for an evolution lasting
for millions of years? Hugo does not bother to answer these questions or
others. Darwin's evolutionism, as well as Lamarck's transformism at a much
earlier date, had disturbed many poets, such as Lord Tennyson and Robert
Browning in England. It did not shake Hugo's faith; the poet did not even
feel the need to exclaim as Michelet did: "Give me back my own being!"
Hugo considered evolutionism a form of materialism, and he rejected evolution as such, but his faith in God was in no way affected by it. In section
49 of *La Légende des siècles* (poem 10), Hugo, upholding his spiritualistic
faith in man, that being who bears archangels' wings upon his shoulders,
proudly rejected both Darwinism and nihilism, the latter being identified in
his mind with German philosophy. Rather humorously—for Hugo certainly
had a sense of humor—he concluded this rather nationalistic poem with the
following lines:

> And when a dignified, very proper, impeccably turned-out
> Englishman
> Says to me: "God has made you a man, but I am making you
> a monkey.
> Now, make yourself worthy of such a favor!"
> This promotion makes me wonder a bit.

In fact, Hugo's attitude towards God, which was expressed in many
different and, perhaps, somewhat contradictory ways, but which was based
on some unshakably solid convictions, cannot be categorized by any of the
usual philosophical labels. In this, he resembles the majority of men, especially those who refuse to adopt an inflexible doctrine once and for all in the
face of the many attractions of life. At certain times, Hugo was greatly
attracted to polytheistic paganism, just as any man is who is struck by the
multiple forces at work in the universe and who refuses to reduce them
prematurely to a single cause. There has been much learned discussion of
the grandiose poem "Le Satyre" and of the relative proportions of pantheism and monotheism found within it, but this kind of discussion is rather
futile. Like any novelist or dramatist, Hugo assumed the role of the monstrous and mischievous rebel who was going to subjugate Jupiter, while he
was composing this fervid philosophical epic. "Crépuscule," mentioned
above, and ten other poems by Hugo would certainly be included in an
anthology of nineteenth-century poems extolling the survival of the ancient
gods, along with poems by Schiller, Hölderlin, Goethe, Keats, and
Swinburne. Hugo slipped a few beautiful sentences, pregnant with meaning,

into his *Promontorium Somnii:* "The pagan sees God as many-sided. His whole religion is protean. The pagan lives in suspense," and "Polytheism is the daydream haunting man." The awareness that Hugo had of mystery, of a Panlike eroticism aspiring to the divine in antiquity, owed little to erudition. He had drawn very little inspiration from Latin writers, with the exceptions of Virgil, Lucretius, and Juvenal. He knew Greek writers even less; Plato, Plotinus, Proclus, and Hermes Trismegistus were virtually unknown to him. But this was of little importance. His feeling for the ancient myths and for the fresh young imagination that had created them was more perspicuous than that of Leconte de Lisle, or even of Goethe, and that of many scholars. In *Promontorium Somnii,* he also alluded very perceptively to the tragic gloom that often veiled the Apollonian light, overvaunted by the Ancients:

> A strange light fell from Olympus on man, animals, trees, things, life and destiny. This halo was around all heads. It was delightful but disturbing, and sometimes cast a tragic ray.

Generally, however, Hugo could not be satisfied with longing for the revival of the dead gods or with portraying, as the Parnassians did, the successive religions in which mortals believed for a while before giving them a royal burial or even going to the point of spurning them by shattering their symbols. Following Hegelianism and the reduction (by Creuzer and Quinet) of all religions to a vast system of symbols, many philosophers of Hugo's day took bitter pleasure in saying that all gods die, including God Himself, even if a vague sense of the divine continues to exist. For Hugo, on the contrary, God continued to survive, and with man's conception of Him purified, He was more resplendent than ever. In *Le Tas de Pierres* (subtitled "Religion"), Hugo noted:

> Religions are the garments that God is made to put on by man. These garments wear out. So the priests become panic-stricken. But they are wrong to do so. God still exists. Through the holes in the robe of religion, He can be clearly seen.

If Hugo had a keen sense of the multiplicity of a world in which everything is in constant motion, is born and dies to be reborn, with his antithetical turn of mind he was even more in accord with the Manichean oversimplification whereby the world is a battleground on which the forces of good and evil come face to face. But once again, it would be imprudent to class the poet in a specific category. For according to him, evil is not coextensive with God. The universe is not divided between good and evil.

Manicheism is rejected in the long, unfinished poem *Dieu,* in the section entitled "Le Corbeau." The ultimate victory of the forces of good and of God, who pardons and accepts the remorse of the archangel of evil, is never in any doubt. To be sure, the psychology of Hugo's characters in his novels and dramas is often simplistic, based as it is on a clear-cut distinction between the good and the wicked, the overbearing and the oppressed. But the philosophy underlying these characters is by no means simplistic.

The essence of Hugo's god is love. This is stated by Satan at the end of the poem that Hugo devoted to him. Satan, the adversary, feels hated and rejected. But he knows that God does not remain aloof from the universe that he has created, that he is not indifferent to his work, which men have ruined:

> But I, the sad enemy and mocking, envious one,
> Know that God is not a soul but a heart.
> God, the loving heart of the world,
> Ties all the fibres of all the roots to his own divine fibres.

However, this god who is love is not the god of the Christians, or at least not the god of the church. Hugo did not accept the principle of original sin, which St. Augustine, in developing his doctrines, read into an ambiguous sentence in the Epistle to the Romans. Moreover, Hugo did not seem to have been very impressed by St. Paul as a person. Nor did he subscribe to the Incarnation, the Trinity, the Resurrection, or the belief that the apostle Peter set up the papacy.

It is not clear whether Hugo's god reveals himself to man, and if he does, whether it is through the Decalogue, sacred books, prophets, or saints. Here again Hugo remains vague. He prefers to repeat in beautiful verses that God is absolute, unfathomable, and unknowable, and that philosophers have never succeeded in figuring out the mystery of the nature of the divine. He prefers to call himself a "dreamer," and the first of the voices heard in *Dieu* (section 2) speaks to the "dreamer" that he is:

> Seeker, will you find what they have not found?
> Dreamer, will your dreams go beyond theirs?

A multitude of philosophical systems are presented, along with entire series of proper names, which Hugo was partial to. Plato, Locke, Lucretius, Swedenborg, Thales, Rousseau, Joseph de Maistre, and several others file past in a disorderly fashion before our eyes and warn the man given to asking questions to recognize his limits:

Do not go beyond them. Seek God. But look for him
In love and not in fear.

It is only in the hour of death that man can receive the revelation that he has anxiously been seeking all his life. Hugo's god, like Pascal's, is more sensitive to things of the heart than to things of the mind. It would be futile to try to prove this. Affirming it is more convincing for men like Hugo, who want to believe or, rather, who cannot help believing. "God's existence cannot be overemphasized," cried the poet, who was impervious to ridicule, in *Religions et religion*. He alternately expresses anger at and pity for those who deny God, those fools who see nothing in the universe but "a vast monument to insanity."

> As their souls stir up the immense depths,
> They are not even aware of the universe,
> Within which the voice of God produces no echo.
>
> ("Pleurs dans la nuit")

This god who is omnipresent is at the same time an entity apart from the universe he has created and this universe itself. All antinomies are integrated within him. He has a limited self, and yet he is the infinite, explained Hugo through the words of an old member of the Convention, on the point of death, in a strange passage in *Les Misérables*. In this passage, Denis Saurat claimed to have detected a surprising similarity with the Zohar and the Cabala, though it is doubtful that there is any connection. Saurat was closer to the mark when he surmised, with complete deference to the esoteric philosophy of the poet, that Hugo needed a god who was universal and free of any constraining religion, so to speak, and who was also, contradictorily, a personal god, for Hugo, a fragment of the divine and endowed with a strong personality, could only conceive of God as similar to himself, also infinite in his own way. Indeed, in *Les Misérables*, Hugo reasons like a dialectician to prove that there are two infinites, one outside us and another within us.

> It can be assumed that these two infinites are superposed, and that the second one underlies the first one. . . . If the two infinites are endowed with thought, each of them has a motivating force, and there is a self in the infinite above, as there is in the one below; the self in the infinite below is the soul, while that in the infinite above is God.
>
> (Part 2, "Parenthèse," 5)

Like many other thinkers of his century, during which it was considered inevitable to give up old religious formulas but essential to maintain the feeling and hope long represented by religion, Hugo did his best to provide a magnificent range of synonyms for the word *god*, but he did not do this in the slightly casual playful manner of men like Renan. Hugo had personal experience of God, experience that he considered as irrecusable as the sign that Pascal, the Jansenist, believed that he had received from Jesus Christ. Just like Pascal, Hugo, too, rejected the god of the philosophers and scholars and preferred to pray to a god who was responsive to human emotions. One of the "Rules for the thinker," found in *Le Tas de Pierres,* states that the great thinker is the one who retains a simple heart in the face of the complications of the mind.

SANDY PETREY

Quatrevingt-treize:
Children Belong with Their Mother

Q*uatrevingt-treize* is clearly a historical novel in the normal use of the
term to designate a work set in a period prior to the author's own. If we
consider history more than chronology, however, this work should in fact
be classified as *anti*historical. It employs a multitude of codes to convey the
single message that human beings must refuse the imperatives put by *historical* existence in order to realize their full *moral* potential. Discussion of
that refusal will be facilitated if we restrict the term "historical novel" to
works which, regardless of their chronological setting, structurally incor-
porate a historical situation. The most nearly perfect examples are the great
realist texts of the nineteenth century. Balzac's and Stendhal's novels depend
for their readability on a specific social environment. They make sense only
because of a historically determined condition whose proximity to the time
of their composition is of no consequence. They are historical not because
they present the past but because they present history.

"Temporal" would be a better adjective for many so-called historical
novels, those in the tradition typified by Dumas's depictions of history as a
form of high fashion in which styles change without affecting what they
clothe. In this tradition, strange fashions can in fact be the most substantive
manifestation of situation in time. In direct contrast are realist works which,
as Auerbach said of *Le Rouge et le noir*, are "almost incomprehensible
without a most accurate and detailed knowledge of the political situation,
the social stratification, and the economic circumstances of a perfectly definite historical moment."

From *History in the Text:* Quatrevingt-treize *and the French Revolution* (Purdue
University Monographs in Romance Languages). © 1980 by John Benjamins B.V.

Eisenstein defined his texts in opposition to temporal works that usurp the label "historical" to disguise a vision of the world which in fact undermines the very concept of a "perfectly definite historical moment." "Everywhere, in America as in France . . . there are always two lovers together in the foreground, and only the background changes. Today it's the French Revolution, tomorrow it's the Commune, but the characters are always the same, and no one is interested in historical events." In temporal fictions, interest centers on individual psychologies to the exclusion of collective structures, and political events attain textual importance only insofar as they affect personal stories. A setting in the past does not suffice to make a historical text. Far from it.

The great interest of *Quatrevingt-treize* is its refusal to fit into either the historical or the temporal traditions. The novel is antihistorical precisely because it first encloses characters in a definite historical moment, then extracts them from it, first weaves the codes of the French Revolution into its verbal texture, then rejects the linguistic forms imposed by its own choice of subject. Its theme is that history can never block humanity's access to non-history. It expresses that theme through an extraordinary series of confrontations between the devices associated with historical and temporal generic conventions.

Entitled with the name of the great year of the Great Revolution, *Quatrevingt-treize* opens with a group of Parisian soldiers on a search-and-destroy mission in a Breton forest. The soldiers are seeking the Vendée rebels whose resistance to the Republic constitutes the Revolution's most serious internal threat. They notice signs of human presence, surround the suspicious spot, and discover not enemy forces but a helpless widow and her three starving children. After convincing themselves that the woman is apolitical, the Parisians adopt the family in the name of the Republic.

The novel then introduces the marquis de Lantenac, an imposing old aristocrat on the way from England to Brittany to weld the various rebel groups into a single army and secure a landing spot for the projected English invasion. Lantenac assumes command of a group of peasants and immediately displays merciless devotion to his cause by massacring some of the Republican soldiers encountered earlier and razing the village which had sheltered them. During the massacre, the Royalists wound the peasant mother and take her children hostage. The first of the novel's three parts ends with a beggar in the smouldering village mediating on Lantenac's ferocity.

Part 2 introduces Cimourdain, an ardent priest turned ardent revolutionary, who is named the Committee of Public Safety's delegate to the

Republican forces in Brittany. Cimourdain's main duty will be to supervise Gauvain, a nobleman committed to the Revolution out of his love for the good, the just, and the true. Gauvain's commitment to those ideals developed from the instruction he received from Cimourdain, the new political delegate, who had once been Gauvain's tutor and who still adores his former pupil. The tutor must now instruct his charge in ruthlessness, however, for Gauvain invariably spoils his many victories by refusing to exterminate the Republic's enemies after defeating them. Cimourdain and Gauvain, embodying the inexorable and the clement sides of the Revolution, debate their opposing principles throughout part 3 of the novel. They agree on only one thing: the future good of mankind demands that the savage marquis de Lantenac be destroyed. Lantenac is Gauvain's uncle, but even this tie of blood does not blind the normally merciful Republican to the necessity of eliminating the Republic's most formidable foe.

The possibility of that elimination comes when Lantenac, a small band of supporters, and their three captive children are trapped in a tower of Gauvain and Lantenac's ancestral castle. Despite the Royalists' threat to kill the hostages, the Republicans attack and win the tower. A dying rebel sets fire to the building, and the three children are about to be burned alive as the marquis de Lantenac escapes through a secret tunnel. On emerging into the open, however, the Royalist leader is transfixed by the scream of the children's mother. Despite the certainty that to do so will mean capture and execution, Lantenac returns to save the children.

Gauvain, his entire concept of his enemy overturned by the Royalist's sacrifice of his life and his cause, cannot accept the thought that such nobility should be rewarded by the guillotine. He consequently arranges an escape by taking Lantenac's place in the cell of the condemned. When Cimourdain learns of this treachery, his devotion to revolutionary discipline forces him to order his beloved Gauvain's death on the guillotine. However, while Cimourdain the political agent must order Gauvain's execution, Cimourdain the human being cannot survive it. The delegate of the Committee of Public Safety commits suicide when the blade hits Gauvain's neck, and the novel concludes with the souls of the tragically opposed Republicans flying heavenward.

In terms of Benveniste's fruitful distinction between "story" and "discourse," between the plot itself and the supplementary information communicated with it, the preceding paragraphs of course summarize only the story. On the level of discourse, the text contains a vast amount of historical description which was not mentioned, such as the breathtaking pages on Paris and the Convention in part 2. The function of historical discourse will be discussed later; for the moment, let us draw attention to the curiously flabby function of history in the story as it stands. Part 1 of *Quatrevingt-treize* introduces Lantenac and the Royalist forces in Brittany; part 2 introduces Cimourdain and the Parisian revolutionaries he represents. The scene is clearly set for a spectacular resolution of the conflict in part 3, but the novel's final section does not conclude with the end of the conflict between Republican Paris and the Royalist provinces. Quite the contrary, political definitions are inoperative in the final narrative sequence, which shows the Republican general first saving the life of the Royalist general and then being decapitated by his Republican ally.

The irrelevance of historical conflict to the final personal stories is matched by the general stasis of the civil war from the beginning to the end of the novel. If we look at the struggle in the west independently of the personalities who wage it, it becomes apparent that nothing happens in *Quatrevingt-treize*. Part 1 opens with the war at a decisive stage. Part 3 concludes with the war at the same decisive stage. This is unusual even for temporal novels. *Gone with the Wind* may convey the impression that the primary effect of the War Between the States was to annoy Scarlett O'Hara, but the war indubitably ends. *Quatrevingt-treize* neither recounts nor suggests the end of the war in which it inserts its characters. If we concur with Greimas and other theoreticians of the subject in defining narrative as a sequence proceeding from a disturbed to a stable situation, then there is no historical narrative in *Quatrevingt-treize*.

In contrast, the novel's personal narrative presents the standard violation and vindication of a stock situation and, furthermore, runs throughout the text. The latter point is significant. Although Lantenac, Cimourdain, and Gauvain are unquestionably the novel's most fully developed characters, their serial introduction makes it impossible for them to furnish the narrative threads which connect the novel's beginning to its end. The characters who do furnish that connection are the ones who, introduced before any of the historically typical protagonists, also motivate the concluding sequence: the apolitical peasant family, Michelle Fléchard and her three children. As the tale of a political conflict, *Quatrevingt-treize* is a nonstory whose end repeats its beginning: *turning point in the war → turning point in the war*. As the tale of family tribulations, it presents a much more satisfactory progression: *children separated from their mother → children reunited with their mother*.

The political conflict is historically specific, a phenomenon of the precise year which the novel's title names and in relation to which its protagonists define themselves. Michelle Fléchard and her children are politically anonymous. They belong together by a timeless imperative independent of historical events. Although the family's dissolution is the effect of historical struggle, the important point is that the novel's basic narrative axis is the disruption and reinstitution of a situation which is eternally valid. History threatens the family unit's sanctity, but that sanctity as ultimately reaffirmed is luminously transhistorical. Children belong with their mother regardless of the year when they were born.

Then what distinguishes *Quatrevingt-treize* from the temporal works which Eisenstein scorned? The Russian filmmaker's precise example of stories to avoid was that of two lovers whose career denigrates historical events. Yet family togetherness is no more pregnant with political significance than the union of a man and a woman in love. If it structures its plot as the timeless tale of maternal impulses, why not classify *Quatrevingt-treize* with thousands of other trivially chronological novels?

The beginning of an answer to those questions is the striking difference between the textual presence accorded the standard lovers and that which *Quatrevingt-treize* assigns the Fléchard family, between the peasants' contrasted functions on the levels of story and discourse. Eisenstein refused temporal fictions because they place personal stories in the foreground and relegate history to the background. *Quatrevingt-treize* reverses that emphasis. The Fléchards' central narrative role does not lead to the extensive delineation reserved for historically typical and conscious characters. Lantenac, Cimourdain, and Gauvain's developed textual presences are inseparable from their developed political consciousnesses. The novel assigns negligible personal and political stature to the characters who unify its narrative; the characters presented as political and personal Titans have subsidiary narrative functions.

Quatrevingt-treize is antihistorical rather than temporal because it refuses to concentrate the reader's attention on characters who act independently of historical movements. It depicts men committed body and soul to historical struggle and recounts the meaningful events of their lives as effects of their political engagement. When those men are inserted into the ahistorical tale of a family reunion, therefore, they must appear there *against* their political definition. Their narrative function requires that they rise above history and act as if their involvement in the war between Republic and Old Regime were a mistake which they fully renounce. Narrative dominance of an ahistorical story corresponds to the thematic dominance of a moral vision in which historical circumstances are insubstantial wisps.

To appreciate the extent to which their participation in the family story denies the value of their political stories, consider the historical consequences of Lantenac, Gauvain, and Cimourdain's involvement with the mother and children. Lantenac is identified time and again as the monarchy's best hope, the one man who can unify the Vendée rebels, open France to the British forces, and restore the Old Regime. "Son nom avait couru dans l'insurrection vendéenne comme une traînée de poudre, et Lantenac était tout de suite devenu centre." The man bearing that explosive name cannot act as an isolated individual. When he returns to certain death for the sake of three children, he is sacrificing the monarchist cause as well as himself. Gauvain's response is even more vilely treasonous. A general of almost supernatural skill, Gauvain alone can withstand Lantenac and save the Revolution. Yet in order to affirm the nobility of the children's rescue, he both releases the Republic's most dangerous enemy and destroys, in himself, the Republic's most successful defender. With Gauvain removed, only Cimourdain might have the strength to organize the Parisian forces; his suicide opens yet another breach.

The chapter which describes Gauvain's conflict over Lantenac has often been compared—the first time by Hugo himself—to "Tempête sous un crâne," the famous chapter in *Les Misérables* in which the real Jean Valjean decides to abandon his secure disguise in order to save a man mistakenly identified as himself. However, while the two chapters are rhetorically similar, the political implications of Gauvain's dilemma confront him with the necessity of a decision wholly unlike Jean Valjean's. The reformed thief condemns himself to assure the safety of an innocent sheep; the Republican general condemns himself so that the wolf will continue to have free run of the fold. Gauvain's sacrifice will lead inexorably to "la mort d'une foule d'êtres innocents, hommes, femmes, enfants, . . . le recul de la révolution, les villes saccagées, le peuple déchiré." Since "sauver Lantenac, c'était sacrifier la France," and since "tuer Lantenac, c'était tuer la Vendée; tuer la Vendée, c'était sauver la France," Gauvain can consider himself only a traitor and a deserter when he decides to liberate his enemy: "Va, fais les affaires des Anglais. Déserte. Passe à l'ennemi. Sauve Lantenac et trahis la France."

Yet this act of black treachery is also an act of radiant virtue. In performing it, Gauvain is bathed in a superior light which, as he goes toward a traitor's death, seems to emanate from his own godlike self. Not only is his face illuminated but the brightness of dawn radiates from his eyes. The deed which history marks as infernal is at the same time divine. Instead of damnation, Gauvain achieves an apotheosis.

The same act thus has opposed meanings, and one of the central ideas of contemporary semiotics is that a single signifying element has two meanings by virtue of two codes. One of the codes in this case is a historical system structured by the oppositions which also name the political conflicts of the French Revolution. The other has a radically different foundation. Gauvain comes to assign meaning by a process which, while making the words of 1793 semantically vacuous, also affirms the majestic plenitude of kinship terms. When Gauvain leaves the Revolution to enter the tale of the Fléchard family, the textual presentation of his decision ceases to divide reality by political categories in order to classify it on the basis of family ties.

Earlier, Gauvain and Lantenac's depictions had emphasized that political definition takes precedence over all other kinds. Lantenac is a Royalist and an uncle, Gauvain a Republican and a nephew. Their political commitments suggest hostility, their family bond affection, and political factors clearly determine their interaction. The two men struggle mightily against one another, vying as to which can swear more strongly to exterminate the other. Lantenac, "ce quasi grand-père," promises to kill Gauvain, "presque un petit-fils," like a dog. Gauvain is no less adamant. In a discussion with Cimourdain, he explicitly chooses political over familial allegiances: " 'Mais alors, si tu prends Lantenac, tu lui feras grâce?' 'Non.' . . . 'Mais Lantenac est ton parent.' 'La France est la grande parente.' " Gauvain's denial is in harmony with the text's overall assertion that ties of ideology are greater than ties of blood. A series of passages establish stylistic fields whose cumulative effect is to annihilate the normal value of family terms, here shown to be politically and hence semantically void. "[C]'est le petit neveu qui se bat contre le grand-oncle. L'oncle est royaliste, le neveu est patriote. L'oncle commande les blancs, le neveu commande les bleus. Ah! ils ne se feront pas quartier, allez. C'est une guerre à mort." The thrice-repeated kinship terms *oncle* and *neveu* are ineffectual in this passage's development toward its concluding war to the death. The operative words are political terms in historically specific oppositon: *royaliste/patriote; bleu/blanc.* Gauvain and Lantenac are enemies not relatives.

But only up to Michelle Fléchard's scream. From then on, not only do Lantenac and Gauvain become allies but the vocabulary of family ties attains unforeseen stylistic stature. No longer is France "la grande parente," for Gauvain sacrifices and betrays France. The family bonds which had been nugatory suddenly become a higher truth than the Revolution, a truth which, by a most perplexing historical judgement indeed, it was the Revolution's task to proclaim: "abolir la féodalité, c'est fonder la famille." Instead of the end of the fatherland's most dangerous enemy, Lantenac's execution comes to mean to Gauvain the distressing loss of a revered ancestor.

> Ce sang qu'il allait répandre—car le laisser verser, c'est le verser
> soi-même—est-ce que ce n'était pas son sang, à lui Gauvain? Son
> grand-père était mort, mais son grand-oncle vivait; et ce grand-
> oncle, c'était le marquis de Lantenac. Est-ce que celui des deux
> frères qui était dans le tombeau ne se dresserait pas pour empêcher
> l'autre d'y entrer? . . . Il s'agissait de savoir si, quand Lantenac
> venait de rentrer dans l'humanité, Gauvain, allait, lui, rentrer
> dans la famille.
>
> Il s'agissait de savoir si l'oncle et le neveu allaient se rejoindre
> dans la lumière supérieure.

The profusion of kinship terminology—*sang, grand-père, grand-oncle, frères, famille, oncle, neveu*—and the absence of political words lexically embody the value system motivating Gauvain. Historical meaning disappears before a form of sense making organized by ahistorical categories. Not a Royalist and a Republican but an uncle and a nephew join one another in the superior light.

On the symbolic level, Lantenac is not Gauvain's only relative in *Quatrevingt-treize*. Cimourdain, the former tutor, is both mother and father to his beloved pupil; mother because "l'esprit allaite; l'intelligence est une mamelle," father by a "profonde paternité spirituelle" that makes him "plus père que le père." As with his natural uncle, Gauvain's bond to his spiritual parent is threatened by political divisions. In the former tutor and his pupil, "deux formes de la république étaient en présence, la république de la terreur et la république de la clémence."

But death itself does not prevent revalidation of Gauvain and Cimourdain's family ties, as the text's final sentence specifies: "Et ces deux âmes, sœurs tragiques, s'envolèrent ensemble, l'ombre de l'une mêlée à la lumière de l'autre." It is as "sœurs," as members of the same family, that Gauvain and Cimourdain leave the Revolution.

Gauvain's reunion with Cimourdain and Lantenac suggests that the opposition between story and history in *Quatrevingt-treize* should be taken farther than was done before. Not only do the three political protagonists have accessory roles in an apolitical tale, they are also the principal characters in stories as resolutely ahistorical as the Fléchard family narrative. The plot and subplots of *Quatrevingt-treize* all display a single narrative axis whose sequence depends for its effectiveness on the supremely nonrevolutionary concept that blood is thicker than water: *family ties broken → family ties reestablished.* Furthermore, the Revolution consistently has the villainous narrative function of keeping families apart. The course of the civil war separates the mother from her children as their respective ideologies separate Cimourdain, Gauvain, and Lantenac. A major component of the textual definition of the Revolution in *Quatrevingt-treize* is its disruption of personal and familial relationships.

Only "a," not "the" major component, however. The Revolution is also represented as the great hope of humanity, the creation in blood and fire of a world where love will reign. By the curious judgement quoted earlier, the same Revolution which destroys family ties also affirms their sacredness. This is the paradox discussed in relation to Gauvain's release of Lantenac: a single signifying unit has contradictory meanings, and such a situation can exist only in the presence of distinct sets of semiotic procedures.

Different semiotic procedures, different ways of encoding and interpreting messages, always manifest different means of representing and understanding existence as a whole. The contradictory values of signifying units in *Quatrevingt-treize*—the rescue of three children, the salvation of Lantenac, the Revolution itself—therefore embody conflicting philosophical assessments of human duty and purpose. *Quatrevingt-treize* authorizes two interpretations of its textual elements, one based on the events of 1793, the other transcending all historical situations to radiate eternal truth. That phrasing suggests the hierarchy by which the decoding possibilities are to be evaluated: historical understanding is inferior. To attain salvation in *Quatrevingt-treize* is to rise above the universe of *quatre-vingt-treize*.

Lantenac is charged with answering two questions. (1) "Should I allow three children to be burned alive while their mother watches?" (2) "Should I destroy the political cause to which I have devoted my being?" If he were presented with either of those questions in isolation, Lantenac's response would be a resounding negative; but they are not presented in isolation. To say "no" to one is to say "yes" to the other, and his choice is to refuse his historical duty for the sake of something higher. Gauvain faces a comparably impossible pair. (1) "Should I release the Republic's most dangerous enemy?" (2) "Should I execute the protector of the innocent?" He too chooses an answer which transcends 1793. The moral duties of a *chevalier sans peur et sans reproche* anachronistically stand above all those urged, however imperiously, by a revolution in process.

> Au-dessus des royautés, au-dessus des révolutions, au-dessus des questions terrestres, il y a l'immense attendrissement de l'âme humaine, la protection due aux faibles par les forts, le salut dû à

> ceux qui sont perdus par ceux qui sont sauvés, la paternité due
> à tous les enfants par tous les vieillards.

That passage's moral hierarchy sets the human soul over and away from earthly questions like a nation's form of government. Analogously, its verbal hierarchy invalidates language grounded in oppositions like that between royalty and revolution. Lantenac and Gauvain are above all historical conflict, and whatever features distinguish political systems from one another are not pertinent to their meaning.

For Gauvain, Lantenac's decision to negate the semantic value of political signs was almost conscious.

> Quoi, être un royaliste, prendre une blance, mettre dans un plateau le roi de France, une monarchie de quinze siècles, les vieilles, lois à rétablir, l'antique société à restaurer, et dans l'autre, trois petits paysans quelconques, et trouver le roi, le trône, le sceptre et les quinze siècles de monarchie légers pesés à ce poids de trois innocences.

The image of the scale is especially apposite to the change of code Lantenac effects. As any English word has meaning by virtue of the oppositions between it and all other English words, so the key political signs *roi, trône, sceptre,* and *monarchie* are meaningful by virtue of their opposition to the signs of the revolutionary regime. And as English words are meaningless in French, so royalist signs are without substance when political discourse is abandoned. Lantenac's decision to save the children was a choice to stop representing his life by a historical code suited for earthly questions.

The Royalist general's acceptance of the higher moral order and of a language adequate to it is transitory. Gauvain's is permanent. When the Republican leader goes to offer freedom to the Royalist prisoner, the latter gives a magnificent speech in defense of his cause. His diatribe both raises the language of Royalist struggle to memorable heights of eloquence and makes acerbically comic metalinguistic comments on the Republic's feeble attempts to create its own language: "ce que nous appelons la boue, vous l'appelez la nation." The response to this eloquence is silence. As if beyond the stage in which political discourse of any kind conveyed meaning, Gauvain speaks only the few syllables required to offer freedom to his uncle. Lantenac has reentered a historical world and uses language capable of speaking it. Gauvain, in a higher world, cannot respond in kind. "L'Ancêtre" is the title given to the chapter containing ten pages which are by far the novel's most compelling defense of the Old Regime and one of its most compelling political statements of any sort, and it is as an ancestor rather than an adversary that Gauvain responds to Lantenac. For those above royalty and revolution, silence is the only answer to historically grounded utterances.

If Lantenac returns to an inferior system of representation, Cimourdain never acquires any other. The political understanding which is his only way of viewing the world forces him to execute his spiritual son. He subsequently finds himself unable to interpret his condition and therefore removes himself from it. Although he used a different vocabulary, Camus defined suicide as the admission of a semiotic breakdown: "killing yourself amounts to confession. It is confessing that life is too much for you or that *you do not understand it*" (emphasis added). Lack of understanding is a lack of representational capacity, an inability to devise an expression of what is that can accomplish the quintessential human goal called making sense.

Hugo originally planned to include in *Quatrevingt-treize* an explanation of Cimourdain's suicide as the response to a moral imperative as strong as the political imperative which forced Gauvain's execution. Two manuscript variants show Cimourdain saying that, while the "law" required that Gauvain die, "justice" demands that he follow his former pupil. The decision not to include any such explanation in the final text and to present the suicide as a stark fact was inspired. Cimourdain does not die because he has alternative means of understanding the world, one structured by political categories such as the laws which vary with time and place (recall that "laws" was one of the words Lantenac perceived as meaningless when he replied to a mother's scream), the other structured by moral ideals like justice which are eternally the same. A prisoner of history, Cimourdain can understand the world in only *one* way, through a representational system marked by historical oppositions. That system is inadequate to his apolitical reaction to Gauvain's death, and he leaves a world without meaning.

Cimourdain's desperately unexplained suicide deserves further comment because it indicates the global failure of historical visions of the world in *Quatrevingt-treize*. When introduced, the priest was presented as the personification of the great political events occurring around him.

"Cimourdain s'était jeté dans ce vaste renouvellement humain avec logique. . . . cette croissance de tout l'avait vivifié. . . . D'année en année, il avait regardé les événements grandir, et il avait grandi comme eux." Completely rejuvenated by the Revolution, Cimourdain understands the world and himself through its development. Only his love for Gauvain prevents him from being an exclusively political creature, and that love is "caché, mais non éteint, par l'immensité des choses publiques."

This immensity of public things is crucial; no less so is the fact that they do not extinguish private things. At the conclusion of the novel, Cimourdain looks at Gauvain and sees a traitor to the cause. That interpretation reverses the one effected when the tutor was forming his charge's mind and the rigorously egalitarian Cimourdain responded not to Gauvain's political meaning but to his childhood. "Que ne pardonne-t-on pas à un enfant? On lui pardonne d'être seigneur, d'être prince, d'être roi. . . . Il est si petit qu'on lui pardonne d'être grand." The final pun on *petit* and *grand*, the former used in its human and the latter in its political sense, perfectly summarizes Cimourdain's semiotic selection. The lexical triplet *seigneur, prince, roi* has no expressive power in comparison to the single word *enfant*. Public things—public names—do not communicate in the private language of love for a child.

Cimourdain's suicide is the result of adopting a converse representational system in which the names of personal affections cannot communicate. Like all characters in *Quatrevingt-treize*, Cimourdain must confront a fearful choice: *either* he understands the world as political, in which case words like *enfant* have no meaning, *or* he responds to children and denies the significance of political signs. After condemning Gauvain to death, Cimourdain went to see him for the last time. Finding him asleep, the former tutor looked at his child in such a way that "une mère regardant son nourrisson dormir n'aurait pas un plus tendre et plus inexprimable regard." The maternal imagery, highly charged in this story of a peasant mother's reunion with her children, states Cimourdain's feeling. But another word in the quoted sentence underlines the devastating effect of Cimourdain's political vision. He has committed himself to a representational system in which maternal love is "inexprimable."

For Cimourdain, therefore, private things cannot be articulated. For Gauvain, who made the opposite semiotic choice, public things like civil war do not exist. "Et l'on pouvait dire: Non, la guerre civile n'existe pas, la barbarie n'existe pas, la haine n'existe pas, le crime n'existe pas, les ténèbres n'existent pas; pour dissiper ces spectres, il suffit de cette aurore, l'enfance." What is the language in which it "can be said" that civil war does not exist? That in which childhood is synonymous with dawn, "innocence" in apposition with "toute-puissance," and all historical imperatives are seen to vanish "devant le bleu regard de ceux qui n'ont pas vécu."

The repetition of words like "n'existe pas" illustrates the all-encompassing quality of the text's representational shift. The graphic sequence s—o—n has one meaning in French, another in English, a third in Spanish, and so on. However, the meaning it potentially bears in other semiotic systems vanishes—does not exist—when we identify the system in which it actually appears. Once the hermeneutic choice is made, alternative meanings are no longer pertinent. Similarly, the nefarious political meaning of Lantenac's release is of no consequence after the decision that children have absolute value.

Quatrevingt-treize can be read as a progressive revelation of children's transcendent significance. Before Michelle Fléchard's scream, characters had made the grievous error of interpreting children within a historical frame. The Royalists assumed the Fléchard family was Republican and took the children hostage. Trapped in the Tourgue, they attempted to make political use of the children by threatening that their defeat would be accompanied by the hostages' deaths. Even Gauvain and the Republicans, although they make (unsuccessful) plans for a rescue, act as if civil war imposes duties higher than those owed to children. While they know that the hostages' deaths could result, they nevertheless attack and conquer. The Royalist who sets the fire intended to burn the Fléchards does so with a speech which definitively asserts that children are political signs. Referring to the imprisoned child king Louis XVII, the monarchist explains his arson by saying that he is responding to Republican interpretation of children as political: "Je venge, sur leurs petits, notre petit à nous, le roi qui est au Temple."

When the mother sees her threatened family, however, Royalists and Republicans stop assimilating children into the discourse which opposes them to each other, recognize that the meaning of a child's blue gaze cannot be expressed in the words for which they are killing and dying, and join to affirm words suited to the majestic truth of that which is above the Revolution. The text concurs. On a stylistic level, the radiance of childish innocence generates a series of words whose sense goes beyond that conveyed by the lexicon of 1793. On the narrative level, the novel which appeared to be about the Vendée rebellion reveals that its subject is the reunion of family members—mothers and children, uncles and nephews, fathers and sons. For stories to be stories, they have to have conclusions. Despite the political circumstances of their beginnings, all the stories of *Quatrevingt-treize* can conclude only by the double move toward affirming the sanctity of family love and rejecting the demands of historical action. To return to Benveniste's formula, both the story and the discourse of *Quatrevingt-treize* begin in history and end by moving out of it.

The great merit of *Quatrevingt-treize* is that it makes the move without presenting the historically formed interpretation as *incorrect*. Rather it is *different*. It is not incorrect to say that the signified of s—o—n is "male child," although that meaning is not pertinent if French is the language in use. Analogously, it is not incorrect to say that Lantenac's return to the children and Gauvain's release of Lantenac have ghastly political meanings. That is a fact which the text repeatedly proclaims. Yet the historical significance of those acts is not pertinent to the signifying network in which they are finally assumed, a network whose concepts are eternal not historical. The text presents the meanings of the French Revolution as simultaneously real and inferior.

Quatrevingt-treize thus arranges its elements so as to announce that they can and must be interpreted by conventions other than those validated by history. The meaning of any sign—words, people, events—varies according to whether it is or is not inscribed in a historical context. Meaning depends on languages; messages communicate only by virtue of codes. While *Quatrevingt-treize* depicts with great force the power of historical codes, it also demonstrates that they can be transcended by an interpretive procedure which nullifies the oppositions structuring the language of 1793.

SUZANNE NASH

Writing a Building:
Hugo's Notre-Dame de Paris

The publication in 1831 of Victor Hugo's novel, *Notre-Dame de Paris*, had such a dramatic impact on the French reading public's attitude towards its historical heritage that the government established in the same year the Commission des Monuments Historiques to save France's buildings from further destruction. Viollet-Le-Duc would devote his life to the restoration of Gothic cathedrals in particular, replacing, for example, on Notre-Dame of Paris, the delicate spire of the Chapel, "amputated" in 1787, and the row of the Kings of Judea above the front portals knocked down in 1789 by the revolutionaries, who had mistaken them (as would Hugo) for the kings of France. Yet, although Hugo himself was a member of the Comité des Monuments et des Arts from 1835 until 1848, he was undoubtedly divided in his feelings about the successful restoration of Notre-Dame when he returned to France in 1871 after twenty years of political exile. On the one hand, he was convinced of the generative power of the written word to shape history, yet, on the other, he must have been dismayed to see its power result in the cosmetic covering up of the disruptive changes wrought by time, man and art that for him constituted a particularly moving and beautiful chronicle of their own. Such a reaction was even more likely, it seems to me, because of a conflict inherent in Hugo's own writing of which he himself may or may not have been aware. Throughout his work, wherever questions of great art or revolutionary action are concerned, Hugo's glorification of the iconoclastic forces of change is rendered ambiguous by a nostalgia, felt on the level of both theme and imagery, for the permanence of an essential order.

From *French Forum* 8, no. 1 (May 1983). © 1983 by French Forum Publishers, Inc.

Nowhere else is this conflict more evident than in *Notre-Dame de Paris*, where revolutionary change is explicitly linked to architectural and scriptural forms of "modern" art and where the story told seems strangely at odds with the values underlying its most powerful narrative techniques.

I will explore this ambiguity by examining the contradictory treatment of the various "Notre-Dames de Paris," that is, the historical stone-and-mortar cathedral to which the authorial voice refers, the structure of Hugo's written narrative entitled *Notre-Dame de Paris*, and the Notre-Dame of Paris which is projected as symbolic space within that structure.

Although Hugo insists repeatedly upon the doomed nature of the historic building because of the destructibility of stone, beginning his novel under the sign of its effacement, he never allows his reader to forget the existence of this referent and the genesis of his book in time. There are three major interventions by the authorial voice which bring that referent sharply into focus. The first is in the introduction: "Il y a quelques années qu'en visitant, ou, pour mieux dire, en furetant Notre-Dame, l'auteur de ce livre trouva, dans un recoin obscur." The second is in book 3, with its two chapters, "Notre-Dame" and "Paris à vol d'oiseau"; and the third occurs midway through the novel in book 5, "Ceci tuera cela."

In the first chapter of book 3, "Notre-Dame," written shortly after the July Revolution, in October of 1830, the conflict between conservatism and radicalism to which I have already referred is the most apparent. Some one hundred pages into the text the narrator arrests his story to describe the monument which inspired his work. The authorial voice is clearly nostalgic about the loss of the old order, which he identifies with the cathedral as it appeared during the thirteenth century. He laments the loss of the structure's original integrity, choosing an organic image to do so. The cathedral is depicted as an old woman whose once-beautiful face and robes have been scarred and deformed by the passage of time and by the carelessness of man, especially of artists. He then proceeds for several pages, through preterition, to restore the church as she used to be, replacing all of the beautiful structures which are missing or defaced. He lingers lovingly on the once-splendid façade depicting the glory and authority of the theocratic era: "les trois portails creusés en ogive, le cordon brodé et dentelé des vingt-huit niches royales, l'immense rosace centrale flanquée de ses deux fenêtres latérales comme le prêtre du diacre et du sous-diacre." The adjectives which he uses to characterize this queen stress her harmony and her unity in diversity: "tranquille grandeur de l'ensemble vaste symphonie en pierre . . . une et complexe, . . . puissante et féconde comme la création divine." With the loss of all that, with the intrusion of new styles, he says the spectator "croirait que le lieu saint est devenu infâme, et s'enfuirait." Then, abruptly, without transition, there is a shift in perspective and in the judgment brought to bear on these culprits of history. Notre-Dame, we are informed, was never, after all, a pure form: "Notre-Dame de Paris n'est point du reste ce qu'on peut appeler un monument complet, défini, classé. Ce n'est plus une église romane, ce n'est pas encore une église gothique. . . . C'est un édifice de la transition." She began as a Romanesque structure, and, with the return of the crusaders, the Gothic arch was grafted onto the original base. There was no organic relationship between the two: "C'est la greffe de l'ogive sur le plein cintre." He has recourse to pre-Christian allusions to describe the phantasm that she was and finally ends with the biblical reference to the Tower of Babel, giving, through the sheer accumulation of images, this traditionally negative figure a strangely positive connotation: "Cette église centrale et génératrice est parmi les vieilles églises de Paris une sorte de chimère; elle a la tête de l'une, les membres de cella-là, la croupe de l'autre; quelque chose de toutes." She is one of the "vestiges cyclopéens, les pyramides d'Egypte, les gigantesques pagodes hindoues. . . . Chaque flot du temps superpose son alluvion, chaque race dépose sa couche sur le monument. . . . Le grand symbole de l'architecture, Babel, est une ruche." Yet, by capping his symbol ("Babel") of the generative potential of absolute relativism with another organic image ("ruche"), he transforms that potential into inner necessity. Finally, after a description which seems to revel in the fertility of the human imagination for change, he returns to his original position at the very end of the chapter to say that all of this is only superficial ornamentation, that the basic design of the church is still Christian and can never be disturbed by these changes; in other words, that the Christian message is always there to be deciphered and believed: "Du reste, toutes ces nuances, toutes ces différences n'affectent que la surface des édifices. . . . La constitution même de l'église chrétienne n'en est pas attaquée." Thus, chapter 1 of book 3 begins and ends on a note of conservative idealism, interrupted in the middle by a brief glorification of the monstrous deformity of an edifice in the process of becoming and whose basic design is no longer discernible.

The third authorial intervention in book 5, the chapter entitled "Ceci tuera cela," which was written about a month later than "Notre-Dame," but withheld by Hugo from the 1831 edition, along with chapter 2 of book 3, "Paris à vol d'oiseau," and chapter 1 of book 5, *Abbas Beati Martini* (these three chapters appeared for the first time in the Renduel edition of 1832), seems, on the other hand, to represent a point of view which transforms the conflict of views apparent in "Notre-Dame" into a rationalized, revolutionary poetics. Here Hugo interrupts his story to make certain we understand the nature of the objectification of Human Thought into its various scriptural forms. The "ceci" to which Frollo had dolefully referred in an earlier chapter is the book or printing, and the "cela" is the stone edifice in which he presides as priest and chief interpretant; but unlike Frollo (who could be said to be representative of the conservative voice beginning and ending "Notre-Dame"), what the authorial voice stresses is the similarity between "ceci" and "cela," that is, the effacement of specific referent, rather than the replacement of one by another. For the narrator there is no essential difference between architecture and books; the latter are simply less destructible than the former because books can be printed in millions of copies and there is only one of each cathedral, just as there was only one of each handwritten parchment before printing was invented. Both architecture and books are forms of writing; it is history which changed the nature of that writing and in precisely the same way for each type of expression. Indeed, Hugo's postrevolutionary novel begun at the end of the Restoration and finished under the July Monarchy has more in common with the Notre-Dame of the fifteenth century, that period of political and social transition, than with any transparently symbolic morality play of the twelfth or thirteenth century. The event which, according to the narrator, caused the radical change in the *nature* of writing—whether that writing be in stone or in ink—was the discovery by the bourgeoisie and the people of the *concept* of freedom, that is, of the advent of democracy and the overthrow of the old monarchical, theocratic structure. The very earliest architectural forms, those which existed before the concept of freedom, Hugo tells us, were like the letters of the alphabet, each letter representing an idea—a kind of hieroglyphics: "On plantait une pierre debout, et c'était une lettre, et chaque lettre était un hiéroglyphe, et sur chaque hiéroglyphe reposait un groupe d'idées comme le chapiteau sur la colonne." In the next stage the structures represented words, and sometimes, as in the case of Karnac, when there was enough stone and enough space, an entire sentence. Finally, the temples represented books: "Tous ces symboles, auxquels l'humanité avait foi, allaient croissant, se multipliant, se croisant, se compliquant de plus en plus; les premiers monuments ne suffisaient plus à les contenir." But what characterized all of these early edifices, according to Hugo, despite their growing complexity, was the unity of message and form. All were modes of what he calls "symbolic" writing, that is, writing that could be deciphered according to one key, of which the priest was the guardian: "L'idée mère, le verbe, n'était pas seulement au fond de tous ces édifices, mais encore dans la forme . . . Sur chacune de ses enceintes concentriques les prêtres pouvaient lire le verbe traduit et manifesté aux yeux. . . . Ainsi le verbe était enfermé dans l'édifice, mais son image était sur son enveloppe *comme la figure humaine sur le cercueil d'une momie"*(my emphasis). One is struck by Hugo's chilling analogy. This kind of monologistic writing had become, in his view, a form of petrification. Later on in the passage he expatiates on this theme: "Les caractères généraux de toute architecture théocratique sont l'immutabilité, l'horreur du progrès, la conservation des lignes traditionnelles . . . le pli constant de toutes les formes de l'homme et de la nature aux caprices incompréhensibles du symbole." Symbolic writing was dead, ungenerative writing. He adds wistfully that every form of deformity even had an inviolable meaning. In Western civilization the Romanesque represented this kind of unified vision. It was, according to Hugo, the crusades which dealt the liberating blow to such an authoritarian structure: "C'est un grand mouvement polulaire; et tout grand mouvement populaire, quels qu'en soient la cause et le but, dégage toujours . . . l'esprit de liberté . . . L'autorité s'ébranle, l'unité se bifurque." Doubleness, rift, ambiguity rather than unity and a decipherable language characterize this new form of writing; seditious pages appear on the storied doors of the cathedrals, pages hostile to the Holy Scripture. The Gothic cathedral and its complex dialectic of relationships replaces the Romanesque—the Gothic, then, is associated in Hugo's mind with revolution and the rise of democracy. Writing is now fundamentally different from what it was: "L'hiéroglyphe déserte la cathédrale et s'en va blasonner le donjon pour faire un prestige à la féodalité. . . . Le livre architectural n'appartient plus au sacerdoce, à la religion, à Rome; il est à l'imagination, à la poésie, au peuple." Form and message, he goes on to say, are once and for all severed; indeed, message has virtually disappeared, and it is form which constitutes the vitality of the structure. The word as truth has been effaced from the wall, and the endless process of questioning and change begins. It is difficult to miss the analogy with Hugo's own neo-Gothic novel as it is described in the introduction of March 1831, written after the novel was completed. Only a few years ago, the author tells us, he saw a word, ANANKE (Fatalité), inscribed on the cathedral wall. That word, already a subversion of the Christian Word (Providence), has now been effaced, and it is on this *missing* word that Hugo will construct his new edifice: "C'est sur ce mot qu'on a fait ce livre." Thus, the sentence ending the introduction and beginning the novel is an ironic distortion of Christ's words, "On this rock I will build my church." In the course of the cathedral's writing, Frollo, the evil priest still caught in the old order and in an obsessive search for the alchemist's Truth of truths, will rewrite the subversive word on Hugo's fictional walls to inspire the series of ironic substitutions which constitute the novel's structure.

It would seem, then, that it was not until he had finished writing *Notre-Dame de Paris,* or, perhaps more significantly, it was in the process of that writing, with the drafting in November 1830 of Book 5, that Hugo came to believe in the value of a text which eludes the "truth" and, in so doing, escapes imprisonment by the message (Fatalité) it projects. The intensity of Hugo's struggle with the conflicting values reflected in his explicit commentaries on the stone-and-mortar referent in books 3 and 5 can be better assessed if we look at the realization of that structure as written narrative and at the Notre-Dame de Paris as it appears thematized within the text.

As I pointed out above, attention to the cathedral as such is deferred for a long while, and, when reference is made, it is in another code—in the historical present, outside of the context of the story. Everything in the first two books suggests the fragmentation, dislocation, indeed destruction, of any form of unifying composition. The main characters are introduced in a series of dramatic and profane spectacles which occur outside the church doors, outside the celestial city. The story begins with a series of negatives, first situating the events in a specific historical moment—the sixth of January, 1482—and then questioning the reliability of any such moment: "Ce n'est cependant pas un jour dont l'histoire ait gardé souvenir que le 6 janvier 1482." We enter the narrative at a carnivalesque time, an anti-day celebrating two festivities each of whose symbolic significance places the other into question: *La Fête des fous* and *Le Jour des rois.* A turbulent Parisian populace has gathered in the streets and is distracted by three events which interrupt each other and stand in contradiction to each other. The first event, honoring *Le Jour des rois,* is the presentation of a mystery play in the great room of the Palais de Justice. The play is late in getting started in this profane theater: it features Jupiter and Venus and is presented to a crowd which pays no attention except to deride it. In fact, the play never gets beyond the prologue because it is interrupted by cries of "Noël," "Noël": the king of fools has been elected. The prize is awarded to the person who can make the ugliest grimace, and Quasimodo is the winner. But, as Hugo succinctly puts it, for this romantic figure of the grotesque, "La grimace était son visage." This is not the vitalistic, topsy-turvy world of the Renaissance, but, to use Bakhtin's formulation, a world of permanent dislocation. Quasimodo's body assures anything but his earth-consciousness. He is condemned to chastity and solitude, cut off even from the populace—Hugo's "new man," whom at times he seems to incarnate. It is not the other side of the healthy body—a buttocks or a fertile belly—which is presented for the crowd's delight, but an outrageously botched head complete with a wart over one eye, wild red hair, broken teeth, and a gaping mouth; and this misleadingly demonic appearance is framed in the broken opening of the rose window of the Palace chapel. Shards of the spiritual world suggested by the novel's title thus constitute the décor of the opening scene. Quasimodo, this "à peu près" who will be our hero, is even described in terms which suggest a building fallen into ruins and put back together again badly, with no notion on the part of the maker as to what the basic design should be. Like the cathedral described at the center of book 3, the bell-ringer who exists as an incrustation within its walls is a grotesque structure, one part having been grafted onto another with no organic rapport. As the crowd shouts "Noël" and Pierre Gringoire, the disappointed author of the ridiculous mystery play, realizes that he will not be able to bring the Holy Virgin on stage because his musicians have left to lead Quasimodo's triumphal parade through the streets of Paris, the third diversion occurs—"La Esmeralda" is dancing in another quarter. We later discover that this is the gypsy dancer of whom the Faustian priest of Notre-Dame will blasphemously say: "Une créature si belle que Dieu l'eût préférée à la Vierge, et l'eût choisie pour sa mère, et eût voulu naître d'elle si elle eût existé quand il se fit homme," of whom the narrator will say: "elle était d'une beauté si rare qu'au moment où elle parut à l'entrée de l'appartement il sembla qu'elle y répandait une sorte de lumière qui lui était propre." There are numerous other references throughout the novel which suggest that Esmeralda represents a secularized figure for the Virgin, yet another Notre-Dame de Paris, a street version, so to speak. It is, for example, she who intercedes on behalf of Quasimodo by bringing him water when he is pilloried, an act which transforms the figure of bodily deformity into a loving, spiritual being. But when we first meet Esmeralda she is surrounded by hellish, rather than heavenly, attributes. She is dancing across the river from Notre-Dame in the Place de Grève, theater for the pillory and the gibbet; it is dusk rather than dawn (the time associated with the Virgin in Christian iconography); Esmeralda and the faces of the spectators are bathed in scarlet light from the reflection of the fires burning at the approach of night; and the male characters watching her are caught in a kind of thralldom which suggests lust rather than worship. Indeed, every time she dances her twirling circular dance throughout the novel, it is for an audience of hidden voyeurs—Frollo and Quasimodo from the battlements of Notre-Dame, Phœbus from the balcony of his fiancée, Gringoire in the midst of the crowd below; all are sexually aroused, all diverted by her from their various pursuits. She becomes an idolatrous obsession rather than a source of faith and peace. Indeed, Quasimodo stops ringing the bells of the cathedral, stops making the Church speak to the city, after he discovers Esmeralda.

Thus we enter a form of writing which is characterized, as far as narrative technique, theme and characterization are concerned, by fragmentation, discontinuity and disfiguration, the very signs of destruction which the narrator sees scarring the beauty of the original Notre-Dame de Paris in book 3. On the other hand, these same characteristics lend the introductory pages their extraordinary energy; they give us the impression that anything may happen as we watch the popular version of traditional romance disappear—the beautiful virgin, pursued by the monster and saved by the handsome knight—and we revel in the piling up of the new tower of Babel rising out of the ruins of the beautiful old cathedral.

It seems that one must be prepared to give it all up, in fact, judging from the violence and savagery with which Hugo destroys our hopes for a redemptive reading. The cathedral as poeticized symbolic space is presented as a gaping, tomb-like void, empty of the faithful, inhabited only by a priest turned alchemist and a monstrously deformed bell-ringer who does not so much dwell in the cathedral as he belongs to it. Every relationship in which we invest our hope for some lasting value is destroyed. Esmeralda is blindly in love with a false god, Phœbus, a hopelessly vapid fop—she never sees beyond his material form. After years of self-martyrdom, Esmeralda's mother, La Sachette, recovers her lost child, only to be rewarded by having her hanged in the Place de Grève in a blaze of ironic light—at dawn, the time of the Holy Virgin, who *never* intervenes for anyone's prayers. All the major characters die a horrible death, except the failed poet Gringoire, who abandons Esmeralda to Frollo and runs away with her goat into the darkness of the city to live out his life writing bad plays for a corrupt officialdom. Deafness or voyeurism relegate every subject to a state of irremediable solitude, and the crowd, that hope for democracy and freedom, turns vicious in the end, forgets its goal to save Esmeralda from the hangman's noose and batters in the great storied portals of the cathedral in which she has sought asylum in order to pillage the wealth of jewels and gold which it holds.

The full measure of the loss of sacred value has been encoded into the text by the way its various narrative strands negate so dramatically the stories of mercy and salvation depicted on the great doors of the stone building that are destroyed by the crowd. Although the narrator mentions the portals more often than any other structural part of the cathedral—nearly every critical event takes place in front of them, and Frollo is constantly examining them in an effort to decipher their meaning—he never tells us precisely what they represent. To know, the reader must look at the restored cathedral still standing today. The narrator does not say, for example, that four of the six doors which open the way to the celestial city inside hold images from the life of the Virgin: her birth with Saint Anne, her marriage, her death, resurrection and crowning by her Son in heaven. We meet only La Sachette, the prostitute mother of Esmeralda, who so idolatrized her baby that one day she lost her to the gypsies while idly vaunting her beauty to a neighbor. Instead of the Virgin's marriage, death and resurrection, we watch the senseless martyrdom of Esmeralda, hanged on a gibbet, twisting like a snake on the rope before being thrown into the ossuary, where Quasimodo joins her as a grotesque bridegroom. The narrator does not say that on the Porte Rouge one can see Saint Louis being crowned by an angel and blessed by Christ. We read only of the cruel Louis XI holding court in the Bastille, from which he betrays his Church by ordering that the victim to whom she has granted asylum be taken prisoner and hanged. And, finally, he does not say that on the Porte du Cloître—the door Frollo always enters to reach his alchemist's tower—is depicted the miracle of Théophile, the learned cleric who sold his soul to the Devil for the gift of philosophical knowledge, but who is forgiven and redeemed through the intercession of the Virgin, shown standing with him, holding the sword which slays Satan. We hear Frollo vainly beg for Esmeralda's mercy, and we follow his transformation from that of a suffering, visionary imagination into the symbol of Satan himself as he falls from the towers of Notre-Dame, pushed by the orphaned monster to whom he had once granted asylum.

In the violence of its satire and the savagery of its ironies, this early novel seems to represent for Hugo a kind of terrible expurgation of his lingering nostalgia for the old order so eloquently described as an aging and majestic queen in book 3, an expurgation which nevertheless generates a radically new style and vision. The old design had to be let go in order to allow the forces of freedom and democracy represented by the people to flood beyond the containing walls of the medieval city. For the novelist in October of 1830 that force has a brutal, even demonic nature, symbolized by the underworld characters of the Cour des Miracles. It is the crowd which gathers eagerly to witness the martyrdom of her own orphaned children, Esmeralda and Quasimodo, when they are tormented or brought to death by the crowd's own oppressors. But it is also the crowd whose hilarity unmasks the dessicated figures of officialdom present at all of these gatherings, and somehow its cruelty is more acceptable than the death-grip of the old order represented so grimly in the Bastille by the torture instruments rationally created to maintain its institutionalized control.

One character, Jacques Coppenole, who appears at the beginning and at the end of the novel, seems to represent all of the most positive attributes of what that people may become. He arrives for the mystery play with the delegation from Holland and immediately wins the crowd's sympathy by refusing to be announced under any fancy title, but simply as "chaussetier." He is a member of the "peuple," the narrator tells us, the new class of bourgeois which is rising out of the lower stratum and penetrating the ruling class:

> Coppenole était du peuple, et . . . ce public qui l'entourait était du peuple. Aussi la communication entre eux et lui avait été prompte, électrique, et pour ainsi dire de plain pied. L'altière algarade du chaussetier flamand, en humiliant les gens de cour, avait remué dans toutes les âmes plébéiennes je ne sais quel sentiment de dignité encore vague et indistinct au quinzième siècle.

He is a long-time friend of the King of the Truands, disguised here as a beggar covered with rags, and he chooses to sit with the beggar rather than with the officialdom to which he has gained access. At the sight of this defiant self-confidence a revolutionary ripple of delight seems to run through the crowd. It is he who interrupts the prologue to the mystery play, denouncing the vapidity of its inflated rhetoric, and proposes to the crowd a different sort of spectacle, the election of the *Pape des fous,* with all of its subversive implications. Jacques Coppenole appears in one other important scene in this long novel, at the end, the scene in the Bastille, where Louis XI decides to use the rage of the populace to achieve his own nefarious ends. The Flemish delegation is there as the sounds of revolt begin to rise from the streets. It is the same crowd which, like the revolutionary vandals of 1787 and 1789, will batter in the portals of Notre-Dame, and Jacques Coppenole calmly announces, in the presence of the King, his pleasure in hearing such sounds. The King allows him to speak, fascinated by his honesty and his unruffled self-assurance, but not before he has insisted that the revolt is not serious and that he can stop it with a mere furrow of his brow. Coppenole answers, prophetically for postrevolutionary France: "Cela se peut, sire. En ce cas, c'est que l'heure du peuple n'est pas encore venue. . . . Quand le beffroi bourdonnera, quand les canons gronderont, quand le donjon croulera à grand bruit, quand bourgeois et soldats hurleront et s'entre-tueront, c'est l'heure qui sonnera." Coppenole disappears from the novel, the truands take over, and the dreadful dénouement where both Esmeralda and Quasimodo die moves irremediably forward. But an optimistic note has nevertheless been sounded, and if we leave the novel with a dreadful sense of loss, we leave it marveling at the inventiveness and energy through which this loss has occurred. It was precisely that inventiveness which provided history with the final ironic twist to the story of Notre-Dame. When Hugo returned from political exile in time for the disaster of the Commune, he found his scarred source of revolutionary inspiration expertly restored to her original untroubled majesty, as if, during the course of seven centuries, nothing had ever happened.

VICTOR BROMBERT

Les Misérables: *Salvation from Below*

The Waterloo episode in *Les Misérables*—consisting of nineteen colorful chapters—may well be the most provocative digression in all of Hugo's fiction. Tangential as it may seem, no digression could be more central. There are other long digressions in *Les Misérables*, monumental assertions of the poet-novelist's ego and of his prerogatives of total vision. But the lengthy discussion of convents deliberately entitled "Parenthèse" and the description of the Parisian sewer system (to take but two examples) are at least bound up with the adventures of the ex-convict Jean Valjean, as he moves from dereliction to salvation. No such claim could be made for the Waterloo episode. Jean Valjean never even comes close to the battlefield. Yet there is every reason to approach this novel from the perspective of this military disaster.

For Waterloo also meant victory. In the late spring of 1861, on the forty-sixth anniversary of the battle, Hugo decided to visit the battlefield. He settled in a small hotel in the village of Mont-Saint-Jean, whence he could glimpse the commemorative statue of the lion. This is the site he chose to finish the novel he had begun some sixteen years earlier, before the events of 1851 drove him into prolonged exile. The importance of the site is tersely inscribed at the end of the manuscript, immediately following the description of Valjean's nameless grave: "Fin/Mont-Saint-Jean 30 juin 1861 à 8 h. ½ du matin." The completion of the book under the sign of Waterloo ("le dénouement est écrit, le drame est clos") harks back, however, to the open-

From *Victor Hugo and the Visionary Novel.* © 1984 by the President and Fellows of Harvard College. Harvard University Press, 1984.

ing pages of the novel. And this not only because at some stages of writing
he had considered placing the Waterloo episode at the very beginning (thus
introducing the epic note at the outset), but because the text as we now have
it opens with an immediate reference to the fateful year 1815. This temporal
signal is repeated at the beginning of book 2, which describes Valjean's
arrival in Digne: "In the first days of October, 1815." The text thus insis-
tently situates itself historically, in the post-Waterloo context of the Restoration.

But Waterloo was also a literary challenge, as indicated by Hugo's
choice of that battleground to complete his novel. To Auguste Vacquerie, he
wrote on that momentous June 30, 1861: "It's on the plain of Waterloo and
in the month of Waterloo that I have fought my battle. I hope not to have
lost it." As for the episode itself, Hugo referred to it in terms that underline
its structural and thematic importance. From Mont-Saint-Jean where he had
just written the word *Fin,* he explained to his son Charles: "The structure is
up; here and there, some part, some architrave has to be sculpted, and the
porch of Waterloo remains to be built." The word *architrave,* connoting a
temple-like construction, suggests monumentality and ample vision. But the
key image is the "porche de Waterloo," leaving little doubt that, even
though he had written it after all the rest and had placed it at the heart of
his text, Hugo considered the Waterloo episode as the spiritual gateway to
his novel.

The section on Waterloo appears well after some three hundred pages
of dense text, and seems doubly incongruous since it opens part 2, which
carries the diminutive title "Cosette." Part 1 (the novel is made up of five
massive parts) has described the saintly bishop of Digne, Monsignor Myriel
(or Bienvenu, as he has come to be known); the dramatic arrival of the
ex-convict Valjean in his house, Valjean's theft of some silver, and his
redemptive confrontation with the bishop; a further crime committed by
Valjean against a child; his subsequent rehabilitation, under the name of
Monsieur Madeleine, in the town of Montreuil-sur-Mer, of which he becomes benefactor and mayor; and his heroic surrender to justice to save a
vagrant, falsely accused of his own former identity and crimes. It is at this
point, as Valjean again disappears into the anonymous world of prison, that
Hugo chose to locate his Waterloo digression, which represents an eight-
year leap back in time.

The tie-in with the story line is almost fortuitous, as though to suggest
some mysterious convergence of pure chance and necessity. Hugo provides
well over fifty pages of elaborate descriptions of battlefield and battle and
indulges in meditations on history, before he launches the reader, *in extremis,*

after the battle has been fought and lost, into a dreamlike sequence: the moonlit, war-torn landscape is visited by an ominous, prowling figure come to rob the dying and the dead, who lie in heaps—some of them buried alive—in the ravine where the French cavalry met its doom. The prowler is the infamous Thénardier, who in the process of stealing the watch, the silver cross, and the purse of the heroic Colonel Pontmercy, unintentionally saves his life. And this Colonel Pontmercy, we later learn, is the father of Marius, the young hero of the novel.

Some preliminary remarks are in order. Since Thénardier, it turns out, is the very individual to whose cruel guardianship young Cosette has been entrusted, the Waterloo episode, blending chance and necessity, also prefigures symbolically all manner of unpredictable conjunctions. At the literal level, the encounter of father and stepfather on the battlefield prepares for the conjunction in love of Cosette and Marius, for which Hugo provides the telling subtitle "La Conjonction de deux étoiles." At the level of metaphor, the confrontation of heroism and villainy signals the permanent interaction of good and evil, an ambiguous system of inversion and conversion. Private obsessions do not suffice to account for Hugo's insistence on the horror of whole battalions buried alive in the ravine. The emergence of Colonel Pontmercy from among the dead, thanks to an act of villainy which, against the perpetrator's will, turns out to be an act of mercy (the pun of the Colonel's name is part of the ambiguity), participates in a larger saga of rebirth. And in this saga, Waterloo itself—a mass slaughter and a calamitous defeat—retrospectively appears as an illumination, or at least as what Hugo, with reference to Marius's political education, calls an "élargissement de l'horizon."

FROM MONTENOTTE TO WATERLOO

On the arm of Valjean's fellow convict, Cochepaille, is the tattoo *1815*. This inscription in the flesh confirms the structural and symbolic importance of the date. Not only does it mark a problematic turning point in history (is it the beginning of a new world or a relapse into the old order?), but the emperor's dramatic return from Elba and his subsequent defeat correspond ironically to Valjean's emergence to social existence from out of his spiritual prison-death. They also correspond, in time, to the confrontation between good and evil in the bishop's house—to the beginning of Valjean's spiritual rebirth.

Dates, always important in Hugo's system, signal far more, however, than coincidence or contrast. The juxtaposition of Napoleon's fall and of

Valjean's spiritual ascent takes on further significance when set against the precise duration of Valjean's imprisonment: 1796 to 1815. This nineteen-year hiatus in Valjean's life spans precisely the years of Napoleon's glory, between the brilliant military campaign in Italy and the Hundred Days. A concrete detail reinforces the parallel: the fastening of Valjean's chain in the prison of Bicêtre, before the departure of the chain gang, occurs on the very day (April 22, 1796) that Bonaparte's victory at Montenotte is proclaimed in Paris. The young general's triumph is thus from the outset ironically contaminated. The link between ignominy and glory suggests the bitterness of a victory that was to signify a reign of tyranny and violence. The choice of Montenotte (Hugo had other Italian victories at his disposal: Millesimo, Lodi, Castiglione, Arcola, Rivoli) allows Hugo to play out etymologically the dialectics of victory and defeat, for Montenotte contains both the suggestion of ascension (*monte*) and of the darkness of night (*notte*). What lurks behind these complex articulations of victory and defeat is not only a discrediting of traditional heroic modes but an affirmation of a nonmilitary kind of heroism.

A similar dialectic affects another crucial date, 1832. For the glorious hours of the revolutionary barricades, even though Hugo invokes Homer, Troy, and the Titans, are marred by the awareness that what is occurring is civil strife and police repression. The words "héroïsme monstre" sum up the last stages of the carnage. Once again—this time quite literally—an exalting downward movement transcends and negates the sordid heroics of war. The deeper heroism of Valjean, whose apolitical role on the barricades is that of a courageous conscientious objector, manifests itself as he rescues the unconscious Marius by lowering him through a manhole, and becomes a saviour-hero in a perilous descent into the labyrinthine sewers. The Fall-Ascent is tersely announced by the subtitle, referring to salvation in the mud: *"La Boue, mais l'âme."*

THE PASSERBY

By disclaimer, preterition, and open statement Hugo multiplies the digressive signals in the Waterloo episode. He begins by referring to himself as a visiting tourist-narrator, walking across the terrain, forty-six years after the battle. This transient figure, this *passant*, takes delight in the bucolic landscape. Self-indulgently, he connects Hougomont—site of one of the fiercest battles—to a putative ancestor, the name *Hougomont* supposedly deriving from *Hugomons*, the name of a manor built by one Hugo, Sire of Somerel. This leisurely, digressive opening is part of a broader discursiveness leading to the appearance of a local peasant, who for three francs offers to explain "la chose de Waterloo"—and who is in turn supplanted by the historian-narrator. This ambling pace is in deliberate contrast to the violence of the battle. But passerby and bucolic landscape are not merely delaying tactics or ironic commentaries on the futility of the war; they function metaphorically, linking the battle to the larger context of the book.

First, a general comment on the word *passant* by which Hugo, as intruding narrator, refers to himself in the opening section of the Waterloo episode. The same substantive is curiously also used to describe an obscure general, Cambronne, who became famous for having defied the enemy, in a hopeless last stand, with the scatological exclamation *Merde!* The unknown officer Cambronne is a "passant de la dernière heure." More significantly still, the returning convict Jean Valjean, when he first arrives in Digne, is also referred to as an anonymous *passant.* But anonymity, in the novel's context, is not a derogatory notion. One of the most moving figures on the revolutionary barricades is a nameless workman ("un passant héros, ce grand anonyme") who speaks up in favor of total sacrifice.

"Un Passant" is a title Hugo considered for part 1 of the novel. Did he give up the idea when he realized that this figure would cast its shadow over the entire work? The recurrent trope of the passerby is in fact wedded to the larger themes of passage, transition, effacement, and becoming. Toward the end of the novel, at the time of the ultimate sacrifice, Valjean understands that as Cosette's adoptive father, he has been a *passant* in her life and must now disappear ("Jean Valjean était un passant . . . Eh bien, il passait"). If, as Marius puts it, Valjean has been a saviour "en passant," it is because as an outsider he is already partially beyond this world. "Je suis dehors" is echoed a few pages later by "je suis hors de la vie." All of *Les Misérables* describes a process of transition in which every threshold is marked by obliteration. Valjean's tombstone, in accordance with his wishes, carries no name. Even the four anonymous lines written on the stone, concluding with an image of departure ("le jour s'en va"), have gradually become illegible— "effaced." And effacement, for Hugo, is always part of a process of transformation.

There is a thematic link between the transient wayfarer and the bucolic Waterloo landscape forty-six years after the battle, for this landscape presents itself in a state of wavelike mobility. The plain is a vast undulating sweep of ground ("vaste terrain ondulant"). A clump of trees "disappears" gracefully ("s'en va avec grâce"). Water images correspond to this undulating landscape. In one of his notebooks, Hugo refers to the "immobile waves" of the terrain. The text of the Waterloo episode mentions in close proximity the flowing of water and the disappearing clump of trees, as well as the "enormous waves" made by the rolling countryside. This liquid imagery is further exploited, as early as the very next paragraph, by a reference to a "flotilla of ducks" in a nearby pool.

Water and liquefaction are, of course, appropriate in the historical context of Waterloo. The unseasonal rain of the night of June 17–18 was in large part responsible for Napoleon's defeat. The French artillery, bogged down in the mire, could not be brought into decisive action early enough. The treacherous landscape, neither solid nor liquid, helped disintegrate the world's most powerful army. When the sun finally appeared, it was a setting sun, whose sinister glow was in contrast to the rising sun of Austerlitz, ten years earlier. The reign of water must further be understood as a signal of catastrophe if one recalls that the chapter describing Valjean's spiritual shipwreck in prison is entitled "L'Onde et l'ombre" ("The Waters and the Shadow").

The metaphorical alliance of water and defeat is sustained throughout the episode. The rout is called a "ruissellement." The last remnants of the Old Guard stand like rocks in "running water." The disbanding army is like a "thaw." Flight and panic liquidate the day. Beyond these images of un-doing, a larger principle is at work. Disintegration is part of the dynamic process of transformation. Not only is the landscape physically and histor-ically transfigured (Wellington, returning to the site, does not recognize his battlefield), but the battle itself, in its chaos and mobility, becomes the enactment of the *truth* of change. The fixity of a mathematical plan immo-bilizes movement. "Geometry is deceptive," explains Hugo—and he calls for a painter who would have "chaos in his brushes." The ceaselessly ero-sive and destructive movement of the sea becomes the model of the battle: the shock of army meeting army creates an "incalculable ebb," the battle-front waves and undulates, regiments form "capes" and "gulfs" and "reefs" as they advance and withdraw. Or rather, it is the battle that becomes a metaphor for the endless toiling of the sea. The mobility of war and the mobility of landscape come to be metaphors for a deconstructive reality of which the sea is Hugo's favorite symbol. One is reminded of the transfor-mational vision, in "La Pente de la rêverie," of huge continents perpetually "devoured" by the oceans.

Disintegration in its diverse manifestations (flowing, melting, thawing, vanishing) is the chief image for the catastrophe of Waterloo. Yet disinte-gration, for Hugo, is always wedded to reconstruction. The wild grandeur of the abandoned garden on the rue Plumet—the happy enclosure of Cosette and Marius's secret love—provides "unfathomable ecstasies" to the contemplative mind, by revealing "decompositions of forces resulting in unity." These laws of constructive decomposition are made manifest throughout Hugo's work, whether in the metaphorical virtuosity of *Les Travailleurs de la mer,* where infinitely changing sea architectures illustrate the principle of constructive effacement, or more explicitly in "Philosophie. Commencement d'un livre," which was planned as a general preface to his works. "Les désagrégations sont des germinations"—this pithy affirmation sums up a development on endings that are beginnings, on beginnings that relate to completions, on death which is birth.

This alchemy of decay and vitality is also the mystery of Waterloo. The wayfarer at Hougomont conjures up visions of petrified horror made visible. The narrator-*passant* on the battleground, like Virgil on the plain of Philippi, experiences the hallucination of catastrophe: lines of infantry undulate; trees quiver; whirlwinds of specters exterminate one another. Yet June 18, 1815, also marks a fresh start. And like all pivotal dates it is Janus-faced: it looks ahead, but also glances back to the past. This double perspective on the military disaster is further complicated by the deliberate epic framework of the episode.

THE END OF THE SWORD-WIELDERS

The battle of Waterloo was an ideal pretext for a bravura piece. Ten years earlier, Hugo had already met the challenge with the poetic tour de force "L'Expiation." In *Les Misérables,* the picturesque elements became ampler, as Hugo indulged in massive evocations of armies of the past and of their paraphernalia. Busbies, floating sabretaches, crossbelts, and hussar dolmans—all in motion—occupy the field of vision. The sheer pictorial exuberance is confirmed by the reference to Salvator Rosa, a painter who specialized in battle scenes.

The literary register is that of the epic tradition. Both sides are glorified, for these are neither ordinary Frenchmen nor ordinary Scotsmen. "These Scotsmen died thinking of Ben Lothian, as did the Greeks recalling Argos." In this modern reenactment of the *Iliad,* every soldier has something of the heroic stature of his general. Every act of valor, every individual death, is a collective event. The death throes of the French army transcend the historical moment. In a typical figure of speech, the agony of the last units is made to signify the death of the great Napoleonic victories: Ulm, Wagram, Jena, Friedland.

The figural pattern remains deliberately epic. So does the process of amplification. The hideousness of the wounds, we are told, has probably "never been seen anywhere else." The military formations are not battalions but "craters"; the cuirassiers are no longer cavalrymen but a "tempest"; each unit is a "volcano"; lava contends with lightning. The mythical nature of such amplifications is made still more explicit by reference to legendary archetypes. The cavalry squadrons are transmuted into "giant men" on "colossal horses." The metamorphosis is completed when horses and men become centaurs. Hugo in fact provides an epic reading of his own text: "These narrations seem to belong to another age. Something like this vision appeared, no doubt, in the ancient Orphic epics which told of centaurs, the old hippanthropes, those Titans with human heads and chests like horses, whose gallop scaled Olympus."

These epic references and devices are not a self-indulgent literary game. They function in a complex manner, serving ambiguously both to magnify and to discredit the historical moment. "The epic solemnifies history," Hugo had written in the famous preface to his play *Cromwell*—making clear, however, that modern times required a dramatic rather than an epic perspective. But the historical line of demarcation is never clearly drawn. Much like his young hero Marius, Hugo had been entranced by Napoleon's battle proclamations, the bulletins of the Grand Army, "those Homeric strophes written on the battlefield." It was through the recorded exploits of the preceding generation that he discovered the link with a privileged past when Action and the Word were seemingly not at odds.

The immediate though troubling link—for Hugo, as well as for Marius—is the father. General Léopold Hugo ("Mon père, ce héros au sourire si doux" of *La Légende des siècles*) is the intercessor between the royalist adolescent and the revolutionary and postrevolutionary glory he came to associate with the figure of Napoleon and with filial piety. In the ode "A mon père" ("Je rêve quelquefois que je saisis ton glaive, / O mon père!"), the twenty-year-old anti-Bonapartist but patriotic poet had already celebrated the imperial army. Soon this celebration was to extend to the emperor himself, and eventually to the political ferment of the revolution which the emperor helped spread across Europe.

But filial piety is also the sign of a feared inadequacy. The "romantic" generation, having reached the age of manhood once all had been played out on the battlefield of Waterloo, exhibited recognizable symptoms of frustration and impotence. Marius, Hugo's contemporary, knows that he can never equal his father's military prowess. The pen, proposed as a glorious rival, was in fact recognized as a not altogether adequate substitute for the sword—at least in the early years. ("Quoi! toujours une lyre et jamais une épée!" the young Hugo wrote in the same ode to his father.) Hugo eventually translated the anxiety of weakness into a vindication of nonbelligerent virtues. But it is noteworthy that his work, even though increasingly committed to a philosophy of progress, consistently suggests generational regression, if not decadence. The son rarely achieves the stature of the father. ◄

The chronologically regressive shift from Napoleon to revolution is at the heart of this nostalgia for epic grandeur. In his early review of Walter Scott's *Quentin Durward*, Hugo, while outlining a theory of the modern novel, betrayed anxiety in the face of a never-to-be-equaled greatness. In an obvious allusion to the French Revolution, and in contradiction to his overtly antirevolutionary fervor, the young poet-critic extolled "the generation that has just written with its blood and its tears the most extraordinary page of all the pages in history." As for Napoleon, whose ties with the Revolution are constantly evoked, Hugo's reception speech at the Académie Française, in 1841, explicitly stated that Napoleon in his imperial excessiveness had the secret of "transforming history into an epic."

By the time Hugo wrote *Les Misérables*, Napoleon had become for him the embodiment of epic action. He had been a despot, yes; but the masses had worshipped him. For them he was *l'homme-peuple,* as Jesus was *l'homme-Dieu.* Balzac's *Le Médecin de campagne* illustrates, in another mode, how deeply rooted the myths of Napoleon's invincibility and immortality were in the popular mind. Hugo himself sees Napoleon as the prodigious architect of a collapse, as a dark genius committed to violence, destruction, and ultimate catastrophe. The terminology is revealing. Napoleon is a fearsome athlete ("sombre athlète du pugilat de la guerre"), a fateful destroyer of men ("grand bûcheron de l'Europe"), an "archangel" of war. But this archangel, in whom good and evil coexist in almost superhuman doses, is above all a genius. He appears—the pun is only half-involuntary—as the "Michelangelo" of war. The comparison is typical of the romantic tendency to juxtapose and blend prophetic, artistic, and political figures. Thus Hugo evokes the "mighty power" by which one becomes Moses, Aeschylus, Dante, Michelangelo, or Napoleon.

Shaper and conqueror of Europe, Napoleon is the man of destiny. Hugo sees him in symbiotic complicity with events, treating destiny as his equal. Mythical images work their way to the foreground. Napoleon is the "titanic coachman" of destiny. Yet he is also destiny's victim (a "condamné du destin"), or, more precisely, he is part of a larger design that the author glimpses when he conceives of Napoleon as an "involuntary revolutionary" and elaborates the metaphor of a defeated Robespierre on horseback, whose defeat prepares the future.

THE EPIC COUNTERPOINT

The year 1815 thus marks for Hugo the point of intersection between the heroic enterprise and a superior design. It also marks the end of the military epic and the beginning of a new spiritual adventure. The symbolic parallelism and contrast between Napoleon's and Valjean's itineraries cannot be overlooked: the convict returns from the Toulon galleys, in October 1815, by moving north through Digne and Grenoble. It is the same road that Napoleon had taken on his short-lived return to power from the island of Elba seven months earlier. Just as the fall of Valjean in 1796 coincided with the rise of Bonaparte, so now the fall of the emperor corresponds to the reemergence of the convict. The contrapuntal motif has distant roots. Years earlier, Hugo the tourist, after visiting the *bagne* of Toulon, meditated at length along the *route Napoléon,* and associated the figure of Jean Tréjean (the original name of Valjean) with the destiny of the emperor. The symbolic contrast is further stressed in the text. Valjean shakes his fist at the church in Digne, in the same square where Napoleon's new proclamations had been printed. The convict-*passant* enters the city by the same street the emperor had come through: "la même rue qui sept mois auparavant avait vu passer l'empereur Napoléon."

Marching, passing, and progressing are all related to the image of an itinerary, and quite specifically to the painful but redemptive road of suffering, the *via dolorosa*. The nightmarish landscape in which Valjean experiences his total abandon—the low hill resembling a shaved head, the dark sky, the sinister light, the one deformed tree—unmistakably brings to mind Golgotha and the Passion of Christ. The agonizing crossing of the sewer, much later in the novel, is further proof of Hugo's obsession with Christ's Calvary. The Valjean-Christ parallel is clearly indicated in the chapter entitled "Une Tempête sous un crâne," which describes Valjean's great moral crisis culminating in the decision to turn himself in to save the falsely accused tramp. Valjean yields to the same "mysterious power" that some two thousand years earlier had impelled another condemned man to "march on." The chapter concludes with a renewed reference to the Man of Sorrows in whom were summed up all the sufferings of humanity, and who also at first had thrust aside with his hand the terrible cup brimming over with darkness.

The allusion to Christ is related to a deeper literary intention. The images of inner struggle and spiritual itinerary are part of a deliberate program to displace the traditional hero in favor of a new conception of the epic. As a preamble to the key chapter "A Tempest in a Brain," Hugo writes: "To create the poem of human conscience, were it only in reference to one human being, were it only in connection with the lowliest of men, would be to blend all epics into one superior and definitive epic." The prism in this moral perspective is, however, not that of analysis but of enlargement and universalization. Hugo retains more than the term *epic;* he conceives the locus of this inner struggle as a mythic battleground. "There, beneath the external silence, battles of giants as in Homer are in progress; skirmishes of dragons and hydras and clouds of phantoms as in Milton; visionary spirals as in Dante." The systematic evocation of the great epic poets further stresses the specific elements of a literary tradition that Hugo wishes at once to emulate and to subvert, as he sets out to explore that "infinity which every man bears within him."

The expression "every man" (*tout homme*) points to an anonymous, collective humanity. The epic dimensions of such a collectivity-were no doubt already on Hugo's mind when, in his early twenties, he published the article on Walter Scott in *La Muse Française* (July 1823) in which he called for epic novels ("grandes épopées") to suit the poetic needs of the modern age. By the time of *Les Misérables,* he had developed the theory of an epic concerned with the great adventure of mankind, in particular with the destiny of the oppressed, redeemable, and ultimately redeeming *peuple,* toward whom his deepest reactions remained, however, characteristically ambiguous. In Hugo's view, all the social and political struggles of the nineteenth century, including mob violence and police repression, occurred within "the great epic field where humanity is struggling."

This collectivization and universalization of the human drama implies that the conscience of a single human being, even the "lowliest," mirrors and reenacts the drama of humanity's "conscience"—and beyond this of the conscience of the world. Hugo repeatedly thinks and writes in terms of an "enlargement of the horizon." Napoleon is impeached by divine judgment, against the backdrop of infinity ("dénoncé dans l'infini"). The cosmic scene is indeed, according to Hugo, the chief subject of his novel. The important digression on monastic life begins with a clear statement of purpose: "This book is a drama whose main character is the Infinite." And in a letter to Frédéric Morin, written a few weeks after the completion of *Les Misérables,* Hugo referred to his novel as an "espèce d'essai sur l'infini."

THE DEATH OF THE HERO

The ambivalent attitudes toward the epic must be read in this ambitious context. Nostalgia for epic virtues is offset by an uncompromising

denunciation of martial horrors. Napoleon is an "archangel of war" because the notion of crime remains attached to his enterprise, and this crime
of violence calls for expiation. Imperial glory no doubt sounded a "Titan's
fanfare" throughout Europe. But the word *fanfare* also makes one think of
fanfaronade: empty boasting. Marius's "epic effusion" is easily deflated by
his politically more mature friends, who convert him to revolutionary ideals.

Demystification of the epic idiom and of conventional epic values was
to be carried out more systematically, by means of parody and association
with archaic violence, in Hugo's last novel, *Quatrevingt-treize.* The undermining process is, however, already at work in *Les Misérables* and is one of
the elements that accounts for the central importance of the Waterloo episode. Popular nostalgia for Napoleonic grandeur was no doubt quite affecting; Hugo himself felt vulnerable to its appeal. But such nostalgia, no
matter how justified by the republican origins of the Empire, was an error;
it implied the glorification of war. And war is carnage. Even the barricade
fighting, though legitimized by revolutionary fervor and explicitly compared
to the exploits at Troy, was ultimately nothing more than a "grand slaughter" ("tuerie grandiose"). There is more than a measure of irony in the
authorial remark that "the epic alone has a right to fill twelve thousand lines
with one battle."

The epic length and the epic tone of the Waterloo section thus find their
deeper ironic justification. The military defeat signals not only the end of
Napoleon and a turning point in history but a major shift in the moral and
intellectual perspective. A new page of the larger text has been set before the
collective consciousness: "Les sabreurs ont fini, c'est le tour des penseurs"
("The sword-wielders have had their day, the time of the thinkers has
come"). And the end of the *sabreurs,* the discrediting of the sword, also
means the death of the traditional hero. There still is room for physical
courage, of course, provided it serves a humane cause. In contrast to glorified acts of warfare and to the "stupid slaughter of the battlefield," Hugo
sets up the unsung bravery of the great servants and visionaries of humanity.

Hugo's own most sustained commentary on the demise of the hero is to
be found in *William Shakespeare* (1864), a wide-ranging discussion of the
nature and destiny of genius. Shakespeare appears in this key text as the
symbol of the genuine conquerors: the thinkers and the poets. The pen is
destined to outlive and vanquish the sword. For Hugo, this is a transcendental reality, as well as a matter of historical evolution. The ascent of the
seer means the downfall of the power-hungry, the annihilation of *hommes
de force.* But this hoped-for twilight of the violent conquerors and this

liberation from hero-worship ("le prophète anéantissant le héros") have their own sad grandeur. Irreverent rejoicing would be out of order; the hero deserves worthy funerals: "Let us not insult that which was great. Jeers would be unseemly at the hero's burial."

The end is thus also a beginning. Napoleon misjudged the vast dawn of ideas which, according to Hugo, characterized the nineteenth century. Napoleon's unredeemable error, in a sense, was not military or political. By adopting the derisive term *idéologue* to discredit philosophers, he became symbolically guilty of the most fatal imprudence: he mocked the future.

THE BRIDGE

If the end is also a beginning, then the catastrophe of Waterloo serves as a vital transition. This paradox of a constructive defeat draws its strength from the interplay of rupture and continuity; it centers on the themes of paternity and temporal progression. For paternity in *Les Misérables* relates both to an origin that has to be found and to a hiatus that must be spanned. The need for a historical continuity is structurally inscribed in the Waterloo episode. The deceptive artificiality that links the episode to the main plot only draws attention to the question of articulation and juncture. The signals speak for themselves. Thénardier, the criminal prowler, and Pontmercy, the wounded hero he robs and saves at the same time, are bonded. The meeting of the "fathers" foreshadows the meeting of the children, the "conjunction of the stars" Marius and Cosette. The digression ends on an ironic yet deeply meaningful note. The wounded colonel gives his name, *Pontmercy,* the two last syllables of which are recorded as an expression of gratitude for a criminal action that turns into a blessing, while the entire name later provides the link with the son. The generational theme is in fact woven into the fabric of the Waterloo digression by means of a wordplay, as the narrator explains that one of the "generative scenes" ("scènes génératrices") of his story is tied in with the great battle.

Other wordplays, especially of an onomastic nature, suggest the notion of a gap to be bridged. Paternity and the image of spanning are, as it were, built into the name of Pontmercy. If the last two syllables point ironically to gratitude, the first one (*pont,* meaning bridge) unmistakably denotes a crossing over. There is further evidence that the bridge is symbolically related to Marius's father. Pontmercy, after the Restoration, retires to the small town of Vernon, which is known for its "beautiful monumental bridge." The metaphor of the bridge would indeed seem to be at the conceptual origin of this father image. A note in the manuscript indicates that Hugo, in choosing the name for Marius's father, hesitated among the following: Pontchaumont, Pontverdier, Pontbéziers, Pontuitry, Pontverdun, Pontbadon, and Pont-florent.

The implied trajectory is not, however, a simple matter of genetic or historical continuity. In a sense, what is being spanned is precisely Pontmercy himself, as well as the historical moment he represents. For the father figure has been hidden from view, forgotten, dismissed. Marius is first presented to the reader in a section entitled "The Grandfather and the Grandson." The title points to a gap: Where indeed is the father? The answer is that, after the fall of Napoleon, he has quite literally been made to disappear. A family sense of scandal (Pontmercy was not only a professional soldier but a fervent follower of the Usurper) forces the ex-cuirassier to keep himself out of sight and to renounce any role whatsoever in the upbringing of his son. This cancellation of the father-presence symbolically reflects a political desire to erase the entire 1789–1815 period as a criminal and irrelevant interlude.

Once again, Hugo plays on the image of the bridge, as the ancien régime grandfather Gillenormand assumes the role of father-substitute in lieu of the repudiated son-in-law. So long as the grandfather successfully influences the political opinions of his grandson, they both meet "as on a bridge" ("comme sur un pont"). But this bridge is a delusion; it is projected over a void. History cannot be denied with impunity. The Revolution and Napoleon cannot be juggled away. Once Marius awakens to the historical reality, when he discovers his father and what he stood for, the false bridge collapses and the void appears: "Quand ce pont tomba, l'abîme se fit."

There is a pathos in this discovery. Marius reaches Pontmercy's death-bed when it is too late; father and son were not destined to make contact in life. But this frustration only heightens the value of a legacy that transcends death. Marius finds a written message—a terse spiritual testament—which he will devoutly carry on his person. The reactionary grandfather's act of father-usurpation must be understood in the light of this newly affirmed spiritual bond with the Empire, and, beyond it, with the Republic. When Gillenormand discovers the note Marius carries religiously like an amulet, and which refers to Pontmercy's elevation to the barony on the battlefield of Waterloo, this leads to a violent confrontation. To Marius's defiant statement "I am my father's son" Gillenormand categorically replies "*I* am your father" ("Ton père, c'est moi").

The eclipse of the fathers in favor of the grandfathers is a recurrent feature in the work of Hugo. Valjean, who at first appears as a grandfather figure in relation to Cosette, becomes her surrogate father after the death of Fantine. In a sense, Fantine must die so he can assume this role. The accession to paternity, signifying also a new life for Valjean, takes place exactly nine months after the death of Fantine. The narrator's language is strong: fate "wedded" ("fiança") these two uprooted lives (the symbolic Widower and Orphan); their two souls meet in a close embrace ("s'embrassèrent étroitement").

Much could be said about the latent incestuousness of Valjean's feelings for Cosette: guilt about their drawn-out seclusion; his surveillance and possessiveness; the exclusive nature of his affections; his sense of terror at the sight of her growing beauty; the jealousy he experiences when he suspects her of having fallen in love; his hatred for Marius, which can be overcome only by an act of total self-sacrifice; the fetishistic attachment to her clothes; his animal-like protectiveness ("C'était un dogue qui regarde un voleur"). The explicit exoneration from incestuous feelings ("Poor old Jean Valjean certainly did not love Cosette otherwise than as a father") only points up the equivocal nature of his feelings for her. On the same page on which Hugo takes the trouble of clearing him from any possible suspicion, he goes on to say that Jean Valjean was a "strange" father indeed—"a strange father in whom there is something of the grandfather, the son, the brother, and the husband."

The incest motif, as André Brochu has shown, subtly reappears in Gillenormand's relation to his grandson, a relation that seems overdetermined by an affective transfer. Marius is the son of Gillenormand's favorite daughter, now dead. The hostility to the son-in-law, Pontmercy, can in fact be explained in terms of jealousy. The transfer to Marius is, so to speak, made visible: Gillenormand is struck by the resemblance between his daughter's portrait and Marius. The text is even more outspoken: "He had never loved a mistress as he loved Marius."

Intimations of incest have an autobiographical resonance, reminding one of Hugo's sense of loss and guilt after his daughter's death by drowning. But the father-substitution, on which the incest motif appears grafted, also signals a symbolic political crime. Gillenormand, the grandfather, is a typical man of the eighteenth century, shaped by, and faithful to, the mores of the ancien régime. His assumption of paternal authority corresponds to the return to power of the monarchy in 1815. The problematic link with the father is thus not a matter simply of tradition (the tie with the past) but of allegiance to history's forward movement. The bridge leads in both directions. The discovery of the heroic father is bound up with the discovery of history as progress. Pontmercy's example reveals to Marius the historic mission of the Republic and the Empire in forging national and revolutionary ideals.

The father emerges as a mediating figure between past and future. Once properly understood, he becomes a principle of conversion. It is significant, however, that the political revelation, though inscribed in a continuum, does not depend on a filiation in direct line. The conversion process requires an outsider: the father comes to the family as a son-in-law. This principle of a dramatic conversion allowing freedom of choice, rather than of a socially or atavistically determined political consciousness, was to be featured even more sharply in *Quatrevingt-treize*.

The idea of progress, coupled with the account of a personal political evolution, is thus articulated in a complex manner on the bidirectional date 1815. The young man's political education requires first the rehabilitation of the father, just as it requires the rehabilitation of Napoleon. In reading history and studying documents,"the veil that covered Napoleon from Marius's eyes gradually fell away." What is unveiled in the process is an even more important historical reality: the French Revolution. Marius begins to understand its true significance with regard to the anachronistic world of the grandfather. Where he formerly deplored the fall of the monarchy, he now sees the advent of a new order: "What had been the setting was now the rising of the sun."

But this inner revolution, these regressive discoveries and rehabilitations of the father, of Napoleon, of the men of the Revolution, precisely because they reveal the truth of progress require ultimately the effacement of the father figure. This would explain not only the self-sacrificing disappearance of Pontmercy but the even more systematic vanishing process that leads Valjean on his earthly journey to a nameless grave. The image of effacement and self-effacement ("Le jeune homme arrivait, le bonhomme s'effaçait") must be read against the other figuration of mobility and transitoriness—the passerby. Valjean, we have seen, qualifies himself as a *passant* in Cosette's life. He knows he must make room for Marius, and for the future.

Marius's moral and political apprenticeship is thus determined by a double movement, regressive and progressive, that first reads (leads) back to the Revolution via the Empire and the Bonapartist adventure, and then proceeds forward to transcend the paternal example. When his fervent readings into the past reveal to him the vitality of the revolutionary figures (Mirabeau, Saint-Just, Robespierre, Camille Desmoulins, Danton), he at first recoils, blinded by the light. But the movement back in time actually represents a steady advance. His dazzlement is a symptom of spiritual progression. He is an "esprit en marche."

Marius's political evolution is seen by Hugo as typical; it is the "story of many minds of our time." The interest in collective history does not, however, account for the detailed evocation of Marius's childhood. There is little doubt that if Hugo took the trouble to retrace step by step all the phases of Marius's political education, it is because he was moved to recall the political climate in which he grew up and to describe his own gradual detachment from royalist views. The personal note appears clearly in the pious chapter "Requiescant" ("Let Them Rest")—a farewell to the past, as well as an evocation of the ultraroyalist days of his adolescence, which are associated with the mother image. The important autobiographical poem "Ecrit en 1846" at the beginning of book 5 of *Les Contemplations* (entitled "En Marche"), which describes his gradual awakening to history and his understanding of the providential role of the Revolution, significantly begins with the memory of his mother ("Marquis, je m'en souviens, vous veniez chez ma mère") and ends with a reference to his mother now in the grave. This is paralleled in *Les Misérables* by the absence of the father in the adolescent life of Marius, and by the early feelings of gloom and resentment associated with him: "il était sombre à l'endroit de son père."

WATERLOO, GOOD OR BAD?

A historically symbolic father who is first eclipsed, then found, and later transcended; a political apprenticeship that moves backward to the Revolution and then sweeps forward to the ideal of progress; a stress on pivotal dates (1815, the year of Waterloo; 1789, the year of the Revolution; 1830, inaugurating Marius's participation in the historical struggle; and, beyond the narrated events of the novel, 1851, the year of Louis Napoleon's coup d'état, which sent Victor Hugo into exile)—all these crisis signals betray an uneasy view of the linearity of history. For if history is a movement forward—and Hugo was committed to the notion of progress—how then is one to explain discontinuities and tragic relapses such as the Restoration and the Second Empire? Waterloo becomes symbolic of the dilemma.

The essential ambivalence of Waterloo is reflected in the title of the didactic chapter 17: "Faut-il trouver bon Waterloo?" Hugo explains in what sense Waterloo can be considered both bad and good. Objectively speaking, Napoleon's defeat marks an interruption in the forward march of history. It means an oppressive and repressive return of the past. The clock has been set back. The event is a counterrevolutionary victory. The monarchies of Europe have seemingly crushed the rebellious, liberating spirit embodied by France. This, several years after the return of Louis XVIII, remains the commonly accepted opinion: "the era of revolutions was forever closed."

But another perspective was possible, in the light of which Waterloo appears as a major turning point on the mysterious road of progress. His mission accomplished, the seed of new ideas having been disseminated throughout Europe, the tyrant had to go. More profoundly, Napoleon's defeat could be interpreted as a victory in the larger battle of which God is the supreme general. Hugo invokes a cosmic battlefield: "Waterloo is not a battle; it is the change of front of the universe." What is involved is nothing less than global destiny. The privileged vision of the author-seer embraces the grand mission of the nineteenth century in the human adventure. Napoleon's victory at Waterloo was simply not "within the law of the nineteenth century." Waterloo was a providential event because it made room for what Hugo calls the "grand siècle" (a polemical expression, since these two words are usually associated with the reign of Louis XIV) and the dawn of new ideas ("vaste lever d'idées"). The mission of this new century is later preached by Enjolras, the young political idealist, from atop the barricades. It is to be "Promethean" in its liberating drive.

The day of Waterloo, June 18, 1815, defined as a "catastrophe," is thus also a day of destiny; more precisely, it is the "hinge" ("gond") of the nineteenth century. It marks the historical articulation in a providential drama which begins with the French Revolution and which, despite apparent setbacks, is not to be arrested. For the Revolution cannot be defeated. Hugo, speaking of the work of the Revolution and of the devious paths of history, plays on the multiple meanings of the word "fateful." The Revolution is "providentielle et absolument fatale"; it brings ruin and death, but is destined ultimately to transcend the violence of history. The apocalypse of Waterloo foreshadows the end of violence in history, and, better still, of history as violence. Hugo's dream, here as elsewhere, is quite literally an exit from what Enjolras describes, in his utopian sermon on the barricades, as "the forest of events." The ideal of such supreme freedom casts light on the uncommon adjectival turn with which Hugo sums up the bewildering significance of the great defeat: "To us, Waterloo is but the stupefied date of liberty" ("la date stupéfaite de la liberté").

THE VICTORY OF CAMBRONNE

Who, under these circumstances, won the battle? History books, according to Hugo, fail to give the right answer. For the victor is neither Wellington nor Blücher. They were mere beneficiaries of chance, and that chance—quite trivially—took the form of water. Had it not rained during the night of June 17–18, the future of Europe might have been different. Yet this chance is hardly of an ordinary sort. The narrator, referring to the "marvelous cleverness of chance" ("prodigieuse habileté du hasard") hints at the intentionality of an invisible plan. *Hasard* is here the mask of concatenation. The text indeed proposes the oxymoronic "enchaînment de hasards." The peculiar "chain" of chance events, before and during the battle, points therefore not to contingency but to necessity. This is sharply signaled by the even more pointed oxymoron "hasard divin."

The conclusion is self-evident: Waterloo is the victory of God. This is implicit in the relation between the infinitely small (the deceptive sign of the peasant-guide) and the fate of the world. It is made explicit in the affirmation that the part played by men was nothing, that all was stamped with "superhuman necessity." Hugo does not hesitate to cast God in the role of supreme protagonist: "Was it possible that Napoleon should have won that battle? We answer: no. Why? Because of Wellington? Because of Blücher? No. Because of God." Hugo has alluded, a few pages earlier, to the "mysterious frown" that became perceptible in the depths of the heavens. There is even a hint that God might have become jealous of the "excessive weight" of Napoleon: "Il gênait Dieu." Napoleon, guilty of hubris, was unconscionably jovial the morning of the battle. The "supreme smile" is God's alone.

Yet God is not the only victor in this catastrophe. There is also a *human* victor ("l'homme qui a gagné la bataille de Waterloo"): the aforementioned General Cambronne, who, when the ammunition ran out and the last units were summoned to surrender, went down in history by defying the enemy with a resounding *Merde!* Lamartine, deploring the occasional "filth" ("saletés") of Hugo's language in *Les Misérables,* specifically protested against Cambronne's obscenity flung in the face of destiny—"Better to die in silence." But what Lamartine failed to understand is that by challenging the power of guns with the lowliest of words, by refusing to be silent, Cambronne-Hugo affirmed not the prestige of the latrine but the power of the word.

Nor is it a minor detail that Cambronne should also be called a *passant*—the very term Hugo as narrator applies to himself as he tours the old battlefield. Cambronne, the unknown hero, is a "passer-by at the last hour," an insignificant participant in the historic event, who, by dint of a single word defying the thunder of war, attains "Aeschylean grandeur." The infinitely small achieves Titanic status, just as the basest word in the French language ("le dernier des mots") becomes the finest word ("le plus beau mot") ever pronounced. In the face of the nothingness of brute force,

Cambronne finds an "expression" (and Hugo a pun): he expresses "excrement." That which is ex-pressed comes, verbally, from what Mikhail Bakhtin calls the "lower stratum of the grotesque" (*Rabelais and His World*). But this grotesqueness is not the negative pole of an antithesis; it remains altogether positive, even lofty. The coarse expletive is qualified by Hugo as "sublime." The scatological utterance here comes from the soul: "il trouve à l'âme une expression, l'excrément."

The reference to the soul or spirit (*âme*) is not in the least ironic. Cambronne, faced with imminent annihilation or surrender, seeks a word the way one looks for a sword; and the word he finds comes to him, Hugo explains, by inspiration from above ("par visitation du souffle d'en haut"). The divine afflatus lifts him to the heights of epic irreverence.

This epic irreverence conveyed by the most plebeian of utterances further undermines the epic sense of hierarchy and distance. Bakhtin's observations on Rabelaisian laughter and *carnavalesque* profanities apply to Hugo's Cambronne, who has the laugh on his side. Such transformational laughter not only exorcises fear and challenges authority; it contains huge regenerative power. Interestingly enough, there is an allusion to Rabelais in the Cambronne chapter, and it is accompanied precisely by a reference to the carnival, the Mardi Gras. More interesting still is the link, in Hugo's mind, between Cambronne's terse exclamation and the title of the novel, with its sociopolitical connotations. In a note found in his papers, Hugo characterizes the word *merde* as the "misérable des mots," and again as the "misérable du langage."

The symbolic victory of *merde* is of course not simply a linguistic matter. In concrete, literal terms, all battles, Hugo would say, end in mud, excrement, and putrefaction. That is the outcome of all violence. The pattern is structurally repeated later in *Les Misérables*. The heroic butchery at the barricades quite logically leads to a descent into the sewers—an immersion that is clearly regenerative.

Cambronne's personal victory is of course also symbolic. At one level, it is a victory against the English general: by uttering the "last of words" (*le dernier des mots*), Cambronne, by a mere dropping of the particle, has the final word (*le dernier mot*). At another level, his is the victorious laughter of defeat which truculently denounces the mockery of meaningless survival ("cette dérision, la vie"). The transcendental, prophetic nature of such a denunciation of the sin of senseless living is illumined by the extraordinary passage in *William Shakespeare* in which the prophet Ezekiel is glorified as an eater of excrement ("il mange des excréments"). According to Jean Massin, Hugo's Ezekiel is the Cambronne of the prophetic mode.

The less obvious victory, however, is achieved against the commander-in-chief, Napoleon. This is implicit in the confrontation of two types of laughter—a confrontation that recurs throughout Hugo's work: the arrogant laughter from above and the grotesque, buffoonish laughter from below. The grin of the satyr forever challenges the laughter of Olympus. Napoleon, still riding high, also laughs. On the morning of the battle, confident that he can still treat destiny as an equal, that this privileged complicity lends him a manner of immortality, he defiantly displays a jocular mood. The chapter entitled "Napoléon de belle humeur" describes the Emperor in high spirits, full of verve, indulging in *bons mots*. At breakfast, before the battle, he has repeated fits of laughter ("accès de rire"), unaware of the divine frown. This Napoleonic laughter connotes not merely hubris and tragic irony; it is related to Napoleon's worst sin, that of having held thinkers in contempt and thus having denied the future. Laughter, in Hugo's work, is almost always politically significant: the oppressive laughter of tyranny is countered by the liberating laughter of the downtrodden—the slave, the faun, the lackey, the clown, the redeeming victim. The gross, plebeian laughter associated with Cambronne's exclamation corresponds to the dynamic laughter of the oppressed who say *no* in order to reaffirm *yes*. Such laughter is revolutionary in nature.

The harsh comedy of street language and the resilient locution of the marketplace do indeed have a rebellious potential. The word *merde* contains the seed of revolt. Cambronne's vigorous utterance links him, in Hugo's mind, to the rebel figure of Prometheus: the single word thrown into the face of the enemy has a "grandeur eschylienne." But Prometheus translated into modern terms means revolution. Nothing could be more telling than the association, in the chapter on Paris entitled "Railler, régner," of the names Danton, Prometheus, and Cambronne. The chapter ends with the elliptical remark that the same fearsome lightning darts from the torch of Prometheus to the clay pipe of Cambronne: "Le même éclair formidable va de la torche de Prométhée au brûle-gueule de Cambronne."

FROM CAMBRONNE TO GAVROCHE: SALVATION FROM BELOW

Cambronne answers the enemy's ultimatum with the most democratic word in the French language. Hugo himself, assessing his linguistic contribution, claimed to have revolutionized the literary idiom. ("Je fis souffler un vent révolutionnaire. / Je mis un bonnet rouge au vieux dictionnaire.") It is hardly excessive to suggest that Cambronne's pungent exclamation corresponds to Hugo's personal intention, as well as to the larger themes of *Les*

Misérables. These themes, in particular the political implications of popular speech and popular laughter, are illustrated by one of Hugo's most striking creations, the slangy street urchin Gavroche—and beyond him, by the personalized figure of Paris, the city of revolutions. Gavroche, the vagrant boy familiar with thieves and prostitutes, the *gamin* who sings obscene songs and has a poet's mastery of argot, is truly a child of the big city: "Le gamin de Paris, c'est le nain de la géante." And of course Paris, the gigantic parent, is the *figura* of the people. The metaphor works both ways. The capital is the populace, and the populace is the *gamin*—with his teasing lightheartedness and irrepressible laughter, but also his grim love of freedom and courage. "To depict the child is to depict the city." If the city populace is comparable to a child, it is because it still has to be formed morally and politically. The mob, the masses, have a potential that needs to be educated, elevated, or as Hugo puts it, "sublimed."

Yet the political potential is there, and laughter is its manifestation. The laughter of Gavroche is the laughter of the city, and the laughter of the city—likened to that which might issue from a "volcano's mouth"—is the laughter of revolution. This laughter is ominous. Gavroche himself may think that he is carefree. He is not. Always ready for a prank, he is also "ready for something else." He will in fact die, singing a mocking song, while gathering cartridges for the outnumbered fighters on the barricades. The imp becomes a hero. The merrymaking populace of Paris is likewise capable of epic anger. But this threatening laughter is not merely a signal of courage and violence; it ultimately serves to build the utopian city of justice. Paris, the capital of revolutionary anger, is also the capital of revolutionary revelation, and as such is destined to become a new Jerusalem. In pages written while in exile to serve as introduction to *Paris-Guide* at the time of the Exposition Universelle of 1867, Hugo denounced the smug and doomed materialism of the Second Empire: "Paris, lieu de la révélation révolutionnaire, est la Jérusalem humaine."

From laughter to epic anger, from argot to the sublime, from *fex urbis*—the dregs of the city—to revelation: Hugo is not interested in irreconcilable antithesis but in the spanning of apparent opposites. The excremental motif reappears in the *gamin*'s warning that the police are coming, which is the signal to escape through the sewage drain: "Ohé, Titi, ohéée: y a de la grippe, y a de la cogne . . . pâsse par l'égout!" It appears even more clearly in the expression *fex urbis*, which etymologically equates the city populace with fecal matter. We are back to the word of Cambronne. Only now the excremental motif is permeated with the realities of social conditions and fraught with revolutionary hopes and ideals. It is the signal that salvation is to come from the filth of the lower stratum, from the depths of misery and crime, from the social *inferi.*

Not surprisingly, the first reference to the *égout* is associated with an image of escape. Salvation is to be found below. Hugo, the polished bourgeois, instinctively apprehensive of mob ignorance and mob violence, here faces some of his most difficult inner contradictions, as he deals with the salvational virtues of the social *cloaca.* This helps explain another digression, one dealing with the criminal gang called Patron-Minette. The appellation derives from *patron-minet,* which in old slang means early morning—a reference to the crepuscular hour when the gang's night work is done and they disband. But it becomes clear that Hugo is playing on the word *mine,* phonetically contained in the word *minet,* and that this word connotes the reality below the surface, the nether regions, the bowels of the earth, with further suggestions of the hellish abyss where the "social Ugolino" (a clear reference to Dante's hell) indulges in vice and crime. Here is the great "cave of evil," oozing with physical and moral pollution.

The image of the mine also connotes arduous work and the extraction of precious ore. The verb *piocher* (to dig with a pick), metaphorically associated by Hugo with the substantive *idée,* means to work or study very hard. The first chapter of the digression on Patron-Minette is entitled "Les Mines et les mineurs." Its idealistic and redemptive overtones are intensified if one remembers that, early in the novel, Bishop Bienvenu extracts saintly pity from what Hugo calls the "mine" of universal misery: "L'universelle misère était sa mine." Salvation from below is indeed the message of the Patron-Minette episode. Hugo reminds his reader that the first Roman Mass was said in the catacombs. Similarly, the new social gospel, the new religion of progress, will spread through the communion of social suffering. The lowest stratum of society is also the revolutionary mine where utopias are elaborated: "Les utopies cheminent sous terre dans les conduits."

This underground imagery remains ambiguous. The figure of Christ is disturbingly coupled with the abhorred figure of Marat, who embodies, for Hugo, all the terror of mob violence. The *fex urbis* can, no doubt, be elevated; that is precisely the mission of the new social prophet. But this prophetic calling first implies a plunging into mud and putrescence. Prophecy and salvation from below are central to Hugo's personal religion. For Hugo's God is no longer the authoritarian divine principle hierarchically and sublimely situated above, but emerges from subterranean darkness, from chaotic and dynamic human suffering and human becoming. That is what police inspector Javert, who lives by the faith that God is allied with law and order, is made to discover through Valjean's magnanimity. The discovery that God rises from the lower depths comes as a great shock to the relentlessly righteous Javert, and leads directly to his suicide. But this same association between God and the dregs of the earth also makes far more meaningful the narrator's somewhat surprising comment that Cambronne's historic cry, which so profoundly shocked Lamartine, came to him by divine inspiration—"par visitation du souffle d'en haut."

THE LANGUAGE FROM BELOW

Slang reflects this paradox at the level of language. Hugo devotes to argot another of his lengthy digressions. His colorful observations may not be of great philological value, but they take on a thematic function and impose a parallel between popular language and the ambivalent nature of the underworld. The first word of the digression is the Latin *pigritia*, from which Hugo derives the French *pègre*, designating the world of thieves considered as a social class. The link between argot and the world of crime suits Hugo's structures. Like the underworld, slang is a pathological "excrescence" ("excroissance maladive"), but at the same time it implies vitality and constant evolution.

The many references to argot as a pathology of language (Hugo calls it a "pustulous vocabulary," a wart-like, ulcerous idiom) are significantly associated with the excremental motif. Slang is compared to a horrible beast made to inhabit the darkness of the cloaca. It is also compared to an underground edifice, collectively built by the accursed race of *misérables*. Willful crime and dehumanizing punishment are inscribed on its walls. The prison imagery is inescapable. The shameless tropes of slang seem indeed to have worn the "iron collar," the *carcan*. The words of this special language appear as if shriveled under the red-hot iron of the executioner. The sense of shame associated with the underworld idiom explains why Eponine, once her love for Marius has illuminated her crime-ridden existence, refuses to speak that "horrid language," argot.

Yet Hugo is fascinated by the forcefulness and vitality of slang and links it to the revolutionary spirit. This vitality, to be sure, remains repellent ("vitalité hideuse") and mirrors the hideousness of criminal faces in the prison and the galleys. Hugo defines argot as the "verbe devenu forçat"—the word become a convict. The double suggestion of force and action implicit in the terms *verbe* and *forçat* reinforces the contention that argot is the language of rebellion and militancy, a "langue de combat." The speech of the underworld expresses the subterranean and perhaps subconscious utopian yearnings associated with the sufferers in the mine.

The power of such a linguistic code is valued by Hugo for strictly poetic reasons. Henri Meschonnic quite rightly sees Hugo's interest in argot—an interest already displayed in *Le Dernier Jour d'un condamné*—as part of a broader reflection on the nature of language and on the poet's will to control it. The "hideousness" of slang, according to Hugo's theory in his preface to *Cromwell,* constitutes a source of aesthetic value: "Beauty has only one type; ugliness has a thousand." The digression on slang in *Les Misérables* is quite explicit. Slang is essentially a poetic construct because of the steady displacement of meanings and the ensuing masquerade of words. Argot's mask-words ("mots masques") serve as camouflage. But conversely, this metaphorical inventiveness brings about a cratylic immediacy, which results in an idiom rich in *mots immédiats.* Argot thus joins poetry in the elaboration of a language designed at once to conceal and to reveal ("tout dire et tout cacher"). In a note accompanying the manuscript of *William Shakespeare,* Hugo elaborated on the relationship between popular language and poetry: "Figurative language is essentially popular language."

The victory associated with the lowliest of words thus transcends praise of Cambronne's indomitable spirit. It does more than hint that salvation comes from unexpected quarters. It signifies the victory of the word as poetic manifestation, the victory of language as poetry—and, by extension, the victory of the supreme master of language, the poet. For the word is more than a sword transforming the vanquished Cambronne into a victor. It is more beautiful than what it represents and has its own opaque reality ("les mots sont des choses," Hugo writes in the poem "Suite," in *Les Comtemplations*). The word's action is militant ("le mot s'appelle Légion"), yet the word's power lies less in its revolutionary potential than in its divine auctorial origin. The concluding line of "Suite" proclaims this all-powerful logos: "Car le mot, c'est le Verbe, et le Verbe, c'est Dieu."

The link between the excremental and religious motifs is suggested repeatedly at the level of metaphor. The Petit-Picpus convent, into which the ex-convict forces his way to escape the manhunt and in which he finds refuge and expiation, is defined by Hugo—together with all monastic enclosures—as a place of putrescence. Conversely, when Valjean, in his ultimate escape, descends into the Parisian sewers, his involuntary memory resuscitates the powerful sensation he experienced when he "fell" from the street into the convent. Spirituality and filth are once again dialectically related.

The revelation of this bond between spirituality and the underworld is in itself a powerful religious experience. The shock turns out to be too much for Javert. His one-track mind, coupling justice and authority, is incapable of accepting the sublimity of the wretch, of assimilating the paradox of a beneficent malefactor, a hideous moral hero, an inverted moral order in which the criminal is redeemable and haloed. When he becomes aware of the superior abyss (the "gouffre en haut"), when he realizes that God is *below* at least as much as above, Javert's machine derails (the section is entitled "Javert déraillé"). He destroys himself, testifying to an intolerable truth.

Les Misérables, in Hugo's mind, grew to be an increasingly religious book. All of human destiny, the narrator explains, is summed up in the dilemma: loss or salvation. In the episode of the barricades, he describes the subject of the book as the unrelenting movement from evil to good, from night to day, from nothingness to God. The *misérables* are in fact the victims of a social damnation, dwelling in what the preface refers to as "hells" on earth. But Hugo rejects the notion of eternal damnation. Satan himself, according to a famous line in *La Fin de Satan*, will be reborn as the angel of light: "Satan est mort; renais, ô Lucifer céleste!" Hugo clearly conceives of himself as a modern Dante—but a Dante who is the prophet of a new religion of liberation. His God is not chief jailer. "No eternal hell!" proclaims the voice from the dark in *Les Contemplations*. Instead, Hugo announces movement toward a higher consciousness through suffering. Redemption, in these terms, implies the transcendence of the prison image.

THE LEADING FIGURE: THE INFINITE

Hugo's most substantial commentary on the religious significance of *Les Misérables* is to be found in a text of 1860 known as "Philosophie. Commencement d'un livre," which was originally planned as a preface to the novel, before it evolved into a lengthy introduction to his entire work. It can perhaps best be described as a spiritual testament. The first sentence sets the tone: *Les Misérables* is meant to be a religous book ("Le livre qu'on va lire est un livre religieux"). The text dwells on some of Hugo's most dearly held notions: dynamic undoing and ceaseless reconstruction, the vitalism of natural forces, the intimate solidarity of the universe, the dialogue with the unseen, the paradox of the irreducible identity of author and God.

But the most interesting aspect of this "philosophical" preface—though it is not so obvious at a first glance—is its polemical intentionality, which illumines the point of intersection between Hugo's religious and political convictions. Hugo writes: "misery being materialistic, the book about misery must be spiritualistic." This somewhat facile opposition of matter and spirit, of subject and literary treatment, takes on its proper meaning only if set against the backdrop of Hugo's private quarrel with his fellow "socialists," at a time when French socialism, abandoning earlier utopian and spiritualistic leanings, tended to link revolutionary virtues with impiety. Pierre Albouy has convincingly argued [in *Mythographies*] that Hugo's real enemies, around 1860, were not at all, as one might believe, conservatives and reactionaries but socialist atheists, who had by then become the predominant force in the socialist movement. Hugo's profession of faith must therefore be read as a protest against what he himself calls "intestinal socialism"—that is, a socialism too exclusively preoccupied with economic realities and economic solutions. Man's needs do not consist merely of filling his belly. The soul is hungry, too, and cannot live on meat and nothingness. Radically opposed to the notion that religion is the opiate of the masses, Hugo attempts instead to associate atheism and conservatism. This is the point of an early chapter in which the bishop confronts the smug, sacrilegious senator. Hugo sees an essential tie between religion and democracy, not simply because republican fervor is compatible with faith but because belief in the Supreme Being legitimizes the principles of equality and justice. In Hugo's metaphysical perspective, infinity is identifiable with progress. Thus, he can assert, in a sociopolitical context, the greatest political misfortune would be generalized atheism: "Le plus grand de tous les malheurs, ce serait tout le monde athée."

There is ample internal evidence of the religious thrust of *Les Misérables.* Some of it is obvious, such as the narrator's declaration, at the beginning of the digression on convents, that the novel's chief protagonist is the infinite ("Ce livre est un drame dont le premier personnage est l'infini"). The dimension of infinity is, however, most often internalized, as during Valjean's first great moral crisis ("A Tempest in a Brain") when it is projected "within himself" ("au-dedans de lui-même"). Hugo's favorite method, in this regard, is allusive. Valjean, facing the abyss of his conscience and about to make a first sacrifice that will lead to resurrection, is compared to another condemned man, the Man of Sorrows.

Opening signals once again are revealing. The novel begins on a religious note, with a lengthy, almost hagiographic account of the saintly bishop of Digne. The ex-convict's confrontation with this "just man" produces a spiritual trauma. Bishop Bienvenu "hurt his soul," just as too bright a light can hurt the eyes. An invisible bond will henceforth tie him to the one who becomes his intercessor, and whom he venerates as a martyr. The suggestion is that of a spiritual family kinship. When news of the bishop's death reaches

Valjean and he appears in mourning, gossip has it that he must be a relative of the bishop.

The polemical intentions underlying the philosophical preface are once again apparent, for Bishop Bienvenu has his limitations. He is a "just man," rather than a visionary or a true martyr. He lacks what might be called a radical dimension. Capable of love and charity, his soul cannot glimpse the apocalypse. He has nothing of the prophet, nothing of the seer ("rien du mage"). This lack of spiritual radicalism is specifically related to a political flaw, royalism—or rather to an undeveloped political consciousness. Hence the importance of the august, persecuted figure of the Conventionnel—the old member of the revolutionary Assembly that governed France in the period of greatest violence. When the bishop and the revolutionary meet, it appears that religion and revolution come into hopeless clash. Yet the confrontation leads to an illumination. The chapter is entitled "The Bishop in the Presence of an Unknown Light." It is the bishop, come to assist the dying political radical, who ends up kneeling in front of him, asking for his blessing.

This act, which so profoundly disturbed some of Hugo's Christian readers, is in reality not the most surprising feature of this scene in which bishop and revolutionary are at first locked in a verbal battle, each accusing the other of responsibility for violence in history. The real surprise is not that the bishop goes down on his knees in front of the old Conventionnel; it is that the Conventionnel speaks the language of religious mysticism. The moment has its peculiar beauty. The death of the outcast in the presence of the bishop and of a child (symbol of innocence and of faith in the future) is illumined by a setting sun and has an iconic quality. Serenity is the prevailing note, and this serenity has much to do with the witnessing of a solemn moment ("Il est bon que ce moment-là ait des témoins"). But the real impact of the scene must be attributed to the unexpected religous rhetoric of the dying jacobin. Words such as *sacre, ciel, infini,* and *Dieu* come quite naturally to him. The articulation between the religious and political spheres is implicit in the comparison between the revolution of 1789 and the advent of Christ. Conversely, Christ is seen as far more radical than Christians such as Bienvenu. Would the bishop take a whip and purge the temple? Is he not afraid to face up to the brutal truths of history? The scene ends with a hint of apotheosis, as the dying man raises a finger toward heaven and refers to the "I of the infinite," whose name is God.

Yet somehow the ultimate message of belief seems no longer addressed to the good bishop. The real interlocutor—absent, but very present in the scene—is the atheistic socialist of the 1850s (Proudhon was very much on

Hugo's mind, but so were a number of fervent Republicans who shared his exile), with whom Hugo felt he no longer had a common language. It is no doubt for the sake of this invisible adversary-ally that he has the old Conventionnel, the former representative of the people, adopt an anti-atheistic revolutionary stance: "Progress must believe in God. Goodness cannot have an impious servant. An atheist is a bad leader for mankind." Matter exists and the belly exists, but the belly, as Hugo puts it later in the novel, must not be the "sole wisdom." Nothing would be more intolerable than the death of the spirit. This resistance to a program for progress founded on a purely economic doctrine helps explain the novel's peculiar perspective on the proletariat, which is seen not as an honest working class but as a hotbed of misery, greed, and crime. Conversely, Hugo's brand of metaphysical socialism, which has its roots in the work of Ballanche, explains why Valjean, as Christ of the people, remains a fundamentally apolitical figure.

"The Last Drop in the Chalice" ("La dernière gorgée du Calice") is the symbolic title of one of the final sections of the novel. Though the mystery of Valjean, the "homme précipice," may strike obtuse inspector Javert as a simple police problem, it is of a profoundly religious nature. Valjean's self-sacrifice and self-abnegation begin with a clear image of separation from the self. This occurs as soon as the conversion following the encounter with the bishop becomes effective. Having, in a trance, stolen money from a little Savoyard boy and thus committed a crime of which he is in fact no longer capable, Valjean sees himself as "séparé de lui-même." His hallucinatory experience amounts to an "ecstasy." His vision projects an immensely aggrandized image of the bishop while his own self seems to shrink and vanish ("Jean Valjean s'amoindrissait et s'effaçait"). This self-effacement is part of a system of transience and transcendence that allows Valjean, while still alive, to become a luminous mediatory figure. He continues to venerate the bishop, but it is he who acquires a halo. When the ex-convict, now a respected mayor, denounces himself to save a falsely accused vagabond, a "great light" dazzles the spectators in the courtroom.

Though Valjean modestly continues to look to the bishop as a model, there can be little doubt that it is he who becomes the chief intercessor. Fantine, on her deathbed, sees him "in a glory," surrounded by celestial forms. Cosette learns through him the joy of prayer. And prayer, for Hugo, is the supreme experience of contemplation and communion. Numerous passages stress Valjean's mediatory role. Little Cosette becomes less afraid in a world that has treated her cruelly, aware that "there was someone there." Walking hand in hand with Valjean, the little child feels "as though she were beside the good Lord." The text becomes more explicit still: "The entrance of that man into the destiny of that child had been the advent of God."

Viewed in a broader thematic perspective, Valjean's spiritual adventure parallels the fall and rehabilitation of Satan in Hugo's mythology of universal pardon. Even the compositional chronology is revealing. Hugo returned to the long neglected manuscript of *Les Misérables* in April 1860, only a few days after abandoning *La Fin de Satan*. The biographical and thematic links are obvious. Yet Valjean is neither a redeemed satanic convict nor a modern apocalyptic visionary, though his name—originally Vlajean— evokes the author of the Book of Revelations. His image quite specifically merges with that of Christ. Allusions and references abound: the Mount of Olives, Calvary, the carrying of the cross. "Lui aussi porte sa croix" ("He, Too, Carries His Cross") is the title of one of the chapters describing Valjean's agonizing progression through the sewers, with the unconscious Marius on his back. His ultimate struggle with his conscience leaves him, after a sleepless night, prostrate in a symbolic position, "his fists clenched, his arms extended at a right angle, like one taken from the cross" ("un crucifié décloué"). And when Marius comes to realize the extent of Valjean's sacrifice, he sees the convict (avatar of Satan) transfigured into the image of the Savior: "Le forçat se transfigurait en Christ."

THE SELF AND THE TEXT OF GOD

The image of the proletarian Christ points to a conceptual difficulty at the core of Hugo's work. For how compatible is the drama of the human soul, always enacted in the singular, with the pressure of collective issues? The spiritual value bestowed on the individual's moral crisis carries politically heretical implications. Hugo himself raises the question just before recounting the heroic revolutionary struggle on the barricades. "What are the convulsions of a city compared with the mutinies of a soul?" And he adds this even more direct challenge to prevalent glorifications (his own included) of the Messianic People: "Man is a still deeper reality than the people" ("L'homme est une profondeur plus grande encore que le peuple"). No authorial statement could proclaim more clearly the precedence of spiritual needs over political commitments.

The priority of selfhood and the "insubmersible" nature of the *I* (as he was to put it in a later novel) are for Hugo directly related to the principle of the Godhead, the supreme selfhood of God. The dying Conventionnel in fact denies divinity as the "moi de l'infini." To be sure, the implicit divinization of the individual soul is not radically incompatible with collective political salvation as understood by postrevolutionary doctrinaires. Neo-Catholic utopian ideologues, in the first half of the nineteenth century, having espoused the controversial idea of progress, worked out the dialectical complexities of their unorthodox stand. Lamennais, one of the most vigorous spokesmen of the new political-religious movement, stated the case with much clarity: "One must beware of thinking that individual salvation is the unique or chief aim of Jesus' teachings . . . It is mankind he wanted to save, and each individual salvation is only a means toward, and an element of, the salvation of all." And again: "Man by himself is but a fragment of being; true being is collective being."

Yet there can be no doubt that for Hugo the priority of the individual soul remained unchallengeable. Politically oriented religions of humanity struck him as limiting and dangerous. The "convulsions of a city" were too closely allied to the violence of the rabble; they carried a permanent threat of *spiritual* death. For death itself should not be allowed to erase identity. Notions of reincarnation, popular with Saint-Simonian thinkers such as Prosper Enfantin and Pierre Leroux, met with Hugo's hostility. He needed to preserve the sense of personal identity.

This concern for the integrity of selfhood logically extends to the realm of literature. It is hardly surprising that when, in *William Shakespeare,* Hugo surveys world literature and discusses the nature of genius, he shows a clear preference for authored texts ("oeuvres nommées") over anonymous, collective works, no matter how impressive. For certain exceptional beings—and this is perhaps the nature of genius—at once embody and transcend collectivities. They *represent* nations, as they represent the abstraction called "the people." Once again the *I* of the individual is valued as larger and deeper ("plus vaste et plus profond") than the *I* of the group.

What is involved is not merely a suprapolitical glorification of the institution of literature but an implicit correspondence between the selfhood of the genius as author and the selfhood of God as the supreme authority. The fine line of demarcation between these identities affects Hugo's narrative technique. His particular type of omniscient perspective posits the essential mystery of fictional characters. Thus, Valjean is no more "explained" than is the nature of good and evil. It is as though Hugo the author believed in the inviolability of his own characters; he comments, observes, and judges—but he remains *outside* them. He may occasionally encroach on their privacy, but he never annexes them. The soul of the protagonist remains private property. As Georges Piroué astutely put it, with Hugo *I* never becomes *He.*

This tendency to be at once on the side of his characters and on the side of God is further complicated as God himself is cast in the double role of witness and participant. The ubiquitous glance is thematized. "White Night," the section referring ironically both to the nuptial joys of the young couple and to the agony of Valjean, ends with rhetoric questioning itself about the impersonal pronoun *one*. The narrator, describing Valjean stretched out on his bed as though crucified, first observes that "one would have said he was dead"; then, as Valjean kisses Cosette's garments, that "one saw that he was alive." He asks: "What one?"—immediately providing the answer: "The One who is in the darkness" ("Le On qui est dans les ténèbres").

Much earlier, during the Champmathieu crisis, the same impersonal pronoun already pointed to a supreme witness—but internalized and made to participate. The *on* is seen as Valjean's conscience, and this conscience is said to be synonymous with God ("Sa conscience, c'est-à-dire Dieu"). The impersonal pronoun thus serves as a bridge between supreme witness and supreme protagonist.

Preterition creates a further bridge, suggesting an implicit cosubstantiality or symbiosis between author and Auctor, between the authorial glance and the glance of God. When Valjean speaks in a whisper to the dead Fantine, Hugo strings together a succession of rhetorical questions about the nature of his words, and concludes on an ambiguous note: "They were heard by no one on earth." The supreme glance is not only the one that sees darkness ("Celui qui . . . voit toute l'ombre," but characterizes the ubiquitous narrator: "the eye of the drama should be everywhere present.")

If the narrative glance is ultimately never extraneous, this is precisely because at a certain level the narrative procedure locates an omniscient, immanent consciousness in the action. God is repeatedly made manifest as the "engaged" author. Or rather, he becomes a protagonist. When Valjean, at a critical juncture, attempts to flee from his conscience, he feels as though "someone" catches him in his flight and brings him back. This "someone" is obviously the same presence that always points its "mysterious indicating finger" at the more difficult road. Not everyone, of course, struggles with this absence-presence as relentlessly as Valjean. His case is, in this sense, tragically privileged. As he himself puts it to Marius toward the end of the novel, he belongs to no family; he remains "outside" ("je suis dehors"). But it is also this apparent exclusion from the human family that makes it impossible for him to silence that "someone" who speaks to him when he is alone. Valjean's secret—his mysterious status as a "tender Cain"—is the "secret of God." Conversely, the supreme author becomes, in the ex-convict's spiritual adventure, as visible as Valjean himself—chief protagonist along-side the modern redeemer figure: "Dieu était dans cette aventure aussi visible que Jean Valjean."

The double status of the Supreme Being—author and protagonist—is far from contradictory for Hugo. God's personal intervention in history (He is the victor at Waterloo) must be read as the obverse of historical necessity—the "force des choses." For this "force" of circumstances, this apparent historical determinism, is described in terms of a "hand" carrying away the "stage set" ("châssis de théâtre") of succeeding political regimes. The theatrical metaphor is appropriate. The stagehand turns out to be the director as well as the author of the scenario. "Scenario divin" is indeed the expression that Hugo uses as he writes of revolutionary turmoil. Ultimately, all of history is viewed as the text of God. In *Quatrevingt-treize,* Hugo was to refer to God as the "rédacteur" of the grim but providential pages of the Terror. But already in *Les Misérables,* the Revolution is described as a "geste de Dieu." And the word *geste,* with a mere variation of grammatical gender, can refer either to action or to text.

Over and above the implicit notion of writing as heroic action, Hugo problematizes the relation of text to ideology, and of ideology to text, by means of a central figure of decipherment. What asks to be *read* is indeed the divine text of history; but this very reading is a form of action as well as a form of writing. In a complex digression on the beginnings of the July Monarchy, Hugo offers the following:

> God makes visible to men his will in events, an obscure text written in a mysterious language. Men make translations of it forthwith; hasty translations, incorrect, full of mistakes, gaps, and misreadings. Very few minds understand the divine tongue. The most sagacious, the most serene, the most profound decipher slowly, and when they arrive with their text, the work has been done a while back; there are already twenty translations on the marketplace. From each translation a party is born, and from each misreading a faction; and each party believes it has the only true text, and each faction believes it possesses the light.

In this crucial passage, translations (based on decipherments and misreadings) appear as new writings—texts on a text; and they represent renewed action in the form of ideological commitments. Thus, writing begets writing. But unless the reading-writing process is enacted by the "few minds" who comprehend the divine tongue, there is the steady danger of discrepancy between the authoritative text of origin (which is also the text of history) and the texts in history, its interpretations.

Hence the privileged status of the magus-poet, of the vatic decipherer. The poem "Les Mages" in *Les Contemplations* lists his virtues. The *mage*, actor-hero in a universal drama, carries from birth, inscribed in his skull, the text of God. Celebrant and revealer, he is fated to write the chapters of the "rituel universel," the Great Book. And this sacerdotal function, this "pontificat de l'infini," in turn leads to the ultimate breakdown of all barriers between transcendence and immanence, to the disturbing celestial fade-out ("évanouissement des cieux") of the final line of the poem. It would almost appear that, by a paradoxical reversal, the deciphering of the divine text implies the writing of it as well.

Hence also the ambivalent readings called for by the key episodes; a historical reading, according to the rationale of progress and linear development; and a cyclical reading, by which the very idea of forward movement links up with a point of origin. Between the two, a complex system of exchange sets up elaborate binary structures.

THE TWO READINGS

The major digressions again best illustrate the compositional principle of the novel. The parallel between the prison from which Valjean escapes and the Petit-Picpus convent in which he and Cosette hide from police pursuit (both are places of "expiation," albeit in a different spirit) provides the opportunity for a sustained thematization of binary opposites. For the concept of monasticism, as Hugo expounds it in a lengthy section entitled "Parenthesis," is filled with contradictions (error and innocence, devotion and ignorance, bliss and inhumanity) requiring the double answer *yes* and *no*: "Un couvent, c'est une contradiction."

To account for some of the negative postures, there is Hugo's recurrent terror of being buried alive, the association of the convent-tomb with the black radiance of death. The yellow teeth of the nuns, as Hugo imagines them (no toothbrush, he claims, ever found its way into a convent), symbolize a spectral "death in life" that is the essence of conventual existence. But this personal revulsion in the face of self-denial and self-laceration must be replaced in a broader ideological context. It is in the name of history and progress that monastic life is here denounced. This abstract condemnation echoes the antimonastic prejudices of the eighteenth-century *philosophes*, as well as the themes of repressiveness and sterility associated with convents in Revolutionary literature. It is the voice of history itself, insofar as history is conceived both as a force and a value, that condemns the convent as a ghost of the past.

The rationalistic perspective merges with personal revulsion. Hugo's terms for censuring monasticism belong revealingly to the realm of pathology. The moral and social noxiousness of conventual existence is seen as a threat to life. Monasteries are a "leprosy," a "consumption" ("phtisie"); monastic withdrawal is castration (Hugo puns: "Claustration, castration"); the world of cloisters is a world of "putrescence" whose infection spreads like a plague. Even worse, ignorance and superstition lead to self-destruction and to the sanctification of cruelty. The monastic excesses of Catholic Spain, exacerbated by fanatical asceticism, bring the world of convents (with their damp *in pace,* dungeons, iron collars, oozing walls) uncannily close to the most punitive forms of incarceration.

The parallel between convent and prison reaches beyond the register of horror into the area of political and moral concerns. The double denunciation operates at two levels. Progress calls for the disappearance of cloisters, as it demands the abolition of the death sentence—and eventually the eradication of all jails. More radical than most of his liberal contemporaries, who merely thought of controlling the carceral world through a more rational system of penology, Hugo had visions of a world in which prison would be as inconceivable as eternal damnation. Social and metaphysical dreams were ultimately to blend in a common utopia. Hell itself was to be effaced, and Satan saved. "Never a chain, never a cell," concludes Saint François de Paule in Hugo's late play *Torquemada.* God in person, as though to confirm this notion of progress transposed to the metaphysical realm, explains in the ultimate lines of *La Fin de Satan* that once prisons are destroyed, Gehenna too will be abolished: "la prison détruite abolit la géhenne." This is, of course, the deep secret of the oracular *bouche d'ombre,* the voice from the dark: "No eternal hell."

Yet there is a striking ambivalence in Hugo's digression on convents. If one of the chapters of this excursus is entitled "Precautions to Be Taken in Censure," this is not to be understood as mere lip service to a venerable institution. Hugo uses the word "respect" several times, but the word acquires a special resonance by contiguity with the word "infinite": "Whenever we meet with the infinite in man . . . we are seized with a feeling of respect." The convent may be a tomb, but it is also the place of luminous spirituality; it oppresses, but also liberates; it is a ghost of the past, yet it is a visionary outpost. The convent, moreover, has all the ineffable charms of the secret garden of love, the *hortus conclusus.*

But this love, cultivated in solitude, is of a transcendental nature; its manifestation is prayer, which brings the infinite within (the "infini en nous") in contact with the infinite beyond (the "infini hors de nous"). Prayer, according to Hugo, is precisely the link between the two infinites: an act of mediation and communion. Valjean's first experience, after the redemptive fall into the convent garden, is to hear a hymn of prayer which brings him and Cosette to their knees. The scene rehearses an earlier one: the ex-convict's kneeling on the pavement, in the dark of night, in front of the bishop's house. The bishop, we are told, raises prayer to the point of "superhuman aspiration." Such praying before prayer suggests an endless spiritual chain which, in the Petit-Picpus convent is ritualistically enacted by the devotion of the Perpetual Adoration. This arduous twelve-hour prayer, which entails kneeling and prostration, is described by Hugo as "grand jusqu'au sublime."

It is difficult to overstate the significance of prayer for Hugo. "One can no more pray too much than love too much," he writes in a chapter devoted to the bishop. One of the chapters in the convent digression carries the terse title "Absolute Excellence of Prayer." More interesting still—especially in the context of a historical denunciation of the parasitic nature of monasticism—is the relation Hugo establishes between a life of prayer and "useful" contemplation. Hugo goes so far as to assert that there is perhaps no more sublime activity and no more "useful work" than that performed by these cloistered spirits.

. Polemical and ideological reasons once again help explain apparent inconsistencies. In the philosophical preface to the novel, prayer is defined as the attempted "dialogue" with the unknown. This contact with mystery takes on full significance when measured against political and economic preoccupations. For Hugo, the self-styled "socialist," disavows solidarity with his fellow socialists, while claiming to praise a common ideal. A simple shift from the first person to the second person plural establishes the rift: "Your economic problems are one of the glorious preoccupations of the nineteenth century." The manipulation of the possessive adjective from the expected *nos* to *vos* ("vos problèmes économiques") keeps atheistic socialism at a distance. The fact is that even before balancing *no* and *yes* with regard to the validity of monasticism, Hugo opted for the latter—in flagrant contradiction of all his strictures. "To *no*, there is but one reply: *yes*." The words that follow make the polemical stance explicit: "Nihilism is powerless" ("Le nihilisme est sans portée").

Beyond the polemical intention there lurks an argument *pro domo*. The notion of a "useful" contemplation is surely related to the poet's views of his own activities as prophetic poet, and more specifically as the visionary author of *Les Contemplations* (1856). "Contemplation leads to action" is the terse summation of the chapter on the excellence of prayer. The desire to reconcile prayer and revolution is paralleled by the urge to vindicate the contemplative mode—and poetic activity in general—as perfectly compatible with moral and political engagement. But such engagement requires separation, distance, abnegation. Exile, political and spiritual, becomes the convenient symbol. Hence the concluding aphorism: "Whoever goes into self-exile seems venerable to us." The sentence, ostensibly referring to the nuns, has also a very personal ring, coming as it does from the one who chose voluntarily to remain on the island of Guernsey—away from the France of Napoleon III. It also confirms, beyond polemics and self-glorification, the deeply religious animus of *Les Misérables*.

MUCK, BUT SOUL

The other major digression thematizing a striking antithesis is the description of the Paris sewer system, which precedes Valjean's ultimate escape. The link between sewer and convent may not be immediately apparent; yet both are places of salvation, and both—one literally, the other metaphorically—are places of putrescence ("Leur putrescibilité est évidente," Hugo writes of convents). But convents at least have gardens; and gardens, especially when protected by walls, are idyllic sites in Hugo's private mythology. In the bowels of the megalopolis, however, there is no visible reprieve from horror. "The Intestine of the Leviathan" is the title of the digression. The terms connote the monstrous as well as the excremental. The chapter heading points to the digestive system of the modern Babylon, filled with "caecums" (an anatomical detail) and infectious cesspools. Here too, as with convents, Hugo marshals the lexicon of pathology. The "evacuation crypt" (*crypte exutoire*) shows "herpetic ooze" (*suintement dartreux*) on its walls. Miasmas pollute the tract.

The other recurrent nightmare image, tightening the underlying link between the sewer and the convent episodes, is that of being buried alive. As Valjean moves deeper and deeper into the mire and is about to be swallowed by a gigantic mudhole, Hugo compares his ordeal to that of a fisherman on some deserted beach being sucked down by treacherous quicksand, condemned to a ghastly burial—"long, infallible, implacable"—in which the grave turns into a tide, reaching from the depths of the earth toward a living human being. Earth, having become as perfidious as water, is capable of drowning a man. This convertibility of solid into liquid is announced, at the very outset of the downward journey to the cloacal world, in a comparison between Paris and the sea. So also the terror of being buried alive ("Inexpressible horror of dying this way!") is prefigured in the cemetery scene, after Valjean agrees to be carried out from the convent in a coffin and subjected to a mock burial.

The escape motif inevitably conjures up carceral metaphors, and those in turn lead to figurations of hell. A narrow passageway that ends in the form of a funnel is "logical in jail" but totally "illogical" in a sewer. Valjean, ironically, seems to have escaped into a prison. When release is finally glimpsed, Valjean—a reincarnation of the archetypal convict—is compared to a "condemned soul" who, from the midst of hell's furnace, suddenly perceives an exit. Revealingly, the "Intestin de Léviathan" section concludes with a most ambiguous image related to the disturbing figure of Marat, who fascinated Hugo both as the revolutionary *ami du peuple* and the embodiment of evil. The episode refers to the astonishing discovery, made during a survey of the sewer system, of a shredded sheet of fine batiste with an embroidered crown, a tattered and filthy remnant of what was once an elegant bedsheet that had served as Marat's shroud and that had been a souvenir of a youthful affair with an aristocratic lady. The antithetical elements (*ami du peuple* and aristocrat, horror and elegance, sex and death) are heightened by the realistic and symbolic setting juxtaposing excrement and salvation.

The association of sewer and revolution is ironic not only because Marat's rag is mixed with vestiges of natural cataclysms (the "shellfish of the deluge") but because violence and survival come into dialectical clash. The allusion to the deluge in the last line of the section has both destructive and redemptive connotations. The linear time of the revolution of men seems denied by the cyclical time of the "revolutions of the globe." Both do, however, function in a salvational scheme. The next section ("Muck, but Soul") in fact opens with a fall into the providential spring-trap of safety. The sewer turns out to be the place of "the most absolute security."

Throughout the long digression, negative elements are in fact consistently translated into positive terms. The purgatorial features of the underworld mean purgation; the voiding crypt in the monstrous digestive apparatus signifies the cleansing of lesions; the burial alive foreshadows salvation; the apocalyptic horrors serve the vision of redemption. The value bestowed on the downward journey to the end of darkness is altogether consistent with the central vision of the novel. The ultimate metaphorical descent is prefigured in the section entitled "Marius Enters the Shadow"; the young man's journey to the barricades is compared to a "descente de marches noires." But it is in the subsequent literal descent to the sewer that the metaphor is most thoroughly worked out: "Jean Valjean had fallen from one circle of hell to another."

Contamination by diverse mythic elements signals, however, the difficulty of a strictly theological reading. The branch of the sewer situated under Montmarte is described as a "dédaléen" network. Elsewhere, Valjean is compared to the prophet Jonah in the belly of the whale. Later still, the police patrol in the sewer network is compared to evil spirits ("larves"), to mastiffs that evoke images of Cerberus-like underworld creatures. Such shifts and blendings of images relate the theological allegory to broader notions of a legendary quest. Valjean's entire career is indeed seen retrospectively as a combination of Christ-like sacrifice ("Voilà l'homme") and initiatory adventure: "il a tout traversé."

But the sacrificial quest is also the poet's adventure. The downward voyage has visionary implications as early as in the poem "La Pente de la rêverie" (1830), not only because of Hugo's reverence for the work of Dante but because he believes that a vertiginal spiral leads to the ineffable "sphère invisible." Only a dangerous voyage into the night can bring one closer to the fateful enigma which it is the poet's mission to confront. In that sense, Valjean is also the *figura* of the visionary poet. During his daydreams in the Petit-Picpus convent (the echoes of "La Pente de la rêverie" are unmistakable), he slowly fathoms the "spirales sans fond de la rêverie."

Valjean's visionary dispositions are at work in a strictly *moral* context. The darkness of the sewer is symbolic of the insight granted Valjean by a life of suffering. Just as the pupil dilates in darkness, so "the soul dilates in misfortune," until at last it finds God. Valjean's salvation, literally and metaphorically, depends on a fall. Hence the terse authorial comment: "Descendre, c'était en effet le salut possible." If Valjean is fated to be a martyr of the dark descent ("O première marche à descendre, que tu es sombre! O seconde marche, que tu es noire!"), it is because espousal of misery is what Hugo calls "sublimation." Unlike inflicted prison sufferings, which made Valjean morally worse, self-imposed sacrifices elevate and liberate him. Having shouldered the wounded body of Marius and reached the bottom of his underground Calvary, shivering, wet, and filthy, Valjean discovers that his soul is filled with "a strange light." Once more he falls on his knees—this time, however, not before an intercessor. God is present to him in the dark. Valjean's foot, in the mire, has found the beginning of the upward slope. He can reascend toward life.

The ambivalences of the sewer episode and its religious symbolization are summed up in the ultimate collapse of the metaphor. Valjean himself, the man-precipice, is described as a human "cloaca" venerating innocence in the form of Cosette. And this metaphor is then telescoped into a larger trope comprising God himself. The figure of darkness, we are told, is "le secret de Dieu."

THE DEATH OF VALJEAN

The logic of the story calls for an apotheosis. When Marius, having discovered the extent of Valjean's sacrifice, rushes with Cosette to his humble dwelling, they arrive in time to witness a scene of death and transfiguration. Hugo does more than compete with Balzac, whose père Goriot also dies as a "Christ de la paternité" (though bitterly, and without the love of his daughters). It is as though Hugo had set out to rewrite this scene of pathos, and to give it an unironic twist. Hugo's chapter reveals the "majesty of the soul"; it confirms Marius's glimpse of a redeemer's destiny: "Le forçat se transformait en Christ." The scene marks a farewell to worldly ties. The little copper crucifix Valjean takes down from the wall is symbolically contrasted with the young couple's recently acquired fortune. Between him and them "there was already a wall."

Yet irony is reintroduced at a level which is not that of pathos. Two difficulties loom over the end of this novel whose preface denounces social damnation, the "hells" of modern society, and the degradation of the "proletariat": not a word is said about social conditions, while private property is justified, indeed sanctified. Is this closing a signal of the profoundly apolitical nature of a book that pretends to be committed to social and political change? What has become of the revolutionary revelation experienced earlier by Marius, whose apprenticeship of historical realities is presented by the narrator as exemplary of the best minds of his time? Enjolras's heroic death as a revolutionary crusader, as well as the presentation of the barricades as a modern Golgotha, surely called for an ending that was not so squarely placed outside history.

Without concurring with Pierre Barbéris's denunciation of Hugo's deep-seated complicity with the bourgeois social order, one must admit that Hugo's revolutionary rhetoric often camouflages the latent yearnings of an *homme d'ordre*. Or rather, revolution itself, in Hugo's private ideology, is made to serve the demands for stability and continuity. Thus, revolution is seen not only as radically different from and even opposed to rebellion and revolt; it is understood specifically as a "vaccination" for any form of *jacquerie* or popular uprising. This revealing unwillingness to understand revolution in terms of class warfare, at a time in Hugo's life when he claimed to have been converted long before to the redemptive virtues of socialism, must be read against his much earlier acceptance speech at the Académie Française (1841), in which he paradoxically invoked the great achievements of the French Revolution as a prophylactic defense against new revolutions—and this precisely in terms of the immunization metaphor: "une vaccine qui inocule le progrès et qui préserve des révolutions."

As for the insistence on money and inheritence in the death scene, it may appear doubly surprising. Materialistic France was earlier criticized by Hugo for its genuflections before the all-powerful *écu*. The bishop, whose immaterial presence hovers over Valjean's death, loved specifically to recall the Church Father's admonition: "Place your expectation in Him to whom there is no succession." Yet matters are not quite so simple. The money motif is from the outset linked to the figure of the bishop, whose accountings of diocesan administration, charities, and household expenses are described in elaborate detail. Bishop Myriel not only handles considerable sums, but it is he who provides the ex-convict with practical advice as to how to make money. It is this advice which is ultimately responsible for the fortune that Valjean accumulates and gives to Cosette. A direct link thus connects the spiritual message to the notion of a material legacy. The closing pages significantly juxtapose terms such as *commerce, argent, fortune,* and *léguer* with Valjean's expressed pride in being poor, his desire to have no name inscribed on his tombstone, and his conviction that it is a mistake to believe that one can *own* anything; for all is part of a larger inheritance. Symbolically, Valjean brought the 600,000-franc dowry in the form of banknotes wrapped in a package that looks like an "octavo volume."

On the other hand, money is also associated, specifically through Valjean's rehabilitation process, with bourgeois virtues and values. In jail, Valjean learns how to save. He is quick with figures. Once settled in Montreuil-sur-mer, he sees to it that his slender capital is "made fruitful by order and care." He helps Fantine to "live honestly by her own labor." It is through his eyes that the "evil poor," typified by Thénardier, are seen as more repulsive and more ferocious than the evil rich. To reduce poverty without reducing wealth seems to be the author's ideal! Valjean's advice to the young couple sounds like a trivial apologia of wealth: "Why not take advantage of being rich? Wealth adds to happiness." But how is this to be reconciled with Valjean's bitter knowledge of the limits of human happiness? Above all, what does this concern for money and legacies have to do with the solemn, transfiguring hour of his death?

Two answers are conceivable—besides the simplistic relegation of Valjean/Hugo to the limbo of petit-bourgeois utilitarianism. The first harks back to Hugo's polemical stance in his continuing debate with his fellow "socialists." The sacralization of property can be seen as a blow at atheistic materialism, as well as at Proudhon's denunciation of private property in *Qu'est-ce que la propriété?* (1840). The other interpretation derives from textual and metaphysical rather than polemical elements. *Les Misérables* is indeed predicated on the idea of redemption (from the Latin *redimere:* to buy back); and the French equivalent, *rachat,* is clearly proposed in dramatic as well as metaphorical terms. Not only is the silver piece Valjean steals from the little Savoyard boy (his last evil action) metaphorized into the staring eye of his own conscience, but the bishop, in offering Valjean a set of silver candlesticks, explicitly glosses this act of generosity: "Jean Valjean, my brother, you no longer belong to evil but to good. It is your soul that I am buying." In the symbolic economy of a text that weaves individual redemptive efforts into the broader theme of collective redemption, it is striking that revolution itself, in its violence, is accounted for in terms of a terrible *price* to pay ("achats terribles") in order to achieve the future. "Une révolution est un péage." But this ideal future, heavily paid for by history, also marks an exit from history.

Such a notion of an eventless ideal future reached through the tollgate of historical catastrophe, such a merger of individual and collective redemption, casts additional light on the special religious nature of Valjean's death. What is suggested—much as in the death scene of the Conventionnel, before whom the bishop kneels—is not a Christian regenerative meeting with the Maker but an effacement signifying a merger with infinity. This obliteration-transcendence, this erasure of all traces, is a recurrent feature in the work of Hugo. The disappearance or absorption into the cosmic whole is repeated in the submersion-death endings of *Les Travailleurs de la mer* and *L'Homme qui rit.* The one-page epilogue of *Les Misérables* confirms this principle of death as effacement. Valjean's tomb in the Père Lachaise cemetery is not only nameless, but even the little poem penciled on the stone by an anonymous hand has become illegible under the effacing action of the rain.

A fundamental Hugolian principle is at work, relating the prophecies of undoing and reconstruction to the dynamics of creation. The literary process itself is symbolized by the image of the dismantled book. In his philosophical preface to *Les Misérables,* Hugo writes of the relentless forces of transformation that depend on destruction, of disintegrations that are germinations. These patterns of cyclical deconstruction are repeated in the later novels; they are related specifically to readings of history that problematize the ideological assumptions of the historical novel. But already in *Les Misérables,* there is the suggestion that Hugo's dynamic vision of history in progress ultimately leads not to a justification of history, but to the dream of an ahistorical point in time where history is denied and there will be "no more events."

Chronology

1802   Birth of Victor Marie Hugo, third son of Joseph-Léopold-Sigisbert Hugo and Sophie Trébuchet, in Besançon, France.

1811   Mother and children leave for Spain, where father is a colonel in the service of the French Empire.

1812   Return to Paris.

1819   Young Hugo publishes first poems in various journals. With Vigny and Emile Deschamps, founds a bimonthly journal called *Le Conservateur littéraire*.

1821   Hugo's mother dies. Publication of *Le Conservateur littéraire* ends.

1822   Hugo marries Adèle Foucher. *Odes et poésies diverses*.

1823   First child, Léopold, dies.

1824   *Nouvelles Odes*. Léopoldine, a daughter, is born.

1827   *Cromwell,* with the long preface that has come to be regarded as a treatise on romanticism.

1828   Definitive edition of *Odes et ballades*. Death of Hugo's father.

1829   *Les Orientales. Le Dernier Jour d'un condamné. Marion de Lorme* banned.

1830   Success of *Hernani,* following the polemical first run at the Comédie française.

1831   *Notre-Dame de Paris. Les Feuilles d'automne*.

1832   *Le Roi s'amuse*.

1833   *Lucrèce Borgia. Marie Tudor*. Hugo takes a mistress, Juliette

Drouet; this liaison lasts fifteen years. Madame Hugo establishes a liaison with Sainte-Beuve.

1835   *Les Chants du crépuscule. Angelo.*

1837   *Les Voix intérieures.*

1838   *Ruy Blas.*

1840   *Les Rayons et les ombres.*

1841   Elected to L'Académie française, after several unsuccessful applications.

1842   *Le Rhin.*

1843   *Les Burgraves.* His daughter Léopoldine drowns in Villequier on her honeymoon.

1848–49   Proclamation of the Republic. Hugo elected to the national assembly.

1851   Following the coup d'état in December, Hugo begins his long exile. He takes refuge in Belgium.

1852   *Napoléon-le-petit*, a pamphlet condemning France's new government. Hugo moves to the Isle of Jersey.

1853   *Les Châtiments* published in Belgium.

1855   Expelled from Jersey, Hugo moves to the Isle of Guernsey and establishes his home in Hauteville House.

1856   *Les Contemplations.*

1859   *La Légende des siècles*, first series. Despite a decree of amnesty, Hugo refuses to return to France.

1862   *Les Misérables.*

1863   *Hugo raconté par un témoin de sa vie*, a biographical work by Hugo's wife, Adèle.

1864   *William Shakespeare.*

1865   *Les Chansons des rues et des bois.*

1866   *Les Travailleurs de la mer.*

1867   Madame Adèle Hugo dies in Brussels.

1869   *L'Homme qui rit.*

1870   Following the fall of the French Empire, Hugo returns to France. He enjoys tremendous popularity.

1871   Elected to the national assembly but expelled after the political unrest of the Commune; travels to Belgium, then Luxembourg, and returns to Paris in September.

1872   *L'Année terrible.* Again, Hugo loses his bid for election to the assembly and leaves for Guernsey.

1873   Hugo returns to Paris.

1874   *Quatrevingt-treize. Mes fils.* Three volumes of *Actes et paroles.*

1876   Hugo is elected to the Senate.

1877   *La Légende des siècles,* new series. *L'Art d'être grand-père.*

1878   *Le Pape.* Hugo has a stroke and henceforth publishes only works written prior to 1878.

1880   *Religions et religion,* written 1870. *L'Ane,* written 1857–58.

1882   *Torquemada,* written 1869.

1883   Juliette Drouet dies. Final series of *La Légende des siècles.*

1885   Hugo dies May 22 in Paris. Following the *funérailles nationales,* his ashes are entombed in the Panthéon. His posthumous publications include *La Fin de Satan* (1886), *Le Théâtre en liberté* (1886), *Choses vues* (1887–90), *Dieu* (1891), *Amy Robsart* (1890), *Post-scriptum de ma vie* (1901), *Le Tas de pierres* (1942).

Contributors

HAROLD BLOOM, Sterling Professor of the Humanities at Yale University, is the author of *The Anxiety of Influence, Poetry and Repression*, and many other volumes of literary criticism. His forthcoming study, *Freud: Transference and Authority*, attempts a full-scale reading of all of Freud's major writings. A MacArthur Prize Fellow, he is general editor of five series of literary criticism published by Chelsea House. During 1987–88, he was appointed Charles Eliot Norton Professor of Poetry at Harvard University.

GEORGES POULET, born and educated in Belgium, has taught at the University of Edinburgh, The Johns Hopkins University, and the University of Zurich. Of his books, *The Metamorphosis of the Circle, Studies in Human Time*, and *Exploding Poetry,* in addition to *The Interior Distance*, have appeared in English translation.

JOHN PORTER HOUSTON is Professor of French and Italian at Indiana University. He is the author of *The Design of Rimbaud's Poetry, The Demonic Imagination*, and *Fictional Technique in France 1802–1927*.

W. D. HOWARTH is Professor of Classical French Literature at the University of Bristol, U. K.

PATRICIA A. WARD teaches French and Comparative Literature at Pennsylvania State University.

RICHARD B. GRANT teaches in the Department of French and Italian Languages at the University of Texas, Austin.

SUZANNE NASH is a member of the Department of French at Princeton University.

JEFFREY MEHLMAN teaches in the Department of Romance Languages at Boston University.

241

ALEXANDER WELSH is a member of the Department of English at the University of California, Los Angeles.

HENRI PEYRE, Professor Emeritus of French at Yale University and Distinguished Professor of French at the Graduate Center, City University of New York, is the author of many volumes of criticism, including *The Failures of Criticism, Literature and Sincerity,* and *What Is Romanticism?*

SANDY PETREY is a member of the Department of French at the State University of New York, Stony Brook.

VICTOR BROMBERT is Professor of French at Princeton University.

Bibliography

Affron, Charles. *A Stage for Poets: Studies in the Theatre of Hugo and Musset.* Princeton: Princeton University Press, 1971.

Albouy, Pierre. *La Création mythologique chez Victor Hugo.* Paris: José Corti, 1963.

———. "Hugo fantôme." *Littérature,* no. 13 (February 1974): 115.

Barrère, Jean-Bertrand. *La Fantaisie de Victor Hugo.* Geneva: Editions du Mont Blanc, 1943.

Baudouin, Charles. *Psychanalyse de Victor Hugo.* Geneva: Editions du Mont Blanc, 1943.

Béguin, Albert. *L'Ame romantique et le Rêve.* Paris: José Corti, 1939.

Brochu, André. *Hugo: Amour/Crime/Révolution: Essai sur* Les Misérables. Montreal: Les Presses de l'Université de Montréal, 1974.

Brombert, Victor. "Hugo, History, and the Other Text." *Nineteenth Century French Studies* 5 (1976–77): 23–33.

———. *"Les Travailleurs de la Mer:* Hugo's Poem of Effacement." *New Literary History* 9 (1978): 581–90.

———. *Victor Hugo and the Visionary Novel.* Cambridge: Harvard University Press, 1984.

Butor, Michel. "Le Théâtre de Victor Hugo." *Nouvelle Revue Française* 12 (1964): 862–78, 1073–81; 13 (1965): 105–13.

———. "Victor Hugo critique." *Critique* 21 (1965): 803–26.

———. "Victor Hugo romancier." *Tel Quel* 16 (1964): 60–77.

Cellier, Léon. *Autour des contemplations; George Sand et Victor Hugo.* Paris: Lettres Modernes, 1962.

de Man, Paul. "Hypogram and Inscription: Michael Riffaterre's Poetics of Reading." *Diacritics* 17 (Winter 1987): 17–36.

L'Esprit créateur 16, no. 3 (1976). Victor Hugo issue.

Gaudon, Jean. *Victor Hugo dramaturge.* Paris: L'Arche, 1955.

———. *Victor Hugo et le théâtre; stratégie et dramaturgie.* Paris: Suger, 1985.

Gély, Claude. *Victor Hugo, poète de l'intimité.* Paris: Librairie Nizet, 1969.

Grant, Richard B. *The Perilous Quest: Image, Myth, and Prophecy in the Narratives of Victor Hugo.* Durham, N. C.: Duke University Press, 1968.

———. "Sequence and Theme in Victor Hugo's *Les Orientales.*" *PMLA* 94 (1979): 894–908.

Greenberg, Wendy. *The Power of Rhetoric: Hugo's Metaphor and Poetics.* New York: P. Lang, 1985.

Haig, Stirling. "From Cathedral to Book, from Stone to Press: Hugo's Portrait of the Artist in *Nôtre Dame de Paris.*" *Stanford French Review* 3 (1979): 343–50.

Holdheim, W. Wolfgang. "The History of Art in Victor Hugo's *Nôtre Dame de Paris.*" *Nineteenth Century French Studies* 5 (1976–77): 58–70.

Houston, John Peter. "Design in *Les Contemplations.*" *French Forum* 5 (1980): 122– 40.

———. *Victor Hugo.* New York: Twayne, 1974.

Maurois, André. *Olympio: The Life of Victor Hugo.* Translated by Gerard Hopkins. New York: Harper, 1956.

Maxwell, Richard. "City Life and the Novel: Hugo, Ainsworth, Dickens." *Comparative Literature* 30 (1978): 157–71.

———. "Mystery and Revelation in *Les Misérables.*" *Romanic Review* 73, no. 3 (May 1982): 314–30.

Meschonnic, Henri. *Ecrire Hugo.* Paris: Gallimard, 1977.

Nash, Suzanne. Les Contemplations *of Victor Hugo: An Allegory of the Creative Process.* Princeton: Princeton University Press, 1976.

———. "Transfiguring Disfiguration in *L'Homme qui rit:* A Study of Hugo's Use of the Grotesque." In *Pretext-Text-Context,* edited by Robert L. Mitchell. Columbus: Ohio State University Press, 1980.

Petrey, Sandy. *History in the Text:* Quatrevingt-treize *and the French Revolution.* Amsterdam: John Benjamins, 1980.

Peyre, Henri. *Qu'est-ce que le romantisme?* Paris: Presses Universitaires, 1971.

———. *Victor Hugo: Philosophy and Poetry.* Translated by R. P. Roberts. University: University of Alabama Press, 1980.

Richardson, Joanna. *Victor Hugo.* London: Weidenfeld, 1976.

Riffaterre, Michael. "La Poésie métaphysique de Victor Hugo." *Romanic Review* 51, no. 4 (December 1960): 268–75.

———. *Text Production.* New York: Columbia University Press, 1979.

———. "Victor Hugo's Poetics." *The American Society Legion of Honor Magazine* 32 (1961): 191–96.

———. "La Vision hallucinatoire chez Victor Hugo." *MLN* 78 (1963): 225– 41.

Rosa, Guy. "*Quatrevingt-treize;* ou, La Critique du roman historique." *Revue d'Histoire Littéraire de la France* 75 (1975): 329– 43.

Schulkind, Eugene. "Hugo." In *French Literature and Its Background, Vol. 4: The Early Nineteenth Century,* edited by John Cruickshank. London: Oxford University Press, 1968.

Seebacher, Jacques. "Gringoire, ou Le Déplacement du roman historique vers l'histoire." *Révue d'Histoire Littéraire de la France* 75 (1975): 308–20.

Simaïka, Raouf. *L'Inspiration épique dans les romans de Victor Hugo.* Geneva: E. Droz, 1962.

Ubersfeld, Anne, ed. *Hugo le fabuleux.* Centre Culturel International de Cerisy. Paris: Suger, 1985.

———. *Le Roi et le bouffon; étude sur le théâtre de Hugo de 1830 à 1839.* Paris: José Corti, 1974.

Ward, Patricia A. *The Medievalism of Victor Hugo.* University Park: Pennsylvania State University Press, 1975.

———. "The Political Evolution of Victor Hugo's Gothic Vision." *Modern Language Quarterly* 34 (1973): 272–82.

Acknowledgments

"The Interior Distance: Hugo's Spatial Imagery" (originally entitled "Hugo") by Georges Poulet from *The Interior Distance* by Georges Poulet and translated by Elliot Coleman, © 1959 by the Johns Hopkins University Press, Baltimore/London. Reprinted by permission of the Johns Hopkins University Press.

"Hugo's Later Poetry" by John Porter Houston from *The Demonic Imagination: Style and Theme in French Romantic Poetry* by John Porter Houston, © 1969 by Louisiana State University Press. Reprinted by permission.

"Hugo and the Romantic Drama in Verse" by W. D. Howarth from *Sublime and Grotesque: A Study of French Romantic Drama* by W. D. Howarth, © 1975 by W. D. Howarth. Reprinted by permission of Louisiana State University Press.

"La Légende des siècles" by Patricia A. Ward from *The Medievalism of Victor Hugo* by Patricia A. Ward, © 1975 by Pennsylvania State University. Reprinted by permission of Pennsylvania State University Press, University Park, Pennsylvania.

"Les Travailleurs de la mer: Towards an Epic Synthesis" (originally entitled "Victor Hugo's *Les Travailleurs de la mer:* Towards an Epic Synthesis") by Richard B. Grant from *L'Esprit Createur* 16, no. 3 (Fall 1976), © by 1976 by *L'Esprit Createur*. Reprinted by permission.

"The Allegorical Nature and Context of *Les Contemplations*" (originally entitled "The Allegorical Nature and Context of the Work") by Suzanne Nash from Les Contemplations *of Victor Hugo: An Allegory of the Creative Process* by Suzanne Nash, © 1976 by Princeton University Press. Reprinted by permission of Princeton University Press.

"Revolution and Repetition in *Notre-Dame de Paris*" (originally entitled "Literature") by Jeffrey Mehlman from *Revolution and Repetition: Marx, Hugo, Balzac* by Jeffrey Mehlman, © 1977 by the Regents of the University of California. Reprinted by permission of the University of California Press.

"Opening and Closing *Les Misérables*" by Alexander Welsh from *Nineteenth-Century Fiction* 33, no. 1 (June 1978), © 1978 by the Regents of the

University of California. Reprinted by permission of the University of California Press.

"After 1852: God" by Henri Peyre from *Victor Hugo: Philosophy and Poetry* by Henri Peyre, © 1980 by Henri Peyre. Reprinted by permission of Renée Spodheim Associates and Presses Universitaires de France.

"*Quatrevingt-treize:* Children Belong with Their Mother" (originally entitled "Children Belong with Their Mother") by Sandy Petrey from *History in the Text:* Quatrevingt-treize *and the French Revolution* (Purdue University Monographs in Romance Languages, vol. 3) by Sandy Petrey, © 1980 by John Benjamins B.V., Amsterdam. Reprinted by permission.

"Writing a Building: Hugo's *Notre-Dame de Paris*" by Suzanne Nash from *French Forum* 8, no. 1 (May 1983), © 1983 by French Forum Publishers, Inc. Reprinted by permission.

"*Les Misérables:* Salvation from Below" by Victor Brombert from *Victor Hugo and the Visionary Novel* by Victor Brombert, © 1984 by the President and Fellows of Harvard College. Reprinted by permission of Harvard University Press.

Index